Agaves, Yuccas, and Related Plants

Agaves, Yuccas, and Related Plants

A GARDENER'S GUIDE

Mary & Gary Irish

Illustrated by Karen Bell

Photographs by Gary Irish except where noted

TIMBER PRESS
Portland, Oregon

Published in 2000 by
Timber Press, Inc.
The Haseltine Building
133 S.W. Second Avenue, Suite 450
Portland, Oregon 97204, U.S.A.

Printed in Hong Kong

Reprinted 2000

Library of Congress Cataloging-in-Publication Data

Irish, Mary, 1949–
    Agaves, yuccas, and related plants : a gardener's guide / Mary & Gary
Irish, authors; illustrated by Karen Bell; photographs by Gary Irish
except where noted.
        p.   cm.
    Includes bibliographical references (p.   ).
    ISBN 0-88192-442-3
    1. Agaves. 2. Yucca. 3. Agaves Identification. 4. Yucca Identification.
I. Irish, Gary. II. Title.
SB317.A2I75   2000
635.9'525—dc21   99-37292
                                                                      CIP

Contents

Color plates follow pages 144 and 208

Preface

Agaves, yuccas, and the other closely allied plants have been the subject of intense, sometimes exhaustive, work by botanists to establish meaningful relationships between the genera and their species. Horticulturists and gardeners have often embraced these plants as wondrous additions to landscapes and gardens, but have frequently had to rely on small sections in generalized publications to help them identify and care for the various species. Often designers and gardeners when they have used these plants at all have tended to see them as similar, undoubtedly because of their very general similarity of form. Because of these situations, gardeners may be unaware of the wide and intriguing range of form, culture, and hardiness exhibited by this unique group of plants.

This book is intended to help gardeners, nursery professionals, and horticulturists ease some of the identity confusion and encourage wider and more creative use of these plants in gardens. The book is focused primarily on the genera *Agave* and *Yucca* of the family Agavaceae. While several other genera of the family also are addressed, the book is limited to those genera from North, Central, and South America. Some taxonomic systems include Asian and African genera, such as *Cordyline*, *Dracaena*, and *Sansevieria*, within the Agavaceae, a point on which we have no opinion except that they are not a part of this work.

We also have included, however, members of the family Nolinaceae within this book for two reasons: these plants are restricted to the Americas, and many of these species have been included within Agavaceae in the past. Many species in both

7

families occur naturally in close association and have similar cultural requirements when grown under horticultural situations. The similarity in growth form and cultural requirements creates a logical horticultural group, despite the awkwardness of dealing with two distinct families.

There are several reasons to utilize agaves, yuccas, and their relatives in gardens and landscapes. As pressure on the world's supply of fresh water increases, designers and gardeners strive to use more drought-tolerant plants for general ornamental purposes. In the western United States in particular the need for water-conserving plant choices has become acute and is expected to continue into the foreseeable future. Most members of both these families are native to arid or semi-arid regions and, therefore, are suited imminently to the needs of less water consumptive designs and gardens.

The past 25 years have seen an ever expanding interest in native plants in American gardens. As the world continues to homogenize, native plants help instill a strong regional look into individual gardens. Members of the Agavaceae and the Nolinaceae provide a strong and vivid regional look when used in gardens of the western United States.

While it has been common to use many of these species as accent plants—placed singly and at a focal point of view where the crisp form can be appreciated—this use is by no means the only application in the garden to which these plants are suited. Many of these plants provide excellent contrast to full, flowering perennial plantings. The linear edges and smooth lines contrast well with the many leaves and billowing forms found so frequently in gardens. There are breathtaking examples of the use of agaves and yuccas in mass, lining a driveway, or following the line of a long bed to question why this dramatic use is not more frequent. Massing of many of these plants highlights the spectacular stem and leaf forms, and increases the interest and sheer spectacle of the garden. The plants also have been used in a western translation of the spare elegance of a Japanese garden to great effect. These plants seem to shift and accommodate to a host of garden styles, and it is only the gardener's imagination that limits their use.

Contrary to popular belief, not all these plants are immense and require palatial gardens for accommodation. Many species are small, well within the size needed for smaller urban or patio gardens. Many species are suitable for containers or for very small gardens that want the distinctive flair afforded by these plants.

Although these plants often are associated with the southwestern United States, they can be effectively used in other regions. The rosette arrangement of the leaves that is responsible for so much of the stunning symmetry of many species, the linear form and hard texture of many species, and the wide range of leaf color can be employed to great advantage by gardeners throughout the world. The use of these plants anywhere, either in the ground or in containers, can provide any garden, regardless of location, with strong structure, texture, and color to relieve the sameness of rounded dark leaves. Experimental plantings of many of these species by innovative nurseries and gardeners in cool, humid regions of North America and Europe show that many of these plants may be suitable for areas with climates very different from that of their natural range.

Throughout this book we have relied heavily on the identification of these plants through vegetative characteristics, using leaves and form more than floral differences. We employed this technique for two reasons. First, agaves live so long and most bloom so briefly that to rely exclusively on flowers, as all worthy botanists must, is discouraging and unhelpful for gardeners and horticulturists. Second, almost all these plants are brought into gardens for their outstanding vegetative character; it is the trait that is most interesting and useful in a garden setting. But, despite our best efforts, sometimes it is nearly impossible to discern one plant from another solely on the character of the leaves or growth form. We can only hope that the differences and distinctions help sort out most of them, most of the time.

We were encouraged in the writing of this book by countless people, many of whom are mentioned in the acknowledgments. Our primary motivation is to help anyone interested in this extraordinary group of plants come to know them better, understand their care, and offer them a place in their gardens.

Acknowledgments

It is hard to imagine how many people it takes to put together a book of this type and how much we owe to all of them for their interest, time, and extensive knowledge of these plants. It is impossible to name everyone, but some must be noted with our deep gratitude. We thank the staff of the Desert Botanical Garden, especially Wendy Hodgson, and the staff of the Huntington Botanical Gardens, especially John Trager, who spent his valuable time showing us around the garden. Bart O'Brien of Rancho Santa Ana Botanic Garden was an enthusiastic participant in agave, yucca, and nolina hunts throughout his garden and provided all manner of other information. We thank Karen Clary for reviewing the species profiles on *Yucca* and give a very special thanks to Greg Starr, who not only reviewed the sections on *Dasylirion*, *Hesperaloe*, and *Nolina*, but always was available to answer questions and offer suggestions for the book.

It is important to us to recognize all the people who took time to give us information about the performance of these plants in their areas or provided additional information or assistance with this book. They include Tony Avent, Randy Baldwin, Mark Dimmitt, John Fairey, Anne Gully, George Hull, Don Johnson, Gene Joseph, Paul and Sarah McCombs, Sean O'Hara, Carl Schoenfeld, Boyce Tankersley, Bud Terrell, and the unsung heroines of the project, the librarians of the Desert Botanical Garden and the Missouri Botanical Garden. And lastly, we thank our dear friends Tom Carruth and the late John Furman for room and board on the trips to California and a host of great times.

CHAPTER 1

History of the Families

Botanists currently assign agaves, yuccas, and their relatives to two families, the Agavaceae and the Nolinaceae. Though they share many vegetative characteristics, these families have significant floral differences. In this chapter we will examine the lengthy, contorted history of discovering, naming, and renaming these plants that has resulted in the current configuration.

Agavaceae

Over the years the family Agavaceae has shifted its definition and composition greatly. The family was proposed first in 1836 by Austrian botanist Stephen Endlicher and included the genera *Agave* and *Furcraea*. In 1866 Richard A. Salisbury expanded the family to include *Littae, Manfreda, Polianthes,* and *Yucca* as well. During the nineteenth century, most botanists continued to assign these genera in varying combinations to either the family Amaryllidaceae, if the ovary was inferior, or to the family Liliaceae, when the ovary was superior. In 1911 Johannes P. Lotsy, following similar work by Adolf Engler in the late nineteenth century, viewed the Liliaceae as a "great group" that needed significant subdivisions. Lotsy divided the plants into two groups. The Dracaenaceae included *Hesperaloe, Yucca,* and genera now considered in the family Nolinaceae, such as *Dasylirion* and *Nolina.* The Agavaceae was separated from the Amaryllidaceae and expanded from Endlicher's definition to include the genera *Beschorneria, Bravoa, Doryanthes*, and *Polianthes*.

In 1934 John Hutchinson reviewed the entire group and advocated the concept of the Agavaceae as a large separate family with 19 genera including plants from the New World and the Old World. Hutchinson basically combined the Dracaenaceae and the Agavaceae into a single large family. Little held the family together beyond the fact that the plants were rosette-forming monocots (containing only one cotyledon in the seed) from similar habitats. Cytological studies during this time confirmed a close relationship between *Agave* and *Yucca*, but other genera in the group, such as *Nolina* and *Dasylirion*, did not show such similarities. In 1981 Arthur Cronquist, in an important work on plant classification, basically followed Hutchinson's expanded description of the Agavaceae, proposing that the family include the genera *Agave, Beaucarnea, Beschorneria, Calibanus, Cordyline, Dasylirion, Doryanthes, Dracaena, Furcraea, Hesperaloe, Manfreda, Nolina, Polianthes, Prochnyanthes, Sansevieria*, and *Yucca*. Cronquist's system became widely accepted and still is utilized in many botanical collections and writings worldwide.

In 1985 Dahlgren, Clifford, and Yeo, in a review of monocots, proposed narrow families and described the Agavaceae as a family entirely contained in the Americas and restricted to the genera *Agave, Beschorneria, Furcraea, Hesperaloe, Manfreda, Polianthes, Prochnyanthes*, and *Yucca*. The genera *Beaucarnea, Calibanus, Dasylirion*, and *Nolina* were removed to the family Nolinaceae. The other genera of Agavaceae from previous treatments, all of which occur outside the Americas, were assigned variously to other families. This configuration of the families is the one used in this book, and using it the Agavaceae can be said to occur in a wide range of habitats from the eastern United States west to the Pacific Ocean, south through Mexico, Central America, Venezuela, Colombia, Brazil, and the West Indies.

Agave is the type genus of the family and is composed of 200–250 species that occur in the arid western United States south through Mexico, as well as Central America, and the

West Indies. Members of the genus can be found growing from sea level to an elevation of more than 7000 ft. (2100 m) in forests, dry hillsides, arid plains, deserts, and the seashore.

The genus *Agave* was established by Carl Linnaeus in 1753, and the name is derived from a Greek word meaning "noble." Since the genus was described for the first time, an extraordinary number of changes and rearrangements has been made in the nineteenth century as more and more plants were brought into Europe and in the twentieth century as more field work in the natural ranges of the plants was conducted.

Early European horticulturists and botanists rarely were able to travel to Mexico or the Caribbean basin to find and study these plants, and had to rely instead on the extensive collections being grown in Italy, England, and other parts of Europe. Extensive use of cultivated plants for taxonomic work often produced misleading conclusions because cultivation practices, cool temperatures, and pot culture can create vegetative characteristics that have little relationship to the true nature of the species. In addition, plants often did not bloom, so minor or culturally derived vegetative characteristics took on more importance than was warranted. Vegetative differences in agaves, as indeed for nearly all members of the family, often are plentiful within one species, and many species were established based on minor distinctions of leaf shape or color, size and shape of teeth, and other vegetative characteristics.

The enthusiastic collector and botanist Count Salm-Dyck, in works of 1834 and 1859, reviewed and annotated the extensive collection of agaves from his garden at Dusseldorf and settled on 45 species for the genus. Later (1864–1867) the Prussian army general Georg Albano von Jacobi described 78 species based on plants in gardens throughout Europe, many of them juveniles in pot culture. Neither of these men used floral characteristics to describe their species.

In 1833 the German botanist Joseph Zuccarini was the first to extensively describe the flowers, but even so they were not used commonly to delineate species differences. Later in the century, American and English workers George Engelmann and John G. Baker revised various species, adding 31 more to the

list. Although Baker did not base his work on floral characteristics, he was very familiar with flowering specimens and described the flowers of many. In 1888 he summarized the current
status of the genus and recognized 138 species.

In 1915 Alwin Berger published his definitive work on the
genus in which he described 274 species. This work was important because it was among the first attempts to organize and
deal with the entire genus taxonomically. Berger was working
from live material, albeit in cultivation chiefly at La Mortola, a
garden on the Italian Riviera renowned for its collection of
Agave, Yucca, and many other related genera.

Berger's contemporary William Trelease from the Missouri
Botanical Garden was the first botanist to make significant observations and records of agaves growing in their native habitat.
Trelease traveled extensively in Mexico, Guatemala, and the
Caribbean, but he still fell prey to the common habits of nine-
teenth-century taxonomists: a reliance on cultivated material,
a casual approach to the location of a given specimen from the
wild, and a need to describe species based on small distinctions.
Trelease published his last agave work in 1924. Between Berger
and Trelease, *Agave* had swelled to 310 species. From 1924 until 1982 various botanists described an additional 35 species.

In 1982 Howard Scott Gentry published his monumental
monograph on the continental North American members of
the genus. He recognized 136 species with the count rising to
197 taxa when all varieties and subspecies are included. He
took a different approach to the study of the genus. He located
all known herbarium specimens and reviewed most of them,
documented his extensive field collections, spent many years
in Mexico and the United States collecting and observing plants
in the wild, and was rigorous about documenting locations for
his source material.

Gentry's organization of the genus *Agave* is based solidly
in floral characteristics. He divided the genus into two subgenera: *Littae,* which included genera with spicate inflorescences
and was divided further into 8 sections with 54 species, and
Agave, which included genera with paniculate inflorescences
and was divided further into 12 sections with 82 species. While

this arrangement makes for some order in a chaotic group, it can cause confusion, particularly to horticulturists and gardeners who tend to encounter the plants for years without the benefit of flowers. There are agaves with extremely similar vegetative characteristics that are in entirely different groups, and agaves with no superficial vegetative resemblance that are related closely.

Figure 1-1. Inflorescence styles in *Agave*: (left) spicate, *A. pelona*; (right) paniculate, *A. scabra*

Gentry's view of the genus is still definitive today and is used as the taxonomic authority for this book. Subsequent botanical work in the United States and Mexico continues to expand our understanding of this highly variable genus. Since the publication of Gentry's work, at least three new species have been added, including one in Arizona, and several more are under consideration.

Another member of the Agavaceae, the genus *Yucca*, is composed of about 50 species and occurs in the southeastern United States, across Texas into the southern Rocky Mountains and westward to the Pacific Ocean, up through the Great Plains, north to Canada, and south through Mexico and into Central America. Yuccas occupy a wide range of habitats from coastal beach communities, prairies and sandy grasslands, forests, and dry hillsides to extremely arid deserts.

Linnaeus first described the genus *Yucca* in 1757. The plants that he described—*Y. aloifolia, Y. filamentosa,* and *Y. gloriosa*—are from the Atlantic coastal plain of North America and had already been known for well over a hundred years in Europe. The name "yucca" is derived from "yuca," the Indian name for *Manihot esculenta,* also known as cassava or manioc. Past and present residents of the Caribbean and other tropical areas consume the large, starchy roots of yuca. The Indian name was applied erroneously to *Yucca* because of confusion in early reports of the plants.

During the ensuing 125 years, several species from the United States and Mexico were described by a large number of botanists. The American physician and botanist George Engelmann did the first major examination of the genus as a whole in 1873. He divided *Yucca* into two groups, *Euyucca* and *Hesperoyucca,* based on floral characters. *Euyucca* was divided further into three sections—*Sarcoyucca, Clistoyucca,* and *Chaenoyucca*—using fruit characteristics. These sections represent the major divisions of the genus today.

From 1902 to 1911 William Trelease divided the group into five separate genera: *Clistoyucca, Hesperaloe, Hesperoyucca, Samuela,* and *Yucca. Hesperoyucca* and *Samuela* contained one species each, the present-day *Yucca whipplei* and *Y. faxon-*

iana, respectively. While these groupings are not accepted today, Trelease did describe several new species and consolidated considerable information on the genus. His work is important and of particular interest to gardeners because he included horticultural forms.

Susan McKelvey, in her work on yuccas of the southwestern United States published in 1938 and 1947, restored much of Engelmann's original groupings and listed 32 species for that area. She described 16 new species, but tended to recognize small differences as sufficient to establish species. In 1953 John Webber, working in the same region, rejected many of McKelvey's species, believing that the genus was highly variable and that many of McKelvey's species consisted of natural hybrids or differences that could at best be considered varieties. Both authors contributed significant ecological information on the genus.

In 1980 the Mexican botanists Eizi Matuda and Ignacio L. Piña reviewed the Mexican species of *Yucca*, contributing considerable information about their distribution, uses, and descriptions of species in the genus. They recognized 30 species of *Yucca* in Mexico.

Today, botanists generally recognize four groups or sections in *Yucca* based to a large extent on the structure and characteristics of the fruit. Two of the groups are large, each with approximately half the total species, while the other two groups consist of one species each. *Chaenocarpa*, one of the large groups, is distinguished by dry capsular fruit that is dehiscent at maturity and by seeds with small wings. *Sarcocarpa*, the other large group, has large, fleshy, indehiscent fruit. On the whole, members of *Chaenocarpa* are small, stemless plants from the northern part of the genus's range, while those of *Sarcocarpa* primarily are arborescent plants from the more southerly parts of the range. There are, of course, exceptions within both groups. The two monotypic groups are *Clistocarpa*, represented by *Yucca brevifolia*, a species of the Mohave Desert with large spongy, rather than fleshy, fruit and tough, leathery, semi-closed flowers, and *Hesperoyucca*, represented by *Yucca whipplei*, a species with a dry fruit, monocarpic flowering, and a unique stigma with small fingerlike appendages.

Classification of *Yucca* species uses a variety of floral and vegetative characteristics. Since many recognized species have considerable individual variation, the resulting confusion within the taxonomic treatment of *Yucca* over the years can still cause havoc in the identification of certain species for botanists and gardeners alike.

The genus *Hesperaloe*, a small group of acaulescent plants distributed in southwestern Texas and northern Mexico, was established by Engelmann in 1871. The name means "western aloe." The plants had been known long before the genus was described, having been originally collected and named by John Torrey as *Yucca parviflora* in 1859 and by Asa Gray as *Aloe yuccifolia* in 1867. In 1894 John Coulter united these two taxa as *Hesperaloe parviflora*. Trelease moved *Y. funifera* into the genus in 1902, and 65 years later *H. nocturna* was described by Gentry. Greg Starr described *H. campanulata* and *H. tenuifolia* in 1998, bringing the total number of species to five.

The genus *Furcraea* was established in 1793 by Étienne Ventenat, a French professor of botany who also served as Empress Josephine's personal botanist. Various members of the genus have been assigned to *Agave* over the years, and many synonymous species were described throughout the nineteenth century. In 1907 James R. Drummond summarized work on *Furcraea* and recognized 10 species as well as 6 additional species that were known poorly at the time but which he thought may have some validity. Today 20 species are recognized in a range that extends from Mexico through Venezuela, Colombia, and into Brazil. *Furcraea* species are found in Cuba and other islands of the Caribbean as well. This genus is one of the most poorly known in the family.

Plants of the genera *Manfreda, Polianthes,* and *Prochnyanthes* were known to European botanists at an early date. Linnaeus described *Polianthes* in 1753. Various botanists through the nineteenth century considered these genera, particularly *Manfreda*, to be part of *Agave*. In 1837, however, Zuccarini described the genus *Prochnyanthes* and separated it from *Agave* and *Polianthes*. Joseph N. Rose in 1899 separated *Manfreda* from the other closely related genera, united *Bravoa* with *Poli-*

Figure 1-2. *Hesperaloe parviflora*

anthes, and added a new genus *Pseudobravoa.* Berger, using material at the Royal Botanic Gardens, Kew, and at La Mortola, reviewed the entire group in 1913 and in an astounding concession to Kew botanists, and apparently against his better judgment, merged *Manfreda* back into *Agave.* Hutchinson in 1934 separated out *Manfreda* from *Agave* and maintained *Polianthes* and *Prochnyanthes* as separate genera in the family Agavaceae. In 1966 Lloyd H. Shinners reversed this designation and assigned all three genera to *Polianthes.* Susan Verhoek-Williams in 1975 reviewed the group but accepted all three as separate genera.

Manfreda as currently understood has 28 species and is distributed mainly from far south Texas through eastern Mexico and into Guatemala with one wide-ranging species, *M. virginica,* occurring throughout the southeastern United States. *Polianthes* has about 13 species, all in Mexico, and *Prochnyanthes* is a monotypic genus found solely in Mexico.

The genus *Beschorneria* was described by the German botanist Karl Kunth in 1850 from a plant then known as *Furcraea tubiflora* and originally described by Peter C. Bouché in 1847. The genus was reviewed by the Mexican botanist Abisaí García-Mendoza in 1987. Currently *Beschorneria* has seven species, all from rocky areas and mountain forests high in Mexico and Guatemala.

Nolinaceae

The taxonomic history of the genera making up the family Nolinaceae is very complicated despite the fact that the four genera have been formally described for a long time. The family was proposed first in 1936 by the Japanese botanist Takenoshin Nakai, but was not accepted by either Hutchinson or Cronquist, both of whom retained these genera in the family Agavaceae. Dahlgren et al. (1985) accepted this separation and listed the family Nolinaceae with the genera *Beaucarnea, Calibanus, Dasylirion,* and *Nolina.* Today approximately 55 species and 60 taxa are recognized in the family.

During most of the nineteenth century, members of the genera of Nolinaceae were included within the family Liliaceae. In 1879 Sereno Watson placed *Dasylirion* and *Nolina* in the tribe Nolineae, separating them from the tribe Yuccae that contained *Yucca* and *Hesperaloe*. In 1888 Engler created a classification of the Liliaceae that included a tribe Nolineae, but within that group taxonomic chaos reigned. In 1872 and 1881 Baker subsumed all species of *Nolina* into *Beaucarnea*, and in 1879 Watson advocated all species of *Beaucarnea* be part of *Nolina*. Several other taxonomic workers, such as William Hemsley and Engler, agreed with Watson's opinion. At the same time *Calibanus* was considered part of *Dasylirion*. In 1906 Rose advocated retaining the *Nolina-Beaucarnea* distinction.

In the twentieth century the taxonomic status of the group continued to be confused. Despite the distinction between the families Nolinaceae and Agavaceae by Dahlgren et al. (1985), it is still common to see genera of Nolinaceae listed in some gardens and publications within the Agavaceae and sometimes even in Liliaceae. As a group these plants were reviewed comprehensively first by Trelease in 1911 as the "desert group" Nolinae, a part of the Liliaceae. Trelease divided all the species known at that time into four genera. He also added several new species to the group particularly from *Nolina* and *Dasylirion*.

The Nolinaceae as recognized today is a family of plants consisting of four genera that occur in semi-arid to arid environments and tropical deciduous forests. Where species occur in moist environments, they tend to be found in rocky or sandy well-drained soils. The range of the family is disjunct; species occur in South Carolina, Georgia, and Florida, from southern Nevada and Colorado to southern California through the western half of Texas into Mexico and Guatemala.

Nolina was described in 1803 by André Michaux, a French botanist who found the first member of this genus along the South Atlantic coast of the United States. He named the genus for C. P. Nolin, the French co-author of an eighteenth-century book on agriculture. Within *Nolina* 25 species occur in the southeastern United States, Texas, New Mexico, Arizona, California, and small portions of Colorado and Oklahoma and into

Mexico. The species are separated into four sections based on combinations of fruit, inflorescence, leaf, and other vegetative characteristics, with one section containing plants with distinct woody trunks.

Dasylirion was described in 1838 by Zuccarini and given its name after the Greek words *dasys* meaning "thick" and *lirion* meaning "lily." The 19 species of *Dasylirion* occur chiefly in Mexico but also in Texas, New Mexico, and Arizona. The genus was reviewed most recently by the American botanist David Bogler in 1994, who recognized four new species.

Beaucarnea was described in 1861 by Charles Lemaire, but the origin of the name is not clear. Rose did significant work on the genus in 1906 and added several species. Currently there are 10 species, which occur only in Mexico and Guatemala. The genus was reviewed most recently by the Mexican botanist Luis Hernández in 1993 who added three species.

Calibanus originally was separated and described by Rose in 1906 and named for Caliban, a monster in Shakespeare's play *The Tempest. Calibanus* is a monotypic genus found only in Mexico.

CHAPTER 2

Description of the Genera

The families Agavaceae and Nolinaceae are monocotyledonous and members of the Liliflorae, a superorder within the monocots. They have some basic similarities with other monocots and the other families of the Liliflorae. The two families also share some common traits in their gross morphology and habit. The plants have a rosette leaf form in which the new linear-shaped leaves emerge from a single growing point on a stem or branch to form a radially symmetrical "head" or rosette of leaves. This characteristic is shared by other monocots, such as *Aloe* and *Dracaena*. The two families share the common monocotyledonous characteristic of having flower parts in groups of six, that is, six stamens and six tepals, the latter a combination of three petals and three sepals that are not distinguished easily from one another. An important similarity is that the families have flowers borne on elongated inflorescences that usually are held high above the rosettes and they have three-celled ovaries that are pollinated by insects or bats. In most plants in these families pollination results in a dry capsular fruit. Finally, the plants generally share a xerophytic habitat where rainfall is scarce year-round or at least seasonally.

Despite these similarities the families differ from each other in some significant ways. The Agavaceae have perfect flowers, that is, both male and female parts are within the same flower, while those of the Nolinaceae are dioecious, that is, the male and female flowers are on separate plants. The flowers of the Agavaceae tend to be variously colored and large, usually at least 1 in. (2.5 cm) long, while those of the Nolinaceae are invariably a creamy white in color and very small, often less than 0.1 in. (2.5 mm) long. In the Agavaceae some genera, such as *Agave* and *Furcraea,* are monocarpic, that is, the individual rosettes die after flowering. In the Nolinaceae all plants are polycarpic, that is, rosettes can produce inflorescences in multiple years. Although exceptions exist, the fruits of the Agavaceae generally are dehiscent, splitting at maturity to release the seeds, while the fruits of the Nolinaceae generally are indehiscent, with the seeds remaining in the fruit. Furthermore, the seeds of the Agavaceae are flat and often black while those of the Nolinaceae are rounded somewhat and generally brown in color.

In this chapter we shall consider the genera of the family Agavaceae first, in their order of importance: *Agave, Yucca, Hesperaloe, Furcraea, Manfreda, Beschorneria,* and *Polianthes.* The four genera of the family Nolinaceae follow: *Nolina, Dasylirion, Beaucarnea,* and *Calibanus.*

Agave

Plants in the genus *Agave* generally are thought of as perennial because it takes more than one growing season to complete the cycle of growth and bloom, but they perhaps are better considered as multiannuals since most of them bloom only once during the life of the plant. Most *Agave* species are monocarpic (blooming once in the life of the plant); only a few species are polycarpic (blooming repeatedly through the life of the plant).

Agaves, in general, have large leaves arranged in a spiral along a small, often invisible, stem to form a rosette. Rosettes are a common adaptation to desert or arid conditions. This growth form allows water to be directed down the leaves, like a channel, to the root zone. During times of serious drought, the small stem of an agave will shrink, allowing a tiny fissure in the soil around the plant base, further increasing the utility of the rosette form in channeling water when it does rain. Rosettes are common in many genera from arid regions including all other members of the families Agavaceae and Nolinaceae, and genera from other families such as *Aloe, Haworthia,* and *Gasteria,* to name a few.

The leaves of *Agave* usually are hard or somewhat rigid and very fibrous inside. Many have prominent sharp marginal teeth, and almost all leaves have a rigid and very sharp terminal spine. A rosette may have fewer than 20 leaves or as many as 200, depending on the species. The leaves are thick and succulent, with specialized cells for water storage. Most leaves are coated with a fine to heavy waxy cuticle. This cuticle is an adaptation to prevent excessive water loss through the leaves, retaining as much water within the leaf as possible to endure long periods of drought. Leaves can be rigid or lax. Teeth, too, are variable, and may be straight or curved, tiny or large, flattened or rounded. The cuticular margin may be smooth, interrupted by teeth, or it may fall away from the edge in long fibers known as filaments. Differences in the leaf margin and marginal teeth make a clear vegetative distinction between agaves and aloes. In agaves the margin and teeth are always of a separate and distinct tissue with a fine line of demarcation. In aloes there is no such border; what look like teeth on closer examination are just elongations of the leaf, like taffy being pulled off the leaf surface.

The leaf margin may be straight along the entire length of the leaf or straight only between the teeth; it may undulate dramatically, rising off the edge in distinctive prominences, or it may gently curve along the edge of the leaf. The terminal spine may be long or short, straight, curved or gracefully cupped, with or without distinctive grooves, but always quite sharp. When the cuticle of the terminal spine continues down the margin of the leaf, the spine is said to be decurrent. The presence or absence, as well as the length of such an elongation, can be useful in separating some agaves.

Leaf color ranges from bright glossy green to dull gray-blue. The varying thickness of the cuticle can affect the color, making the leaf appear horizontally banded, as in *Agave zebra* and *A. sobria.* In some species, such as *A. franzosinii,* the waxy cuticle is fine, like a blush, and will rub off with pressure or scratching. Nearly all leaves are glabrous, that is, without hairs

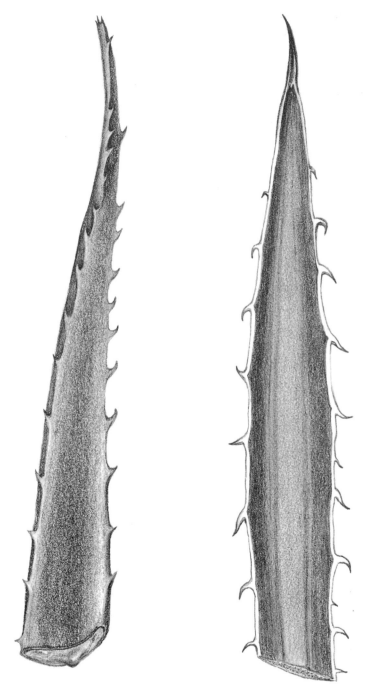

Figure 2-1. Leaf comparison: (left) aloe and (right) agave

or pubescence, although the leaves of *A. scabra* have minute tubercles that give the leaves a rough, or scabrous, feel.

In all agaves the vascular system elongates through the leaf, creating fibers that run the entire length of the leaf. In some species, such as *Agave sisalana* and *A. fourcroydes*, this feature is very strong, making the fiber an important and useful economic product of the plant. This fibrous leaf makes a clear distinction between agaves and the superficially similar aloes. Aloe leaves are gelatinous in the interior, never with the fibers present as in agaves.

The combinations of these leaf characteristics can help determine one species from another, especially without the flowers, but they are general and sometimes unreliable. Leaves of a single species, particularly one with an extensive range that covers wide geographical and ecological areas, often show enormous variation. When all the leaf characteristics are taken together, most agaves can be either identified or choices limited to a few species by leaf differences, but without the flowers or fruit, identification is often uncertain.

The leaves of *Agave* live a remarkably long time, generally 12–15 years, often the entire life of the plant. All the water-storage and energy-storage capacity of the plant is in the leaf, so it is advantageous to retain the leaves as long as possible to provide sufficient energy for the bloom. Therefore, on any one plant, there will be leaves held in bud, juvenile leaves, and very old mature leaves, adding further to the variation so common in agaves. Most leaves are held in bud a long time, usually 2–3 years, and in some species the teeth of the surrounding leaves impress themselves on the surface of another. This pattern can be faint or clear and is known as a bud imprint. In *Agave colorata* and several other species it is among the most ornamental aspects of the plant.

The stem of *Agave* usually is small, merely a base, hidden beneath the mass of leaves. A few species form trunks of significant size, but they are rare. Rhizomes, or underground stem extensions, however, are fairly common. Small buds occur along the rhizome, then reach the surface and form one or many new rosettes that eventually can form extensive clonal colonies in some species. Plants formed from the rhizome are called offsets or pups, sometimes suckers, and arise, depending on the species, only when the plant is young, only at or directly after bloom, or during the entire life of the plant. In some species offsets are produced prolifically while in others only one or two offsets are produced. Mechanical injury to rosettes can also induce the production of offsets in some species.

The roots of *Agave* are wide-spreading and fibrous, growing radially from the plant. The oldest roots become thick and slightly woody, while the younger ones are extremely fine and heavily branched. The roots die quickly when soil moisture decreases and regenerate just as quickly when water is available. This style of root is a major adaptation to low and erratic rainfall and is found in many succulents. The vast number of fine roots allows for water uptake quickly, and the fact that the roots are very shallow permits even small rainfall events to provide significant water to the plant.

The flowers of *Agave* have petals and sepals that are nearly indistinguishable and are referred to as tepals. The six tepals are tough, often leathery, and held in two sets of three. The color of the tepals is most often yellow or gold, but white and wine-red occur (Plate 16). The tepals flare in certain species, and not at all in others, and are fused in the lower section. This fused segment unites with ovarian tissue and connects the base of the tepals to the top of the ovary. This structure is called the tube. The tube may be long or short and may have a tight constriction above the ovary. The inferior three-chambered ovary has numerous ovules. Six long, exserted stamens with two-chambered flat anthers and a three-part style may be held either below or above the anthers, but nearly always above the tepals.

Flowering is a multistage event. In the first stage the tepals open to reveal the folded anthers. The next day or two the anthers emerge, pollen ripens and is dispersed, and then the anthers dry (dehisce). Just as the anthers dry, the stigma is elongated fully and opens with a sticky coating to be receptive to any pollen that is delivered. The pollen tubes form after pollination and fertilization is possible. This sequence takes a week or longer depending on the species.

Blooms are held on tall, often spectacular inflorescences rising a great distance from the plant, up to about 6 ft. (1.8 m) in small species and more than 40 ft. (12 m) in the largest (Plate 5). The inflorescence style separates the genus into two large subgenera: *Littae* where the inflorescence is a spike or infrequently a raceme, and *Agave* where the inflorescence is a panicle. The inflorescence is formed in most species at the apex of the rosette. These plants are then monocarpic, and the rosette dies once flowering is completed. A few species flower from the axils of the leaves, and these plants continue to live beyond blooming. Flowers on the inflorescence begin opening from the bottom of the inflorescence to the top. Flowering may continue for up to two months or more depending on the species.

The flowers of *Agave* are pollinated by a host of agents: bats, hummingbirds and other nectar-eating birds, bees, moths, and other insects. Many species, especially paniculate forms, hold their flowers upright and the tepals are very firm and hard. This habit is probably an adaptation to the visits of bats or large birds, which could tear more fragile flowers apart. Generally, the flowers of spicate-blooming agaves are held less upright, are less durable, and are more likely to be pollinated by insects. Many agaves have prolific amounts of nectar when in flower and some have distinctive aromas. In *Agave* it is thought that a musky, deep smell attracts bats, while the sweeter fragrances attract insects.

The fruit of *Agave* is a capsule with three chambers. The capsules generally are woody, and many dehisce longitudinally when mature, but remain on the plant for months. The seeds are flat, black, and numerous in the capsules.

The 200–250 species of *Agave* are found only in the Americas. Mexico is the center of diversity for the genus and has more than 125 species throughout the country. The United States has about 15 species, and the remaining species are distributed through Central America, Baja California, and the Caribbean basin. Most agaves grow on dry sites, rocky hillsides, and graveled plains, rarely in forested areas, although when found in forests the soil is usually limestone or sand. Where rainfall is abundant, plants often are found on rocky hills, cliff faces, or limestone outcrops. Certain species are found in oak woodlands and even in mixed tropical and temperate forests, generally on the hillsides or where the soil is thin and rocky. Agaves grow where temperatures regularly exceed 106°F (41°C) in the summer, and where winter lows are regularly 15°F (−9°C) or lower. They occur at elevations from sea level, including coastal beaches, to mountainous areas over 8000 ft. (2400 m).

Yucca

The genus *Yucca* exhibits a variety of forms from short stemless grasslike plants to towering, branched treelike plants with one to many rosettes. Yuccas are polycarpic with one exception.

The leaves of *Yucca* are linear and usually numerous on the plant. Individual leaves are very fibrous, and many have extensive numbers of filaments peeling from the margin. Size and shape of the leaves vary considerably. Leaf size, however, does not correlate well with plant size. For example, the small stemless *Y. filamentosa* has very small leaves only a foot (30 cm) or so long, yet the enormous tree-sized *Y. brevifolia* has leaves of nearly the same length.

Leaf color is remarkably variable, ranging from a bright glossy green to a fine gray-green and even a pale blue. Some species have cuticular coatings that create a blush, or the blue-gray color. Leaves are glabrous but like *Agave* species, some *Yucca* species have a scabrous surface while others are smooth.

The arrangement and number of leaves also vary in *Yucca*. In some species the leaves are held rigidly on the stem in dense rosettes, while in others the leaves are pliable and in a few species the leaves are lax, appearing to fold in the middle. The number of leaves held on a plant varies from only a few dozen to 100. Some species shed dead leaves; in other species the dead leaves cling to the stem and remain on the plant for a very long time, often the life of the plant.

Leaf margins generally are smooth, but in a few species the margins have fine serrations. Approximately half of all *Yucca* species have marginal filaments. These filaments vary in thickness and the amount of curl, characteristics that can assist in the identification of species. Caution, however, must be exercised because the characteristic of filaments and the arrangement on the plant vary significantly. In many species the leaf margin is marked with a thin stripe colored yellow, brown, or brown and white. Taken with other leaf characteristics, this color stripe can be helpful in the identification of several species. Most species of *Yucca* have a terminal spine that varies from heavy and strong to weak and blunt. A few species are entirely without the spine.

Yuccas can have single or multiple trunks or be trunkless. The trunkless species tend to occur in the colder, northern parts of the range of the genus, the forests of eastern North America, the Great Plains, and the southern Rocky Mountains. The trunked species are from tropical or subtropical areas in the eastern United States, the arid parts of the western United States, or throughout Mexico to Guatemala. In some species the trunk is not upright and tends to run along the ground, extending the plant into a wide, low colony. Trunks can branch or not and the oldest part of the trunk can become fissured and woodlike. In the largest species the trunk base extends for many feet and is like a small platform on which the gargantuan plant rests. Like *Agave* species, some species of *Yucca* spread by underground rhizomes to create low colonies. The "wood" of *Yucca* is typical of other woody monocotyledons such as palms in that it is fibrous with many air spaces. This structure makes the wood strong and light. In some trunked species the large main stem terminates underground in a flat or rounded structure from which growth nodules may form. These growth areas occasionally give rise to new stems above ground. Field observations on *Yucca faxoniana* and *Y. schidigera* have shown that, after wildfires, new stems can be formed from the base even if the aboveground stems were destroyed. An analogous situation may occur in gardens, when stems are killed by extraordinary cold weather and new stems are likely to develop from this basal growing point. *Yucca baccata* combines both strategies of shoot development: basal growth nodules give rise to new aerial stems and underground rhizomes.

The roots of *Yucca* are strong, fibrous, and cordlike. In species that form rhizomes, roots develop along the underground stem. Roots can also form along a stem that bends and touches the ground. In *Yucca elata* one or two large rhizomes form vertically downward, and roots emerge along the entire length. This habit makes this species particularly difficult to move when plants are large because damage to the large rhizomes can result in death of the individual. In *Y. whipplei*, seedlings develop a swollen underground bulblike structure from which the roots grow.

The flowers of *Yucca* have three sepals and three petals that are very similar and often are referred to as tepals or segments. In some species the three inner tepals differ slightly in shape and size from the three outer tepals, and in *Y. faxoniana* the floral segments are united at the base to form a short tube. In most species any union of the perianth segments is at the base, with the top part of the segment free. Most flowers are more or less bell-shaped (Plate 87). The tepals are thick and leathery and range in color from creamy white to greenish white to clear white. In many species the outer tepals are colored with streaks of pink, maroon, brown, red, or purple. This coloring is pronounced particularly when the flower is in bud. Horticultural selections of *Yucca filamentosa* have been made based on the streaks and colors of the tepals. Some clones of *Y. baccata* var. *vespertina* show very dark tepal coloration so that the entire bud is a deep maroon color, which contrasts vividly with the light blue-green leaves.

The ovary of *Yucca* is superior and has three chambers that contain the numerous ovules. The flowers have six stamens that are attached at the base of the tepals. The three stout styles are higher than the stamens, presumably to prevent self-fertilization. The stigma is divided into small dense heads with one exception, *Y. whipplei*, which has distinct capitate heads.

The inflorescence in *Yucca* is a raceme or, more commonly, a panicle. Most panicles are oblong, but may also be long and narrow or round and ball-shaped. The arrangement of the inflorescence in relation to the leaves varies: it maybe held entirely within the rosette, halfway within the rosette, or high above the leaf rosette on a long stalk.

Figure 2-2. Inflorescence styles in *Yucca:* (above left) fully outside
the leaves, *Y. elata;* (above right) embedded in the leaves,
Y. baccata; (below) partially imbedded in the leaves, *Y. recurvifolia*

The pollination of *Yucca* flowers is a striking example of biological mutualism. The plant depends on small moths in the genus *Tageticula* (synonym *Pronuba*) for pollination. In turn the moths depend on the yuccas for part of their life cycle. *Tageticula yuccasella*, a small white moth, acts as the pollinator for yuccas throughout eastern North America into the Great Plains, the southwestern United States, and parts of Mexico. In the far western United States *Y. brevifolia* is pollinated by *Tageticula synthetica* and *Y. whipplei* by *Tageticula maculata*. It is possible that other moth species act as pollinators for some Mexican species of *Yucca*. The mutually dependent relationship between the moth and the yucca was discovered in 1876 and published in 1892 by Charles Riley, an entomologist for the state of Missouri. When yuccas bloom, an adult moth hides in the flower during the day, emerging at dusk to pollinate the night-opening flowers. The female moth collects the sticky pollen from one flower and carries it to another, forcing the ball of pollen down the tube of the stigma. During this process the moth thrusts her ovipositor into the wall of the ovary and releases her eggs. The developing larvae feed on seeds as they develop. As the larvae mature, they eat through the yucca fruit and drop to the ground. At this point it is assumed that the larvae burrow into the soil to pupate. Eventually moths emerge and begin the cycle again. The moth lays only a certain number of eggs in each flower, thereby regulating how many seeds will be consumed by the developing larvae and allowing a portion of the seeds to mature and thus continue the yucca into successive generations. Exactly how the moth controls egg laying to ensure enough seed survival is known poorly, but this complex relationship obviously is well tuned.

Yucca whipplei is pollinated by a moth, but may be able to take advantage of other pollinators as well. This species secretes nectar and so is visited often by bees and other day-active insects, suggesting it may be able to accommodate day and night pollinators.

Approximately half of all *Yucca* species have the typical woody capsules of the family Agavaceae, while the other half have fruit that is large and fleshy (see *Y. treculeana*, Plate 98).

One species (*Y. brevifolia*) has fruit that is large and spongy-textured. The fleshy fruits are eaten undoubtedly by animals and still are relished by native peoples in the areas in which these fruits naturally occur. The variation in fruit type in *Yucca* has been used as an important taxonomic characteristic in the genus. The seeds are small, flat, and black. Packed tightly into capsules, the seeds can take one to three months to develop, depending on the species.

The natural distribution of the genus *Yucca* is very extensive, ranging from the Canadian prairie provinces through large parts of the United States, from the Atlantic and Gulf Coastal regions west to the Pacific Ocean, through most of Mexico south to Guatemala, as well as some Caribbean islands. Yuccas are plants of arid or semi-arid regions, but where climates are humid, such as in the eastern United States, yuccas generally occur in sandy or gravelly soils that tend to dry out quickly. The eastern species occur either on the beach or sandy coastal islands or inland on sandy or gravel soils, often in clearings in forested areas. Yuccas of the Great Plains and those of high desert grasslands and the open shrublands of the Colorado Plateau generally are acaulescent or with very short trunks and tolerate cold and drought. The western species occur on gravel, rocky, or sandy soils, in plains and slopes, as well as high desert grasslands. All the deserts of the United States have yuccas, as do the mountain ranges and plateaus along the Mexican border in Arizona, New Mexico, and Texas.

Mexico is a center of diversity for *Yucca* with a wide range of forms. The immense trunked forms occur principally on the dry interior tablelands, deserts, and dry mountains of northern and central Mexico. Several of these large species range further south into the tropical zones of Mexico and Guatemala. Mexico also is the home to two unique species. *Yucca endlichiana* from the deserts of the state of Coahuila has short rigid leaves that emerge directly from the ground to form thick clusters of plants similar in appearance to *Agave lechuguilla*. Another interesting species, *Y. lacandonica,* is from the state of Chiapas, where it grows as a true epiphyte in large trees in the tropical forests.

Hesperaloe

Plants in the genus *Hesperaloe* grow in a stemless rosette, which may be either tightly congested or very loose. All may spread by rhizomes, a characteristic most prominent in *H. parviflora*. Plants are polycarpic but monocarpism may exist, at least occasionally, in the genus.

The leaves of *Hesperaloe* are hard, rigid, and often deeply guttered along their length. They generally are straight, although one species has a slight arch. The leaf margins are smooth, and they have abundant marginal fibers that detach readily from the leaf. There is no terminal spine, but the leaf tip is acute and can be stiff. Leaf color ranges from a dusky dark green to a bright yellow-green.

The stems of *Hesperaloe* rarely are visible, although stem tissue is found at the base of the plants. Plants form short underground rhizomes from which numerous rosettes develop. The roots of *Hesperaloe* are like those of *Agave*. They form radially from the plant and are shallow and very fibrous.

The flowers of *Hesperaloe* are composed of six floral segments, or tepals, which are generally the same length and nearly the same width. The tepals are separate or only slightly united at the base, and in most species they flare open towards their ends. The flower is either campanulate or nearly so. The stamens and pistil are rarely much outside the tepals. Flower color ranges from white and green-white to two-toned with a pink to red exterior and a pink, white, cream, or yellow interior. The flowers are held on a large inflorescence that is either a raceme or a loose, few-branched panicle. The flowers are pollinated by hummingbirds, bees, bats, and hawk moths. The fruit is a capsule with numerous flat, black seeds (Plate 68).

Hesperaloe is distributed in southern Texas and northern Mexico. Plants prefer dry grassland, desert shrublands, and oak-pine forests.

Figure 2-3. Filament styles: (from left to right) regular,
coarse, and curly, *Yucca baccata*; regular, thin, and curly,
Agave filifera; irregular, thin, and curly, *Hesperaloe parviflora*;
irregular, thick, and straight, *Hesperaloe funifera*; irregular,
thin, and straight, *Yucca elata*

Furcraea

Plants in the genus *Furcraea* are large and have the rosette formation typical of the family, in many ways resembling *Agave* vegetatively. Many species are stemless but those that have stems are huge, rising more than 20 ft. (6 m) in the air with spectacular rosettes of leaves held at the very top. Like *Agave* rosettes, those of *Furcraea* are monocarpic and die after blooming.

The leaves of *Furcraea* are large and linear, and are positioned either low on a short stem or on a very tall stem. They are smooth to slightly scabrous, with some leaves having a slightly glossy appearance. The leaf margins have no filaments, but the leaves of most species have marginal teeth, some of which may be large and prominent, or fine, making the leaf margins serrated.

Most species of *Furcraea* grow close to the ground on very short stems or on stems that virtually are invisible. The stems of some species, such as *F. macdougalii,* are spectacular, rising more than 20 ft. (6 m) in the air. They are unbranched and topped with the large rosettes of leaves. When in flower, the inflorescence can stretch the height of the plant to more than 40 ft. (12 m).

The roots of *Furcraea* are similar to those of *Agave.* They form radially from the plant and are shallow and very fibrous.

The flowers of *Furcraea* have characteristics of *Yucca* and *Agave.* The identical tepals are arranged in two rows of three and are fused for at least half their length into a long tube. Like the flowers of *Yucca,* the flowers of *Furcraea* are generally white or sometimes cream at least on the inside but often green on the outside. Also like *Yucca,* the stamens and pistils of *Furcraea* are held within the tepals or barely exserted. The flowers are held in a tall inflorescence that is a loose panicle. Unlike *Agave* flowers, which are held upright, *Furcraea* flowers are pendant, hanging like long-stemmed bells. Pollination biology is not well known in this genus, but considering the floral position and minimal nectar-production, pollination is probably by bees or other insects.

The genus *Furcraea* is found in deciduous tropical forests and open areas from Mexico south to southeastern Brazil and the Caribbean. The greatest concentration occurs in Venezuela and Colombia.

Manfreda

Plants in the genus *Manfreda* form small rosettes that rarely are held on a visible stem. The leaves are quite distinctive: they are very fleshy, brittle, and deeply guttered, and occur in a loose, often floppy rosette. Leaf color varies from dark dull green, light dull green, or a light celadon-green to a blue-green. The leaves of some species and of some populations within a species can have an attractive maroon-colored or dark green-colored mottling. The leaf margins are either smooth or lined with tiny weak teeth, and they lack a terminal spine.

Manfreda species generally are stemless or have a tiny stem that is more of a basal plate at the bottom of the rosette. *Manfreda guttata* has a short, visible stem, but it is the exception in this genus. The roots of *Manfreda* are like those of *Agave*. They form radially from the plant and are shallow and very fibrous.

The flowers of *Manfreda* are a fusion of six tepals with a variable-sized tube between the base of the tepal and the top of the ovary. The ovary is inferior and has three chambers with numerous ovules. Tepals are colored variously from a light green to white and cream. A few species have pink to dark red tepals, and one species has nearly brown tepals. In most species the stamens and pistils are highly exserted from the tepals and are often a bright maroon-red in color. As in *Agave,* the timing of the maturation of the pollen and the maturation of the stigma is staggered, presumably to prevent self-fertilization. Many flowers are fragrant, some delightfully so, but others have a musky or chemical odor. The flowers are held on an inflorescence that is extremely tall for the size of the plant, generally 10 times the height of the plant or more. The inflorescence is a spike or a raceme with a single flower in each node. Pollination is by a host of insects and occasionally birds. Many *Man-*

41

freda species have receptive stigmas at night and are pollinated by hawk moths and similar night-flying insects.

Manfreda occurs in the United States from West Virginia to Missouri and Florida to east and south Texas, in central and eastern Mexico including the Sierra Madre Occidental, and south into Central America. Manfredas can be found in moist forests, prairies, and in desert regions.

Beschorneria

Plants in the genus *Beschorneria* have large rosettes without a stem. Many look like the large tropical members of *Agave* and *Furcraea*. The leaves of *Beschorneria* are very similar to those of *Furcraea* and to several tropical species of *Agave*. The leaves are large, generally sword-shaped, somewhat fleshy, and fibrous. They typically are smooth-margined or have minute teeth and rarely have a terminal spine. Leaf color ranges from a dark glossy green to a pale blue-green.

The stem of *Beschorneria* is visible rarely, although stem tissue is found at the base of the plants. Short rhizomes are formed from which numerous other rosettes develop. The roots of *Beschorneria* are like those of *Agave*. They form radially from the plant and are shallow and very fibrous.

The flowers of *Beschorneria* are tubular with six narrow tepals that usually are bright green in color, but may be partially colored red, purple, or brown in some species. The flowers are borne in pendulous groups on a loose raceme. At the base of each group of flowers are green, red, or purple bracts. Because the plants are polycarpic and create numerous offsets, old plants can be spectacular when flowering.

Beschorneria is found in Mexico and Guatemala especially along the Sierra Madre Occidental. The plants prefer rocky soils in mountainous areas.

Polianthes

Plants in the genus *Polianthes* are small and stemless. They do not form clear rosettes. The leaves of most species are thin and succulent, linear and grasslike. They come to an acute tip but are not sharp-pointed and have no terminal spine. They are glabrous and dark green, although they can have red dots or marks near their base.

Polianthes species are stemless, but in some species the leaf bases unite, forming a bulblike structure. Bulblets form annually around this structure.

The flowers of *Polianthes* have six fused tepals that form a very long, curved tube, which flares and opens at the end. The flowers are white, sometimes red or orange, and often with a strong sweet fragrance. The stamens and style are within the tepals and, like *Agave* and *Manfreda*, the flowering sequence of *Polianthes* is staggered to forestall self-pollination. The flowers appear to be mainly pollinated by night-flying insects.

Polianthes occurs in Mexico from the states of Chihuahua to Michoacán. Species are found in grasslands, oak forests, and wet meadows.

Nolina

Plants in the genus *Nolina* are stemless rosettes with hundreds of leaves, or tall trunked plants. The genus has been separated into four sections based on combinations of fruit, inflorescence, leaf, and other vegetative characteristics. One section contains plants with distinct woody trunks.

The leaves of *Nolina* range in color from light blue-gray to dark olive green. Like leaf color in most members of both families, the leaf color of *Nolina* is quite variable, depending on cultural and environmental conditions and on age of the plant. As is typical for the family, the individual leaves are long, linear, and pliable, and held in multiple, occasionally single, rosettes. The leaves have very small teeth, which virtually are invisible to the naked eye, but create a distinct edge that can be felt if a hand is run along the leaf margin. Although marginal leaf fibers are uncommon in the genus, *Nolina bigelovii* has brown to tan fibers, a characteristic that separates it from other species in the genus.

Several *Nolina* species are arborescent with trunks that can be up to 15 ft. (4.6 m) tall. These trunks are unbranched until the very top, where one to several branches can result in multiple heads of leaves. In the stemless species of *Nolina*, bundles of long linear leaves arise from the base of the plant. The plants increase in diameter by developing new bundles of leaves. Some stemless species of *Nolina*, including the three native to the southeastern United States, produce grassy leaves from a bulb-like structure.

Flowers are tiny, dioecious, and cream-colored. The loosely paniculate inflorescence bears thousands of them. The ovary is three-celled and produces a two-seeded or three-seeded fruit. The fruits are small but often numerous, and they generally dehisce at maturity.

Nolina is the most widespread genus in the Nolinaceae. Species occur in the South Atlantic states and the southwestern United States, and in large parts of Mexico. The habitats of the plants vary from tropical deciduous forests, open dry woodlands, shrublands, and open grassland areas to the very dry Mohave Desert.

Dasylirion

Most species of *Dasylirion* are stemless or have a very short trunk usually no more than 3–5 ft. (1–1.5 m) tall with the plant appearing low and shrublike. One species, *D. quadrangulatum*, has a trunk to 17 ft. (5 m) tall. *Dasylirion acrotriche* commonly forms a short trunk as can other species when very old. In many cases a long shag of dead leaves helps prop up the short trunks that tend to recline in old age.

The leaves of *Dasylirion* are long, linear, and pliable, ranging in color from yellow-green to dark glossy green or blue-gray. The leaf margin is lined with large, hooked teeth, except in *D.*

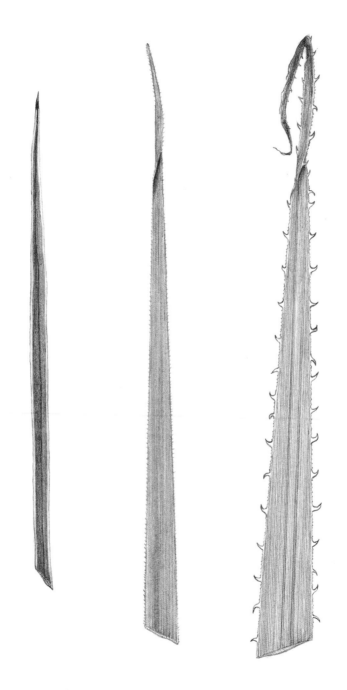

Figure 2-4. Leaf comparison: (left) smooth margin, *Yucca rostrata*;
(center) finely toothed or serrulate, *Nolina nelsoni*;
(right) toothed margin, *Dasylirion wheeleri*

quadrangulatum, which has tiny, straight teeth. It is common for the direction of the hook to be toward the end of the leaf, but in *D. leiophyllum* the teeth are curved towards the base. The teeth usually are yellow to brown and small. Between the large teeth are minute ones, nearly invisible to the naked eye, that form a serrated edge.

The inflorescence is narrow and dense with small finger-like branches called fascicles. Thousands of tiny cream-colored flowers are borne on a single inflorescence with male and female flowers on separate plants. The fruits of *Dasylirion* are pale yellow to cream and have three wings, with one, occasionally two, seeds. The wings presumably assist in wind dispersal of the seed.

Dasylirion is distributed in Texas, New Mexico, and Arizona and throughout much of northern and central Mexico as far south as Oaxaca. Plants occur on rocky or gravel slopes and cliff sides where soil drainage is extremely good. In higher and moister environments they occur in grasslands and open woodlands, including oak and pine forests at very high elevations.

Beaucarnea

Beaucarnea is an arborescent genus with all its species developing woody trunks. The leaves are very similar in appearance to those of *Nolina*—long and linear. The teeth, however, are very small and create a distinct edge that can be felt when a hand is run along the leaf margin. The number and size of the teeth vary.

A variety of stem types and branching arise from a swollen base. Some *Beaucarnea* species have many small twisting and branching stems, while others have a few, thicker and relatively straight branches. The trunks develop a large swollen woody caudex at their base. The size, shape, and bark of the caudex vary with species and their habitats. Species from more arid and inland climates often have very wide caudexes. Plants from more coastal and generally moister environments have narrower caudexes.

Figure 2-5. Flower and inflorescence, *Beaucarnea recurvata*

The inflorescence is a short-stalked, multibranched panicle. The flowers are tiny, white, and campanulate or rounded. Each inflorescence bears thousands of flowers. Male and female flowers occur on separate plants. In some species the young fruit is red and can make an extremely attractive display. The mature fruit has three wings, presumably for wind dispersal. The seed is red to brown and rounded with three irregular lobes.

The genus *Beaucarnea* is distributed only in Mexico and Guatemala. The plants are found primarily on steep, rocky slopes in tropical deciduous forests. A few species are found in drier habitats with *Agave* and *Yucca.*

Calibanus

Calibanus is a monotypic genus and perhaps the most unusual member of the Nolinaceae. The leaves have teeth so small and scattered that the leaf edge feels merely rough. No stem is present; the leaves emerge directly from the woody caudex. The leaves occur in bundles and are long, coarse, and linear, which gives the plant a most unusual appearance, especially when old. The flowers are small and purplish, and are held on a branched panicle that arises from the tuft of leaves. The small tuft dies after blooming. *Calibanus* has had little reported on its natural habitat and distribution other than that it occurs in dry mountains in north central Mexico.

CHAPTER 3

Horticulture and Cultivation

Members of the Agavaceae and the Nolinaceae have been in cultivation for centuries, some arriving in European gardens with the first explorers of the Americas. An even longer history exists of cultivation and ethnobotanical use in Mexico, Central America, and the Caribbean islands. Despite this long interest in the plants, very little explicit cultural information has been published. This chapter will address the history of cultivation and offer detailed cultural information based on our personal experience, that of other gardeners, and published sources.

Ornamental History

No clear record indicates whether plants in the Agavaceae were used ornamentally in Mexico or elsewhere in the Americas before the Spanish conquest of 1521. *Polianthes tuberosa* is the one exception with clear evidence that it was grown by the Aztecs for ornament and its fragrance. While Mexico, and in particular the area around Mexico City, was full of exquisite, carefully planted gardens at the time of the conquest, the exact composition of those gardens is unknown. Europeans, however, were enchanted with these plants, as well as so many others from the New World, and brought back species of *Agave*, *Yucca*, and *Furcraea* almost immediately upon reaching the Americas. The plants quickly began to be grown in all important gardens of Europe early in the sixteenth century. The distinct nature of these plants, with long rigid leaves rising on few or many stems, so different in shape and form from anything previously known, must have intrigued early European horticulturists.

Clusius, a Belgian botanist, provides the first tangible record of European *Agave* cultivation in 1576 with a drawing of a plant that he had received as an offset from a plant growing in Spain. The plant was probably *Agave americana.* Another drawing, by Jacapo Ligozzi, was painted shortly thereafter and records a flowering individual of *Agave americana* in Florence, Italy.

As the East Coast of the American colonies and the Caribbean basin began to be explored and settled, *Yucca* species native to those areas began to appear in European collections. The sixteenth-century gardens of the famous English plantsmen John Gerard and John Parkinson, as well the gardens of John Tradescant and his son John, both royal gardeners, contained yuccas, especially *Y. filamentosa.* The first yucca flowering was recorded in England in 1604 in the garden of William Coys. By 1605 *Y. aloifolia* also had appeared in garden records, and by 1620 it was reported to have bloomed in the Vatican gardens. Drawings of the Villa Pia at the Vatican gardens in 1736 clearly show agaves in the large urn pots. In photographs of the same garden in subsequent centuries the planters still are occupied by agaves.

In North America the extent to which these plants were used in early horticulture is not well known. Thomas Jefferson was interested in the group and many other native plants. His 1794 plant list for the garden at Monticello includes *Yucca filamentosa,* which he called bear grass, and *Manfreda virginica,* the Virginia aloe.

As England began to play a greater role in the exploration of the Americas, English gardeners began to grow agaves as well. The records of the garden at Cliff House in Salcombe detail what is probably the first bloom of an agave in England. The plant was *Agave americana* and was known to be 28 years old at the time of its blooming in 1774. Subsequent agave blooming was recorded over the next 50 years at this garden.

Interest in the agaves and yuccas, especially the agaves, increased as the plants spread. Long known and grown in Mexico for fiber, species such as *Agave angustifolia, A. fourcroydes,* and *A. sisalana* were introduced early to tropical areas such as Indonesia, the Philippines, and Africa for the commercial production of rope and cordage. *Agave fourcroydes* and others were brought into Florida during the late eighteenth century as fiber crops and from there were dispersed widely. *Furcraea foetida* also was introduced into many tropical areas as a fiber crop, and *Furcraea* species appear in early garden records. Most plants listed in seventeenth-century garden catalogs referred to plants of *Furcraea* as belonging to *Agave,* but because *Furcraea* is more tender than most members of the family Agavaceae, its use was limited to the warmest areas of Europe.

The mid to late nineteenth century saw an explosion of interest in the cultivation of many members of the Agavaceae in Mediterranean and English gardens, as well as isolated greenhouse collections in Germany and St. Petersburg. In many cases, particularly in Victorian gardens, the plants were valued highly as fascinating novelties. Italian gardens tended to use them as excellent foliage plants in large containers and to accent the highly stylized evergreen gardens popular at the time. By the end of the century, a hundred or more species of *Agave* alone were known in cultivation, and *Agave* and *Yucca* were listed in every serious gardening book or encyclopedia of the time.

The European desire for exotic plants reached a crescendo in the second half of the nineteenth century as yuccas and many other members of the family Agavaceae and other unusual plants from the Americas, Asia, and Africa streamed into European gardens. By the mid-nineteenth century most yuccas native to the eastern United States were being used in horticulture, although apparently not in great numbers. An article from the *Horticulturalist and Journal of Rural Art and Rural Taste* in 1852 praised the use of yuccas as ornamental subjects: "[T]here are few plants so ornamental as several of the yuccas, and yet we seldom see them employed in any conspicuous way, in our pleasure grounds or flower gardens." The useful evergreen nature of the yuccas for winter gardens also was realized at the time as it was recommended that groups of yuccas be planted to "cheat the season out of its dreariness."

In the late nineteenth century the Royal Botanic Gardens, Kew, sent several botanists to the Riviera to report on the kaleidoscope of exotic plants being imported into those gardens. One of these men, William Watson, reported in 1889 that seven species of *Agave*, four species of *Beschorneria*, six species of *Furcraea*, and six species of *Yucca* were grown commonly in Mediterranean gardens. He found many species in bloom including *Y. whipplei* with hundreds of 3 ft. (1 m) leaves. Watson reported magnificent specimens of *Y. filifera* at Villa Valetta and one at Antibes, France, with a stem 3 ft. (1 m) in diameter and which reportedly flowered every year.

In 1891 John G. Baker toured the Riviera again for the Royal Botanic Gardens, Kew, specifically to study *Agave* and allied genera, as well as what were then known as the arborescent Liliaceae, many of which now are considered in either the Agavaceae or the Nolinaceae. Baker reported that the gardens at La Mortola in Italy and the Jardin d'Acclimatisation at Hyeres on the French coast contained the largest numbers of such plants. Like Watson before him, he found a wide variety of these plants growing on the Riviera. He reported twenty-seven species of *Agave*, two species of *Furcraea*, one species of *Beschorneria*, and eleven species of *Yucca*.

The wealth of these plants inspired early attempts at horticultural development. At La Mortola in Italy, Thomas Hanbury became so interested in the propagation of yuccas that in the 1890s he imported yucca moths to pollinate his plants. Although the experiment was not well documented, the curator of the garden found seed capsules on what he called *Yucca flaccida*. Some capsules had what appeared to be exit holes, presumably of the yucca moth larvae. By 1874 a Mr. Deleuil of Marseilles had made several purposeful crosses of *Yucca*. In Naples another grower, Carl Sprenger, produced many crosses that appeared in his 1901 and 1902 lists.

Members of the Nolinaceae, particularly *Beaucarnea*, were introduced and had much the same history in European gardens as those of the Agavaceae, with many plants being imported in the nineteenth century. By 1861, when Charles Lemaire described *Beaucarnea*, those plants had been growing in Europe for at least 27 years. In the second half of the nineteenth century, plants of *Dasylirion* and *Nolina* began to show up in European conservatories and outdoor gardens on the Mediterranean. As early as 1857 a plant of *D. glaucophyllum* had flowered at the Royal Botanic Gardens, Kew, and by 1911 this species was found in Italian gardens at La Mortola, Palermo, and Naples. During Baker's visit to the Riviera in 1891, he found three species of *Dasylirion* growing commonly in the gardens there and a particularly large specimen of *Beaucarnea recurvata* at San Remo, the trunk of which was 6 ft. (1.8 m) in diameter at the base. He also recorded *Nolina longifolia*, which later was seen in flower in Genoa.

Modern-day Italian gardens and other Mediterranean gardens still grow a significant number of species from both families. The Orto Botanico in Florence, Italy, grows at least 29 species of *Agave* today, mainly in containers outdoors, and the Orto Botanico of Padua has at least 23 species under similar culture. Various species of *Beaucarnea, Dasylirion,* and *Yucca* still are found commonly throughout the region. *Beschorneria* grows in all the warmest parts of Europe including the Italian Lakes region and into the warmest parts of Switzerland including the incomparable Lake Como region.

Like their European counterparts, American gardeners were not immune to the pleasure of gardening with these plants in the late nineteenth century and began to become more acquainted with all members of both families, particularly *Agave* and *Yucca*. Gardening catalogs and encyclopedias of the time give a clue to how many were known, although it is harder to know how popular or common they were. By the time William Trelease produced his landmark work entitled *The Yuccae* in 1902, many horticultural selections of yuccas native to the eastern United States were known. Trelease listed several selected varieties and garden cultivars of *Yucca aloifolia, Y. filamentosa, Y. gloriosa,* and *Y. recurvifolia*.

In the United States almost all records of the Nolinaceae

occur after the turn of the twentieth century. Individuals of *Beaucarnea recurvata* at the Huntington Botanical Gardens in San Marino, California, date from before 1920. The genus *Beaucarnea* was reported from gardens in the warm parts of Florida in the first half of the twentieth century. In 1913 Liberty Hyde Bailey set out to catalog and describe what were the known plants of horticulture at the time. His monumental *Cyclopedia of Horticulture* listed 150 species of *Agave* with cultural notations and identifications. Of these, 48 still are recognized as species. Most of the rest became varieties or were subsumed into other taxa. Other members of the family were well known as well: 28 species of *Yucca*, of which 11 still are recognized, 6 species of *Manfreda*, and 9 species of *Furcraea*. In the Nolinaceae, 6 species of *Dasylirion* were known, one of *Nolina*, and 4 of *Beaucarnea* (although Bailey considered these to be in *Nolina*).

Agaves and related plants and members of the Nolinaceae, with the possible exception of potted *Beaucarnea recurvata* and various smaller yuccas, fell somewhat out of favor as the twentieth century progressed and American gardeners turned increasingly to voluminous color displays and the delights of perennial gardens. Ironically, two of the best collections in the United States of many of these plants were built from 1920 to 1980, one in southern California at Huntington Botanical Gardens and the other in Phoenix, Arizona, at the Desert Botanical Garden. At present the Desert Botanical Garden has 235 taxa in the Agavaceae and 21 in the Nolinaceae. The collection at the Huntington Botanical Gardens is even more extensive with 492 taxa in the Agavaceae and 45 in the Nolinaceae. The Missouri Botanical Garden in St. Louis has long held very important agave, yucca, and other related collections, mainly as herbarium specimens from early explorers and collectors, but because of its climate it is unable to display living collections more thoroughly.

In coastal California gardeners maintained a strong interest in agaves throughout the century chiefly because of the Mediterranean climate that is so amenable to outdoor cultivation of the plants. *Agave attenuata* is nearly wild in the Los Angeles area, maintaining itself in derelict homes and vacant lots. *Agave americana*, *A. angustifolia*, and *A. salmiana* are found throughout the coastal region as are *Yucca elephantipes*, *Y. gloriosa*, *Y. recurvifolia*, *Beaucarnea recurvata*, and *Furcraea foetida*.

In the later part of the twentieth century, as American gardeners began to turn increasingly to native plants and plants with characteristics suitable for a given region, interest in agaves, yuccas, and their relatives increased dramatically. In the arid West, particularly in cities such as Phoenix, Tucson, and Las Vegas, the need for high water conservation in the choice of ornamental plants and the work of interested growers have united to build a wider base of agaves, yuccas, dasylirions, and nolinas in cultivation. Today, in the most arid parts of the West, native agaves, such as *Agave deserti*, *A. lechuguilla*, *A. lophantha*, *A. murpheyi*, *A. neomexicana*, and *A. parryi*, are being used throughout the region. This increase in availability mirrors the population growth of the southwestern states, as well as an increased interest in using agaves and other native plants.

Although many *Yucca* species have been known to collectors and specialty growers for more than 100 years, these plants only became widely available to the gardening public in the twentieth century. Today a large proportion of the yuccas native to the United States are being propagated and offered for sale, including *Y. baccata*, *Y. elata*, *Y. rostrata*, *Y. torreyi*, *Y. treculeana*, and *Y. whipplei*. *Dasylirion* species, particularly *D. texanum* and *D. wheeleri*, also have become very popular in modern landscapes, and *D. acrotriche* and *D. leiophyllum* are increasing in use. Many species of *Nolina* have become more available in recent years, particularly *N. microcarpa*, *N. parryi*, and *N. texana*.

Economic and Ornamental Distribution

As agricultural crops for fiber production, *Agave* species are found in Africa, especially Tanzania, parts of Indonesia and the Philippines, and other tropical areas such as Mexico and the Caribbean. None of the other genera, save a small number of

Furcraea species, enjoy success as a significant agricultural fiber crop. Recent research indicates, however, that *Hesperaloe funifera* may have good potential for agriculture production of fiber in arid areas. Some plantings of yucca for fiber production have been made in Mexico.

Polianthes species are grown in Mexico and other tropical regions for their cut flowers and in France as an ingredient in the making of perfumes. A tiny interest in the chemical properties of some species of *Agave* for medical research is emerging. Future agricultural and other economic uses will probably continue to develop over time as more research is expended to search for drought-adapted crops and viable economic activities in arid lands.

As ornamentals, the members of the Agavaceae and the Nolinaceae have drawn attention from gardeners since the first introduction to European gardens in the sixteenth century. *Agave* species are grown throughout the world as ornamental plants as are many species of *Yucca*. Many Mediterranean and tropical gardens are graced by species of *Furcraea* and *Beschorneria*, although they seem to be less common in the United States. Even though most *Manfreda* species still are uncommon anywhere, *M. virginica* has been grown since the eighteenth century in North America and is today most common in southern gardens. The tuberose, *Polianthes tuberosa*, is grown in gardens throughout the world both for its lovely flowers and its luscious fragrance.

Except for *Beaucarnea recurvata*, which is grown in warm climates worldwide, and a few species of *Dasylirion*, members of the Nolinaceae are infrequently used in gardens. Along the Mediterranean coast of Europe and coastal California, some species are evident, but never in large numbers. In the desert climates of the southwestern United States, *D. wheeleri* has become a very popular landscape plant in recent years. Many species of *Dasylirion* and *Nolina* can no doubt be grown in more humid climates. Successful cultivation of plants in England and North Carolina has shown that, given good soil conditions, the ornamental range of many plants in the Nolinaceae can be extended beyond what it is thought to be today.

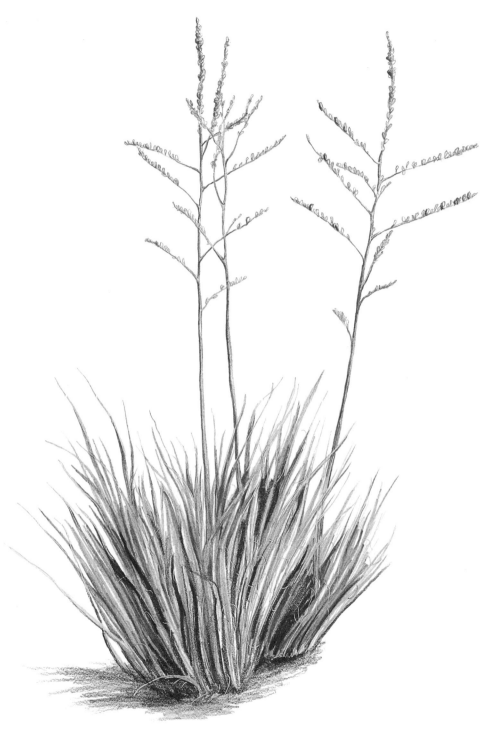

Figure 3-1. *Hesperaloe funifera*

Figure 3-2. *Dasylirion wheeleri*

Ethnobotany

Members of the Agavaceae and the Nolinaceae have provided a long and varied list of useful products for the peoples who have lived alongside them for a very long time. Archaeological records indicate that *Agave* species have been used for fiber since 7000 B.C. Cultivation of various agaves, presumably for fiber but possibly for food as well, is thought to have occurred since at least 5000 B.C. Agaves, yuccas, and their near relatives have been used for making cloth, sandals, rope, straps, fishnets, cradle lashings, rope ladders, baskets, sleeping mats, brushes and brooms, medicine, food, soap, beverages, and building materials. Every part of the agave plant and the yucca plant has been used by one or another of the various peoples who lived alongside them, both historically and in the present day.

The primary use of agaves and yuccas is for fiber, which is strong but flexible. Although fibers along the leaf margins are common in many species, the usable fiber is hidden inside the leaf. It is extracted by roasting or boiling the leaf to break it down, then soaking it to separate the fibers, and finally washing and drying the resulting fiber.

The finest agave fibers come from leaves still in bud. Weaving with this type of agave fiber is practiced still in parts of Mexico today, and items made from it are extremely pliable and smooth. The fiber can be woven so tightly and small that it will roll like cloth. Less fine fibers are used, particularly in northwestern Mexico, for widely woven bags and mats.

Some agaves were cultivated for their fiber and possibly for food when the Spanish explored Mexico. *Agave fourcroydes*, known as henequen, is grown in the Mexican state of Yucatán and the Caribbean islands for commercial fiber, as are species of *Furcraea*. Henequen represents a small fraction of the long fiber of this type grown in the world. By far the largest percentage of this type of fiber comes from *A. sisalana*, which is grown in East Africa, Asia, and Brazil. Both of these *Agave* species are sterile hybrids that probably originated as selections by local farmers in Mexico long before the Spanish arrived.

Like *Agave* species, some *Furcraea* species such as *F. ca-*

buya and *F. hexapetala* have been used as agricultural crops for fiber production. The best-known species for fiber production is *F. foetida,* commonly called the Mauritius hemp, as it is cultivated on the island of Mauritius in the Indian Ocean. The plant also is grown in other tropical climates throughout the world because it is better suited to moist tropical climates than are many commercial fiber-producing agaves.

The entire leaf of many *Yucca* species is cut into fine or wide strips and worked into baskets. In fact, baskets of exceptional quality still are made from split yucca leaves in Mexico and the southwestern United States. To provide distinctive red accents, the small roots of yuccas such as *Yucca brevifolia,* Joshua tree, and *Y. baccata,* banana yucca, are incorporated into the basket. Yucca leaves were used also as thatch for shelters created with yucca trunks. The end of a fresh or dried leaf can be chewed or pounded with a rock to fashion a paint brush with which to decorate pottery and other implements.

European settlers from the Spanish in Mexico to the English in North America learned many of these techniques and put agave and yucca leaves to use for their own products. Rope and twine were made from the fibers, and in the southeastern United States the leaves of several *Yucca* species were used to weave chair seats and to make cord from which to hang meat. In the 1890s Messrs. Densmore, Means, and Fleming operated a factory in Los Angeles where medical splints were made from the trunks of the Joshua tree. The wood was ideal: it was light, pliable, and extremely sturdy, and allowed considerable air circulation. Thin sheets of the product could be cut with scissors to custom fit a splint. These same sheets also were used in the manufacture of bookcovers. In the early twentieth century there was an abortive attempt at large-scale paper production from the leaf fiber of Joshua tree. Handmade paper from yucca fiber is produced still and is of exceptional quality. In 1936, in response to increased pressure on these yucca populations and to protect some of the most spectacular stands of the plant, President Franklin Roosevelt created Joshua Tree National Monument, now Joshua Tree National Park. It is one of the few American national parks created primarily to preserve an individual plant species.

Agaves and yuccas have been an important food source for thousands of years in Mexico and the southwestern United States. The evidence is ample, particularly in Arizona, that agaves were cultivated for food. The remains of roasted plants are found in sites as old as 1000 A.D. *Agave murpheyi* is found in Arizona only with archaeological sites that include roasting pits and rock walls. The walls formed terraces on which agaves could be cultivated on the steep hillsides. Agaves still are eaten infrequently in parts of their range. The entire plant is harvested, the leaves cut away to the base, and the resulting large cabeza or head is roasted by laying hot stones or coals in a bed at the bottom of the pit, and covering it all with dirt and brush. The roasting can take days depending on how many heads are roasted and how large they are. Once done this delicate and sweet food is eaten right away or pounded into a cake and dried for storage.

The fruit of the banana yucca, *Yucca baccata*, named for its large fleshy pod, was used extensively by the Navajo, Hopi, Apache, and other peoples of the American Southwest for food. The fruit was eaten raw or cooked down into a conserve that makes a fine beverage sweetener. The fruit also was dried and stored for future consumption or roasted and ground into small cakes for winter food. In the Chihuahuan desert region, fruits of several species were fermented into an intoxicating beverage.

The flowers and buds of *Agave, Beschorneria,* and *Yucca* are eaten either raw or cooked with other foods, particularly with eggs. European settlers in the southeastern United States cooked yucca flowers like cabbage and sometimes even pickled them. Yucca flowers of certain Mexican species have been canned and sold commercially. Yucca flowering stalks are reported to have been roasted, peeled, and eaten like sugar cane. In addition, cooked stalks were ground into a pulp for making cakes.

Agaves have been used for centuries to obtain various types of beverages. The Aztec culture of central Mexico knew how to make the alcoholic beverage pulque and used it extensively in daily life and as a necessary component of a variety of religious and ceremonial activities. Pulque was so important that its production and use, at least in the city, were controlled tightly and the penalties for abuse were severe. It is still made today in a limited region of central Mexico. This fermented beverage is made by finding the agave just before it is ready to bloom and cutting out the central portion where the stalk is forming. The timing is important, and those who can identify the exact moment possess a respected skill. The wound is allowed to heal over and sit for up to a year as the plant continues the physiological transformation of carbohydrates to sugars that was begun by the onset of blooming. After this time has elapsed, the agave is reopened and the ensuing liquid is drained from the plant. Known as aquamiel, this liquid is sweet and in some plants is reputed to be very tasty. It is a valued beverage in some remote parts of arid Mexico where water is very scarce or intermittently available. When aquamiel is fermented, it becomes pulque, which is mildly alcoholic. Often herbs are added to flavor the product and to increase its potency. Pulque is made from a selected number of species, principally (listed in their order of importance) *Agave salmiana* and *A. mapisaga*, but also *A. atrovirens*, *A. hookeri*, and *A. americana*.

The Spanish brought the process of distillation to the highlands of Mexico, and over the centuries a significant industry in a distilled agave beverage, known as mescal, has flourished. Mescal is made by taking the head of the agave minus the leaves, cooking and chopping it to a mash, then fermenting it, and finally distilling the liquid. In the state of Jalisco, near the town of Tequila, this process is so well developed and the plants used are so closely kept secret that, like the name of certain French wines, the name tequila for this product is restricted by law to only mescal made in this area. Plants used for tequila are selected clones of *Agave tequilana*, but mescal can be made from a host of other species including *A. angustifolia*, *A. palmeri*, *A. potatorum*, *A. shrevei*, *A. weberi*, and *A. zebra*.

The roots and stems of several species of *Agave*, *Beschorneria*, *Manfreda*, and *Yucca* contain a mucilaginous substance high in saponin, which is a laxative and a soap. In Spanish the word *amole* is used for plants, regardless of genus, that are used to make soap. The process is the same regardless of the type of plant. Roots are used either fresh or dried and are soaked and pounded with water until lather forms. The resulting soap was used to clean anything, but particularly hair and fiber. Yucca soap is prized especially for its ability to give black hair a deep, glossy sheen. In the Pueblo cultures of northern New Mexico hair washing with yucca soap often precedes ceremonial dances. The English common names soaptree yucca and soapweed, for *Y. elata* and *Y. glauca*, respectively, are derived from this use.

There are other specialized uses for these plants. The trunks of tall species such as *Yucca valida* or *Y. filifera* were used in the past as palisades to control cattle. Numerous *Agave* species have been used and still are today in Mexico as fences or borders for fields. In hard times yucca trunks are split open so cattle can eat the soft, pulpy interior. Agave leaves and flowering stalks often are used as cattle food, especially in the arid parts of northern Mexico. Yucca leaves have been used in the United States as cattle feed. Early in the twentieth century, whole plants of *Yucca elata* and *Y. glauca* were chopped and ground, sometimes mixed with cottonseed meal, and fed to starving cattle. For a short time, this practice was so extensive that machines were manufactured with whimsical names such as "The Ideal Yucca Chopper" and the "Krack Jack S. S. Cutter" to assist ranchers in the tasks of chopping and grinding.

Plants in the Nolinaceae have had many of the same traditional uses as those of the Agavaceae. Native peoples and early settlers in the areas where these plants grow wild made good use of the fibrous linear leaves for a variety of purposes. The leaves of *Nolina* were used as thatching for small shelters and for making brooms, baskets, hats, and mats. In northeastern Mexico the long straight leaves of *Dasylirion quadrangulatum* were used as thatching for small houses.

Fibers were extracted by the same method as for agave and yucca fiber and used mainly for cordage. Fiber from *Dasylirion* also was used to create rope and sandals. Some of these articles, such as mats and baskets, still are manufactured today in northwestern Mexico for local use and for sale in the tourist trade. Entire leaves of *Dasylirion* are used extensively for the creation of mats, baskets, toy dolls, and paintbrushes. In rural Mexico, leaves and leaf bases are used in a folk art tradition known as the "flor de sotol." In this art, the leaves are wrapped around a circle of string to create a variety of multipointed ornaments. The ends of the leaves radiate either inward or outward from the circle, similar to the idealized rays of the sun. These "flor de sotol" pieces are used to decorate poles, crucifixes, arches near churches, graves, and cemeteries.

It probably is safe to assume that the long fibrous leaves of *Beaucarnea* species were used for thatching, making baskets, and other similar uses, but such use is poorly documented. It has been documented that the leaves of *Calibanus hookeri* have been used as thatching and scouring materials.

Parts of *Dasylirion* species have been used in the construction of shelters. The Apache used the strong but flexible dried flowering stalks as framing elements, which were lashed together at the top to create the rounded, conical form of a wickiup. The wickiup then was covered with leafy branches and hides.

The trunks of some species such as *Nolina matapensis* sometimes were used as building posts. Some trunks also were roasted and eaten, and the Apache roasted and ate young flowering stalks of nolinas. In other locations the flower and fruit of various *Nolina* species are reported to have been used as food, and the roots of *N. palmeri* reportedly have been used as a substitute for soap, similar to such uses for several species in the Agavaceae.

The large tender crowns of *Dasylirion* species were prepared as food in exactly the same manner as agaves by removing the leaves and burying the head in a pit of hot rocks and coals, which is then covered by brush and dirt. New flowering stalks were baked on coals to create a succulent dish. The stalks also were crushed and mixed with water to create a fresh beverage that was allowed to ferment, creating a wine. After distillation became known, a distilled liquor made from dasylirions, known as sotol, began to be manufactured. The liquor often is mixed with herbs and used as a medicinal potion to treat symptoms of flu and colds.

Just as with agaves and yuccas, during times of drought, dasylirions were used as supplemental cattle feed. The tender leaf bases are fed to cattle and sheep, and the trunks often are split open to allow animals to consume the tender interior parts.

Planting

For virtually all members of the Agavaceae and the Nolinaceae the timing and techniques of planting are the same. Tropical members of any of the genera and all species of *Furcraea* do not tolerate freezing temperatures and probably cannot be grown out of pots in cold winter climates. Where winters are cold and freezing temperatures are common, these individuals should be planted in the spring as the weather begins to warm. Because all the species grow in moderate to warm weather, a spring planting begins root growth in sufficient time to establish the plant before the next cold winter.

In Mediterranean climates where winters are very mild with very few freezing events, the timing of planting is not as critical. Care must be taken, however, that the plants are watered sufficiently during the dry summer to ensure that the root system becomes established.

In mild winter climates that have hot summers, particularly hot and dry summers, fall planting is best, so that root systems establish through the mild winter before the onset of the stressful summer season. If planted in early spring, plants must be carefully watered and shaded from the sun during the summer to prevent sunburn and debilitating heat stress.

All these plants need a well-drained soil for best performance and to insure that roots do not rot when the weather is cold and damp. The species of *Yucca* native to the eastern United States are more tolerant of damp soils, but still do best with excellent drainage. Species of *Yucca* from the Great Plains, such as *Y. glauca*, have been shown to perform well in cold, wet, tighter soils. Specific species that can be grown outdoors in colder climates are noted in the profiles.

Many species, particularly of *Agave, Hesperaloe,* and *Yucca,* are native to very arid areas with rocky, often mineralized soils. These plants can be easily rotted by the addition of too much organic matter or too much clay in the soil. The infrequent addition of small amounts of compost or other organic amendment can help open up a very tight soil. In areas with very poor drainage or very tight soils, it is advisable to locate these plants in a raised bed or up on a short berm or mound to improve the drainage. Amendment of poorly drained soils with gravel, sand, or crushed bricks improves drainage and maximizes success in cool, humid climates.

Proof is ample that many species in the Agavaceae and the Nolinaceae can be grown in cool or humid climates if proper care for their growing conditions is taken. Successful planting from such disparate but humid climates as coastal British Columbia, North Carolina, Massachusetts, England, and the Netherlands indicates that many species can be grown successfully well outside their native ranges if soil conditions are good and the plants have sufficient cold tolerance. It cannot be assumed, however, that all cold-tolerant species will survive and prosper in cool damp climates even if soils and drainage are improved. More species will need to be used and evaluated to create a clear picture of growing these plants in such climates.

Planting techniques should take into account characteristics of the plants and their needs. When planting agaves, regardless of the soil type, raise the center of the hole slightly, just an inch (2.5 cm) or so, and plant the center of the plant at the top. The crown of the agave particularly is susceptible to infections and, when the soil inevitably subsides after planting, the crown can sink below the soil line. The practice of raising the center of the planting hole slightly is helpful in all the stemless members of both families to prevent crown rots.

For all plants, begin by digging a shallow hole no more than the depth of the root system and four to five times wider than the container in which it is growing. The roots of agaves can be significantly pruned when planted. A good general rule of thumb for how much to prune is to hold the roots in your hand like a flower bouquet and then prune at the bottom of your hand. The roots of most other plants in these families are not pruned as easily and much more care should be taken with the roots to avoid damage, breakage, and future rotting problems.

Backfill the planting hole without soil amendments or with a very small amount of compost. Tamp the soil lightly as it is backfilled to prevent excessive settling later. In very dry climates create a small berm around the plant for holding water. This berm allows water to be applied directly to the root zone and to percolate slowly into the soil. Soil amendments or fertilizer at the time of planting are unneccssary. Most of these species, particularly the most drought-adapted species, rarely need fertilizer when planted in the ground. A light enrichment of the soil once or twice a year is sufficient. Yuccas from the eastern United States can tolerate much richer conditions, as can *Polianthes* species and some *Manfreda* species.

When planted in very hot summer areas, agaves, furcraeas, manfredas, and yuccas often benefit from a mulch of rocks or stones. The rocks need not be small or cover the ground entirely. One or two well-placed rocks can cool the soil at the root zone sufficiently and hold a tiny amount of moisture, which is beneficial to the plant in the hottest part of summer. Organic mulches can create problems for these plants unless used carefully. Straw, leaves, and other organic mulch can hold too much moisture for many species, and the mulch can easily work into the crown of the plant where it encourages rot.

Agaves and other low stemless plants in the Agavaceae and the Nolinaceae that are grown under trees, particularly the leguminous trees of the desert, catch and hold the tiny leaves, flowers, and pods of the trees. This debris should be removed regularly and kept to a minimum. Otherwise it decomposes and rots right on the surface of the leaf, causing lesions of dead tissue and infection that can lead ultimately to the death of the plant.

Moving agaves from one site to another requires no special techniques. Simply remove the plant from one location, dig a hole, and put it in another. If the new location is much sunnier than the previous location, artificial shade should be provided to prevent sunburn during the first summer. Agaves benefit from having their roots dry out for a week or so between plant-ings, but even that precaution is not absolutely necessary. On the other hand, if required, bare-root agaves can be left dry and in the shade for weeks or even months between plantings with no ill effects.

Moving mature arborescent plants, such as some members of *Beaucarnea, Furcraea, Nolina,* or *Yucca,* is more difficult. These large plants are sensitive to root and stem disturbance, and wounds of the basal growing platform in *Yucca* can intro-duce a host of infectious agents into the plant. If possible, it is much more advisable to move such plants when they are young and nearly stemless. All other stemless plants of either family move readily, although *Dasylirion* species can be hard to es-tablish when moved in warm weather. Plants tend to rot easily with watering, yet watering is necessary to reestablish the root system. Moving dasylirions in cooler weather, but not cold, usually helps maximize their chances of survival.

Watering

Watering agaves depends on the temperatures and light condi-tions under which the plants are growing. As a general guide, agaves grow when it is warm, but rarely when it is very hot, over 106°F (41°C), and rarely when it is cold. Because they are succulent and able to store water for future use, they should not be overwatered, especially when the plants are dormant. Cool, damp soils host several diseases that rot agave and, per-versely for gardeners, so do hot, moist soils. Agaves that come from extremely xeric conditions are particularly susceptible to overwatering during their "off" season. Tropical agaves and most of the larger cultivated species tend to accept much more water than one would expect as long as drainage is very sharp.

As is true for all desert plants, and perhaps all plants, it is a poor practice to water agaves in the ground frequently with a small amount of water. It is better to water them well. If a plant is in a basin, fill up the basin. Otherwise, water agaves twice a month if the weather is hot, and let the water percolate slowly into the soil. In moderate climates or during the spring and fall in the hot desert climates, watering every three weeks generally is sufficient. In the hot deserts, water every 10 days in the summer, more frequently if it is very hot. Agaves are better kept quite dry when it is cold regardless of the climate.

Agaves signal water stress by having a wrinkled or withered appearance on the surface of the leaf. Leaves that fall or flop often indicate much more serious problems, or such extreme water stress that one needs to act immediately. Wrinkling will correct with a good watering.

Drip irrigation often is used for watering in desert regions. It is a good practice for watering agaves if there are adequate drip emitters to reach all around the plant and the station timing can be adjusted to meet the low water use requirements of these plants. If automated watering cannot be adjusted to infrequent application because of other plants on an irrigation system, agaves are watered best by hand when they need it. Agaves in a dense perennial planting need never have a dedicated dripper, as there is plenty of soil moisture in the vicinity.

Infrequent overhead watering of agaves can be successful, but if the water is too strong, it causes pits on the surface of the leaf. This mechanical damage is most extreme on soft-leaved agaves and generally is cosmetic, but every opening is an opportunity for bacteria, fungi, or viruses to enter the plant. In addition, in areas with very salty or mineral water, salt deposits can accumulate on the leaf, causing a wound that looks like burn on the surface of the leaf or discoloration of the leaf.

Watering of yuccas, likewise, is dependent on the local climate and the individual species. In humid and rainy climates, such as the eastern United States, most yuccas can survive on natural rainfall. New plantings should be watered during the warm summer months to ensure establishment if rain does not occur regularly. In semi-arid areas, in higher elevation areas, such as much of the western United States, and in cool coastal areas with dry Mediterranean climates, yuccas rarely need more than just occasional watering in the driest periods to help insure the health and vigor of the plants. When summer drought is extensive, as can occur in Mediterranean climates, watering every two to three weeks is necessary to maintain a healthy plant. Again, new plants need to be watered more often until they are established fully. In the driest and warmest desert climates, supplemental watering of yuccas not only maintains their health, but may be necessary for their survival. Such watering is important particularly for yuccas that are native to rainier areas, but even the most drought-adapted species benefit from at least intermittent watering in the summer.

Beschorneria, Furcraea, and *Manfreda* species need regular summer irrigation in the hot desert regions. In addition, it is best to plant them in light but constant shade and to provide some organic or inorganic mulch. All of them easily accept watering every four to six days in summer, but can go for up to three weeks between watering in cooler temperatures. In more moderate summer temperatures, water much less often, one to three times a month, depending on the temperatures.

Plants of the Nolinaceae naturally are tolerant of dry conditions and, if planted in rainy climates, they need little or no supplemental irrigation once they are established. In the hot, dry low desert, supplemental water is needed about every 10 days in summer, but care should be taken to insure that the plants dry out between irrigations. Hot and damp soils for long periods of time encourage root rots in these species. In milder climates and in Mediterranean climates little supplemental water is needed once the plants are established. If summer drought is particularly long or severe, provide water once a month to insure health and continued growth.

Supplemental irrigation for plants in both families is best done by hand and only when needed. In the low desert, plants can be placed on automated drip systems but the station must be dedicated to plants of this type to avoid severe overwatering and to assure soils dry out between irrigations. Particular care should be taken with these plants to insure that irrigation or rainwater does not stand near any woody bases, increasing chances of bacterial or fungal infection to the plants.

Containers

A relatively small root system, a great tolerance of root crowding, and the stunning variety in both families make these species excellent candidates for container culture. Many of these plants have a strong sculptural or symmetrical form that is compatible near buildings and in courtyards. Potted plants create a distinct and sometimes even dramatic accent in a planted landscape, often adding an exotic, tropical touch to a garden. Container plants often are desirable around pools because the litter is reduced greatly.

Various species work well in containers. Very small species, such as *Agave parviflora, A. pygmae, Manfreda maculosa,* or *Yucca pallida,* can be featured and enjoyed closely in a container, and larger species, such as *Agave desmettiana, A. vilmoriniana, Yucca filamentosa, Y. rostrata* (Plate 93), *Beaucarnea recurvata,* or various species of *Furcraea* (Plate 61) and *Beschorneria,* can make dramatic focal points in pots. *Calibanus hookeri* is among the best species for containers. Its small size, enlarged base, and upright or slightly arching linear leaves make it an interesting and well-behaved container plant. *Beaucarnea recurvata* and *Yucca elephantipes* are ubiquitous container plants with their tolerance of the dry and dusty conditions of indoor culture. All plants in the two families should be slightly underpotted to insure that soil does not stay moist constantly and can dry out between waterings.

Soil for container plants needs to have adequate nutrients for good growth without being too rich and needs to provide excellent drainage. A mix of three parts forest mulch or compost, two parts sand, and one part pumice to which a light fertilizer such as dried poultry waste (3–2–2) is added works well. Mixes are as plentiful as growers and gardeners, so you will want to experiment to find the best mix for your plants and conditions. The principles of good drainage and light fertilizer should be adhered to for all plants in both families.

It is important to plant agaves and other stemless species a little high in the pot. All leaves should be above the lip of the pot, and the crown should be above the soil line. The soil will

Figure 3-3. *Manfreda maculosa*

subside as it is watered and can move into the crown of the plant, where it usually leads to infection.

Plants in containers are restricted in size by the amount of room for their roots. Plants that have been seriously underpotted for a long time have masses of roots coiled around in the pot, but have not grown in size appreciably. It can be a useful trait to keep the plant a bit smaller than normal. Eventually a plant in a container that is too small uses up all the soil and begins to discolor, fade, and wither because the roots have no soil to provide water and nutrients to the plant. If at all practical, plants should be repotted at least every three years. If the plant and container are too large to repot, add soil mix, including a light fertilizer, annually to the soil surface, just below the leaves.

Containers should be sized to match the size of the plant plus some growing room. To keep young plants or seedlings growing steadily, move them up one pot size at least annually. Once the plants are near full size, choose a container big enough to accommodate the ultimate size of the plant. Care should be taken to select a pot that is not too large because it is important that agaves, yuccas, and their relatives be slightly under potted compared to most other plants. If the plants have too much soil in relation to the plant's ability to absorb the water, the roots can rot during cool or damp weather. Pot culture keeps plants much smaller than if they are grown in the ground, so estimating the ultimate size of the plant can be tricky. A good rule of thumb is that container plants reach about half the ultimate size they could have reached in the ground.

When repotting it often is necessary to remove some of the overgrown roots. Prune with a very sharp cutting tool, and take as many roots as necessary to fit the remaining roots easily in the pot. If practical, dry the roots of *Agave* for a few days. If that is not possible, lightly dust the roots with powdered sulfur or plant in dry mix and water a week after planting to help prevent infection. All other genera should be planted immediately.

Containers can be made of any clay or plastic, but clay has definite advantages in growing these plants. It allows air to enter the pot on all sides and allows the pot to dry out quickly.

A dry pot is a particular advantage in cooler, more humid climates, but can be used anywhere.

In general, very xeric members of any of these genera can grow in full sun or partial shade in the low desert, but demand full sun in other climates. Eastern plants (that is, those from more moderate climates) demand some shade in the low desert when grown in containers and can be grown in either full sun or partial shade in more moderate climates. Only *Agave* species from the most xeric regions can be placed in full sun in containers in the low desert. In milder climates, or along coastal areas, all species can be placed in full sun or partial shade. *Yucca* species in containers generally can be placed in either full sun or partial shade, with the western species most tolerant of full sun in the desert. In very cold climates where container plants are outside only during the summer, the plants do best in full sun.

Plants in containers need more water, especially in the summer, than plants in the ground. Because there are so many variables of soil, pot, and weather, it is difficult to generalize how often to water plants in pots. Test the soil: it should be dry nearly to the bottom of the pot before watering. Water thoroughly, letting water drain out the pot. In the hottest part of the summer, with temperatures regularly over 106°F (41°C), water twice a week. In temperatures below that but still hot, water once a week. When highs are 70°F (21°C) or lower, be very careful that the plant is not overwatered; most plants need water only every two to three weeks in these temperatures. Again, check the plants before watering, and do not water if the soil still is moist regardless of the temperature. Plants in full sun may need more than this recommendation, and plants in the shade, in coastal situations, or where weather is cool and humid or cold may not need water this frequently.

Do not use self-watering mechanisms when these plants are grown in containers. They inevitably provide too much water for the plant. Saucers are useful to protect floors, patios, or tables, but should be removed when the plant is watered so that drainage is free and no water remains standing in the saucer.

It is best that containers placed outside do not come in direct contact with the soil. These plants will live in their pots for a long time, so preventing the infestation of crickets, pillbugs, and a host of other soil and root-eating creatures that thrive in the cool moist conditions at the base of a pot helps keep the plant healthy.

In areas where regular freezing occurs, pay careful attention to container-grown plants. Even very cold tolerant species can be damaged in containers if the temperature gets low enough for a long enough time. Containers lack the insulating quality of the ground, a fact that can be compensated for by placing them adjacent to buildings to gain protection from cold winds. If severe cold is expected, the pots should be brought inside or covered with artificial insulating materials.

Frost Protection

Plants of the Agavaceae and the Nolinaceae as a group exhibit a puzzling array of resistance to cold. In general, knowledge of the natural distribution helps or at least offers clues regarding a species's frost tolerance, but in the end experimentation and experience are the only true measure.

Most agaves come from the subtropical and tropical regions of the Americas where winter lows are rarely below 20°F (–7°C), but those from higher latitudes and elevations generally have more cold tolerance. This situation, however, is complicated because high elevations in northern Arizona, where some very cold tolerant agaves are native, experience very cold temperatures, while high elevations in southeastern Mexico are extremely moderate. Species with enormous ranges or those that cover wide elevational ranges are even more difficult to predict. Plants from the most northern extent of the range might have significantly more cold tolerance than the more southerly members of a species. *Agave parryi* is a good example of this phenomenon. Plants from northern Arizona are extremely cold hardy, tolerating temperatures down to –10°F (–23°C), while plants from the border of Zacatecas-Durango in Mexico can only tolerate temperatures down to 15–20°F (–9 to –7°C). As a general rule, agaves with soft, pliable leaves are more frost tender than those with rigid, hard leaves. Another general rule is that the larger the plant, the more tender it is. More detailed information on cold tolerance of agaves is given in the profiles and in Table 3-1.

A few techniques help to extend the cold tolerance of plants. If grown in a container, for example, a plant can be moved to a covered porch, covered house, or greenhouse if frost is imminent. This strategy is most reliable for northern gardeners or for those who demand perfection in the leaf. In areas where radiant cooling dominates in the winter, a simple covering of frost blanket, old sheets or linens, or plastic on a frame prevents frost damage. For plants that are marginal or not overly tender, the overhead protection of a dense evergreen tree, porch, or eave of the house is sufficient. In gardens where there are small, but significant elevational differences within a very small site, put the most tender plants at the highest point of the garden to allow the cold air to drain away from the plants.

Most plants in the Agavaceae and the Nolinaceae tolerate cold better if the soil is dry. The most difficult impediment to growing these plants successfully in many parts of the country is not the absolute cold, but the combination of long periods of cold with wet weather. Damp soils are difficult for these plants to overcome. If winters are very cold and very wet, plants in containers may be the best option.

Cold damage is evident in a leaf that has changed color quickly, from a light and dull or glossy look to a dark but glassy, almost translucent appearance. Very soon the leaf begins to blacken, usually at one end, and the damage can continue any distance down the leaf. If damage is severe or throughout the plant, the leaves become flaccid and appear to have melted, particularly in agaves, or rapidly dry and turn brown, as in yuccas and many plants in the Nolinaceae. Do not prune the leaves, as it is much better to let them die and become brittle before cutting them off. If the damage is not extreme, the plant seals the frozen leaf and any rot or infection will not spread.

Yucca is the most northerly distributed genus of the Agavaceae, and many species have evolved in areas where regular freezing occurs. Although yuccas vary considerably in their tolerance to freezing temperature, most species can tolerate moderate amounts of freezing weather. Because of these variations in frost tolerance, the best way to avoid frost damage of yuccas is by selecting appropriate species that can tolerate the pattern of freezing weather normally found in the area where they are to be planted. Frost tolerance information on yuccas is presented in Table 3-1. If an extremely severe freeze is expected, yuccas can be wrapped with cloth. It is particularly important to protect the growing points on the individual rosettes. Only the growing tips of large yuccas and nolinas need protection, while smaller plants need to be covered completely. If freezing weather destroys the rosette, leave the stem until warm weather returns. New rosettes may sprout from the stem or the base.

Furcraea and *Polianthes* species are unable to withstand temperatures much below freezing, especially in wet soil conditions. Unless the garden is in a nearly frost-free climate, it is advisable to keep *Furcraea* species protected throughout the winter. If the climate has only light freezing weather, then planting under evergreen trees, near buildings, or in other warmer microclimates in the garden can help the plants survive spells of light freezing weather. *Polianthes* species can be overwintered if the ground does not get too cold. All that is needed is to heavily mulch the bulblike structure with leaves or brush.

Hesperaloe and *Beschorneria* species can tolerate some freezing weather, but they should be protected if temperatures threaten to exceed their cold tolerance for long periods of time. Because they are unarmed, these plants easily can be protected by bundling up their leaves and tying them together with a rope. The tied-up leaf mass then can be covered with burlap or some other cloth. The cloth should be removed as the weather warms.

Tolerance to freezing temperatures varies considerably within the Nolinaceae. *Beaucarnea* is a strictly tropical genus that does not tolerate severe or prolonged freezing weather.

Generally these species should be planted where temperatures rarely fall below approximately 25°F (−4°C). Although large beaucarneas have survived freezes down to 20°F (−7°C), damage to the stems is severe and plants lose considerable mass.

Dasylirion and *Nolina* species have a much wider range of cold tolerance. Many are able to tolerate temperatures below 15°F (−9°C). *Nolina texana* reportedly tolerates temperatures down to −15°F (−26°C). Protecting nolinas and dasylirions from cold damage can be difficult because of the large, often armed rosettes. They can be protected in the manner described above for the genera *Hesperaloe* and *Beschorneria*, but more care must be taken to avoid sharp cuts from the serrated or toothed leaf edges.

Table 3-1 indicates the approximate cold tolerance of some species in the Agavaceae and the Nolinaceae. Little published information exists on the cold tolerance of many of these plants. This list was constructed by examining published reports and the natural distribution of the plants, from personal experience, and from personal communication with individuals who grow the plants. The temperatures listed are conservative and should not prevent gardeners from attempting to grow the plants at slightly colder temperatures, particularly if protection can be provided when temperatures plunge.

Gardeners should be aware that tremendous variabilities in microclimate and soil conditions affect survival in freezing weather and that plants in warm microclimates are able to survive at temperatures seemingly below their cold tolerance. Genetic variability also can affect dramatically the cold tolerance of many species. For example, gardeners have reported wide variation in the tolerance of *Dasylirion wheeleri*: plants originating in southern Arizona are damaged at 5°F (−15°C) while those originating in New Mexico occasionally tolerate temperatures to −10°F (−23°C). Thus some large ranges of cold tolerance can be found within individual species. If gardeners are concerned about growing a plant that might be considered frost sensitive in their area, then obtaining a plant from a colder part of its range and planting it in a warm microclimate will certainly maximize its chances of survival.

Table 3-1. Approximate cold tolerance of selected species.

Species	Temperature	
Agave americana	15°F	−9°C
A. americana var. *expansa*	20°F	−7°C
A. americana var. *medio–picta*	15°F	−9°C
A. americana var. *variegata*	25°F	−4°C
A. angustifolia	25°F	−4°C
A. attenuata	28°F	−2°C
A. bovicornuta	20°F	−7°C
A. cerulata	10°F	−12°C
A. chrysantha	17°F	−8°C
A. datylio	25°F	−4°C
A. deserti	15°F	−9°C
A. desmettiana	25°F	−4°C
A. filifera	17°F	−8°C
A. fourcroydes	25°F	−4°C
A. geminiflora	25°F	−4°C
A. havardiana	−10°F	−23°C
A. lechuguilla	0°F	−18°C
A. lophantha	10°F	−12°C
A. macroacantha	25°F	−4°C
A. marmorata	25°F	−4°C
A. murpheyi	10°F	−12°C
A. neomexicana	−20°F	−29°C
A. ocahui	15°F	−9°C
A. palmeri	10°F	−12°C
A. parrasana	15°F	−9°C
A. parryi	−20°F	−29°C
A. parryi var. *couesii*	0°F	−18°C
A. parryi var. *huachucensis*	15°F	−9°C
A. parryi var. *truncata*	15°F	−9°C
A. parviflora	10°F	−12°C
A. pelona	20°F	−7°C
A. salmiana	5°F	−15°C
A. salmiana var. *crassispina*	25°F	−4°C
A. scabra	10°F	−12°C
A. schidigera	15°F	−9°C
A. schottii	10°F	−12°C
A. shawii	25°F	−4°C
A. sisalana	25°F	−4°C

(continued)

79

Table 3-1 (continued).

Species	Temperature	
A. striata	15°F	−9°C
A. tequilana	25°F	−4°C
A. toumeyana	10°F	−12°C
A. utahensis	−10°F	−23°C
A. utahensis var. eborispina	−10°F	−23°C
A. utahensis var. kaibabensis	−10°F	−23°C
A. utahensis var. nevadensis	0°F	−18°C
A. victoriae-reginae	10°F	−12°C
A. vilmoriniana	22°F	−6°C
A. weberi	12°F	−11°C
A. zebra	20°F	−7°C
Beaucarnea gracilis	25°F	−4°C
B. guatemalensis	27°F	−3°C
B. recurvata	25°F	−4°C
B. stricta	25°F	−4°C
Beschorneria yuccoides	15°F	−9°C
Calibanus hookeri	17°F	−8°C
Dasylirion acrotriche	15°F	−9°C
D. leiophyllum	0°F	−18°C
D. quadrangulatum	15°F	−9°C
D. texanum	5°F	−15°C
D. wheeleri	0°F	−18°C
Hesperaloe campanulata	12°F	−11°C
H. funifera	10°F	−12°C
H. nocturna	10°F	−12°C
H. parviflora	−20°F	−29°C
Manfreda maculosa	10°F	−12°C
M. virginica	−20°F	−29°C
Nolina bigelovii	15°F	−9°C
N. erumpens	0°F	−18°C
N. longifolia	15°F	−9°C
N. matapensis	15°F	−9°C
N. microcarpa	−15°F	−26°C
N. nelsoni	10°F	−12°C
N. parryi	10°F	−12°C
N. texana	−15°F	−26°C
Yucca aloifolia	0°F	−18°C
Y. baccata	−20°F	−29°C
Y. brevifolia	−10°F	−23°C
Y. elata	−10°F	−23°C

Species	Temperature	
Y. elephantipes	27°F	–3°C
Y. faxoniana	0°F	–18°C
Y. filamentosa	–20°F	–29°C
Y. filifera	20°F	–7°C
Y. flaccida	–20°F	–29°C
Y. glauca	–35°F	–37°C
Y. gloriosa	22°F	–6°C
Y. grandiflora	20°F	–7°C
Y. harrimaniae	–20°F	–29°C
Y. pallida	0°F	–18°C
Y. recurvifolia	0°F	–18°C
Y. rigida	5°F	–15°C
Y. rostrata	5°F	–15°C
Y. rupicola	0°F	–18°C
Y. schidigera	0°F	–18°C
Y. schottii	–10°F	–23°C
Y. torreyi	5°F	–15°C
Y. treculeana	10°F	–12°C
Y. whipplei	0°F	–18°C

Seed Propagation

Propagation by seed is highly successful for all members of the Agavaceae. Whether the seed is fresh or out of storage, germination occurs within one to three weeks of sowing, often much faster. Seed of *Agave* and *Yucca* species is viable for a long time —up to five years with shelf storage and longer if frozen. *Hesperaloe* and *Manfreda* species have not been studied for viability, but reports indicate that seed at least five years old produced excellent germination results.

The most difficult part of growing these species from seed is to be sure that the seed is pure. *Agave* species, in particular, easily hybridize, and unless absolutely no other species is in bloom within the range of a hummingbird, or unless you have hand-pollinated the plant, it is impossible to be certain the seed is pure. Hand pollination can be easily accomplished by brushing pollen onto the stigma when it is sticky and glistening. In night-blooming species the stigma generally is receptive into the very early morning. This very temporary state often lasts only one day per flower. Closing off the flower with a cloth or mesh bag prevents other pollinations.

To propagate agaves and most other plants in the two families, sow seed closely in shallow dishes or flats and cover it very lightly. We use a mix of half perlite and half vermiculite with a small addition of compost. Water to keep the medium moist, but be careful that the soil is not saturated. Too much moisture will rot seedlings quickly. Grow the seedlings in strong but indirect light. In the low desert it is necessary to provide some shade for seedlings. Although not highly temperature dependent, most species germinate faster and grow faster after germination if the soil and air temperatures are above 80°F (27°C).

The seedlings of these plants vary somewhat depending on the genus. In *Agave, Hesperaloe,* and *Manfreda,* seedlings are very succulent and cotyledons look very much like true leaves. The rosette form is established immediately, and even tiny *Agave* seedlings have a minute terminal spine. Most very drought adapted *Agave* species can take up to six months to grow leaves after the initial seedling leaves appear. In *Yucca,* seedlings are somewhat succulent, but as they mature look very grasslike, particularly in certain species.

The plants also vary some in the rate at which they grow and mature. It can take five to five and a half months for yucca seedlings to grow a full complement of juvenile leaves, which usually are succulent, flexible and a blue-green color. Yuccas have a full compliment of adult leaves and the general form of the mature plant in one and a half to three years, but may take five to seven years to achieve full maturity and begin to bloom. The age of maturity in *Agave* is much more variable and species dependent, but most plants have complete rosettes within three years from seed. *Hesperaloe* species take about the same amount of time, although in *H. parviflora* the process can be as short as 18 months. In *Manfreda,* within a year after germination the plant has grown significantly but will take another two years to bloom.

Although seedlings of these plants tolerate transplanting well when very small, it often is advantageous to leave them crowded for up to two months before transplanting them to be sure the root system is sturdy. In addition, small plants are highly susceptible to root rot if overpotted and watered too frequently. After initial transplant, seedlings grow rapidly and need to be transplanted often to maintain steady vigorous growth.

While mature members of the Agavaceae need light and infrequent fertilization, seedlings and young plants respond dramatically to a richer environment. A mix that is four or five parts inorganic matter, such as gravel, pumice, or fine rock, and one part compost or potting soil, with a slow-release fertilizer works well for transplanted seedlings. Liquid fertilizer works equally well.

Seeds of the Nolinaceae can be planted in the same way as described above. Like seedlings of the Agavaceae, those of the Nolinaceae must be kept moist but not saturated, and do best in very strong light, although the full sun of the low desert is too intense.

Plants of either family must be introduced gradually to growing in very strong or full sun. The genera *Dasylirion, Hesperaloe, Nolina,* and *Yucca* can begin to tolerate full sun once plants are 2–6 in. (5–15 cm) tall and growing in separate pots. In very hot summer climates such as the low desert it is best to begin full sun treatment in the fall. For the other genera, partial shade will be necessary in the low desert all the time. For all species, once a clear rosette has formed, the plant should be able to tolerate the most sun it will take as an adult in the climate in which it is being grown.

Vegetative Propagation

Vegetative propagation of many of these plants is an important method used to increase their numbers in a garden or nursery setting. Several vegetative techniques can be utilized depending on the species. Although not all the plants in the Agavaceae and the Nolinaceae can be propagated vegetatively, at least one vegetative technique is available for many species. The most common methods of vegetative propagation for both families are the removal of bulbils, division of rhizomatous clumps, or removal of stem suckers.

Bulbils are small plants formed from the axillary bud at the base of the flower. These plants are clones of the blooming plant. Bulbil formation is common in about 17 *Agave* species, all *Furcraea* species, and has been irregularly documented in *Yucca*, particularly *Y. elata*, and *Hesperaloe*. Many bulbils develop quickly after the flowers die, but can remain on the inflorescence for one to two years before falling to root in the ground. Bulbils can be removed at any time after formation, but the small plants develop much faster if they can be left on the stalk until at least four leaves appear. The size of the bulbil depends on the species, but take the largest and most vigorous when selecting bulbils for propagation. Many species develop adventitious roots while still on the plant, and all grow to a size ranging from 2 to 6 in. (5–15 cm) if left to mature. Bulbils should be removed when they separate from the stalk without difficulty. A small basal plate at the bottom of the bulbil must be intact for the plant to grow roots.

Place the bulbils in a bed of sharp sand or a pumice and sand mixture and keep them moderately moist and shaded at this time. Bulbils set roots very quickly, usually within two to four weeks, and are ready for transplanting to separate pots in two months or less or when they have doubled in size.

At least some species in all genera of both families create new rosettes from shoots of underground rhizomes. These are known as offsets, and they sometimes are called pups in *Agave*. Offsets are formed underground from the buds along the rhizome or occasionally along the upper stem of the plant. Like bulbils, offsets too are clones. In *Agave*, some species never form offsets, while others grow offsets only once when young or throughout the life of the plant, and still others form offsets only at the time of flowering. In some species of *Agave*, notably

Figure 3-4. Bulbils, *Agave desmettiana*

A. victoriae-reginae and *A. cerulata,* specific populations form offsets freely, while other populations are solitary.

Some species of *Manfreda* form offsets so aggressively that the plant becomes a dense colony of rosettes. In these colonies, when one or several individual rosettes are in bloom, others are just in the formative stages. This phenomenon also occurs in several *Agave* species and is very common in *Beschorneria, Manfreda, Polianthes,* and *Prochnyanthes* as well. There is ample anecdotal evidence that many offset-forming species of *Agave* form offsets extensively and often more quickly if crowded in a container, although the exact inducement that crowding affords for offset formation is not understood.

Offsets can be removed at any time from the original plant by digging carefully around the plant and gently pulling and lifting until the offset comes free. If the offset does not come free easily, continue to dig, pull, and prod rather than cut it off. The small plants should have their own roots by the time they are large enough to be seen and need only be set in either a sand or sand-pumice bed, or directly potted to continue growth. Offsets often are highly distorted and asymmetrical from the crowding that can occur when growing near the original plant. This distortion will correct quickly once plants are growing individually in uncrowded situations. If it was necessary to cut any of the large rhizome while removing the plant, treat the rhizome with sulfur dust to help retard the introduction of infectious agents, or let the entire plant dry out for a week or two to heal the wound before repotting.

Besides *Agave* species, *Hesperaloe* species and many *Nolina* species commonly are propagated by division. In *Hesperaloe* and the so-called grassy nolinas, *N. texana, N. microcarpa,* and *N. erumpens*, offsets from the clumps can be separated and potted separately. This division is best done in the fall or early spring when the weather is cool. Although not common in *Dasylirion,* clumps and small individuals are formed in some species that can be removed and propagated. This removal also should be done in fall or early spring.

Many *Yucca* species also produce offsets by spreading rhizomes or aboveground stems, depending on the species. Many species root along the stem if it bends or is broken, thereby laying on the ground and growing a new, seemingly disconnected plant. Removal and planting of these offsets are similar to the methods described above, but particular care should be taken with *Yucca* species to remove as much root as possible with the offset rosette to maximize its chances of survival. In *Y. gloriosa* and *Y. elephantipes* small offshoots that develop into new growth directly from the stem can be removed and propagated.

A final method of vegetative propagation involves the taking and planting of stem cuttings. These stem cuttings are best taken during the growing season. Cuttings may be set in sand or a sand-pumice mix until roots form. Root formation can take up to three months depending on the species and conditions. The propagation medium should be kept moist, but care must be taken to not keep it so wet that the stem rots.

Stem cuttings can be taken by cutting off a piece of stem with or without leaves. For a cutting with leaves, the lower

Figure 3-5. *Nolina microcarpa*

leaves should be cut off, and the stem should be planted as described above. Although this technique works well for the species that are from coastal and more humid environments, it is much less successful for species from drier environments.

In large-trunked yuccas, plants have areas of active growth at the base of the trunk just at or below the surface of the soil. These suckers eventually become more or less vertical and can be removed and planted in the same manner as stem cuttings.

Pest, Disease, and Cultural Problems

Relatively few pests and diseases affect plants in the Agavaceae and the Nolinaceae. The most severe pest of these species is the rabbit, both cottontail and jackrabbit. Rabbits eat the leaves and even the blooming stalk in very small individuals. Luckily, these voracious pests rarely eat the central bud, but can cause so much damage to a young plant that it will die. In non-garden settings cattle also can be an extreme pest of *Agave* in certain parts of the plants' range. The most destructive damage occurs when the animal eats an emerging flowering stalk. In small or limited natural populations this destruction can cause havoc for seed production. It is a rare problem, however, in a garden setting, and the eating of flowering stalks or leaves generally is a cosmetic problem that rarely endangers the life of the plant. Cages and fences are the only controls that truly work to deter cattle or rabbits.

Among the most serious insect pests is the agave snout weevil (*Scyphophorus acupunctatus*), which affects many *Agave* species (Plate 3) and occasionally *Yucca* species. This dark brown to black weevil is 1 in. (2.5 cm) long. The female weevil inspects agaves by boring tiny holes in the leaves to "taste" her way to a suitable site where she can deposit her eggs. This sampling produces an acidic substance from the plant that heals the tiny wound and deters the female from laying eggs. By some as yet unrecognized mechanism, this defense breaks down when the agave is near blooming, so that undeterred the female lays eggs near the base of the leaf.

The vast concentrations of sugars and carbohydrate in the bud at this time make a feast for the emerging larvae. With an advanced guard of tissue-destroying microbes to soften the tissue, larvae proceed through the leaf, eating out the heart. In addition, entry is provided for a wide range of bacteria, fungi, and viruses into the tissue of the plant. While there is great physical damage to the plant, it is these agents that introduce lethal infections.

Damage from agave snout weevils is hard to notice until it is too late. Careful and close examination will reveal the small punctures by the female, but more often the older leaves of a fine healthy plant suddenly collapse, drooping erratically, and leaving the central bud as a spike. Soon that too falls over. All this damage can take place in a matter of weeks. At this point there is nothing to do, as the plant is all but dead.

Diazinon may be used on the plant throughout its life as a preventative measure. Because, however, this practice is expensive, not to say poisonous, it is a frustrating solution. It would be more effective if it were possible to notice the loss of a plant's natural defenses and treat it then, but we know of no such method. Weevils are most active and engage in egg-laying in warm weather, so plants are most susceptible at that time.

Agave snout weevils have traveled the world with agaves and are found wherever agaves are grown. While the weevil could infest any agave, some plants seem more susceptible than others. As a very general rule, hard-leaved medium to small agaves are less susceptible than large, softer-leaved species. *Agave americana*, *A. chrysantha*, and *A. palmeri* are particularly susceptible to this insect's infestation.

Some interesting research on the natural history of the insect, however, has revealed a possible avenue of work to help select for better resistance in ornamental populations. Not all agaves, even of susceptible species, are prone equally to weevil infestation. By examining ornamental populations in bloom and looking for weevils on these plants and in populations that are not in bloom, researchers have found that a small percentage of highly susceptible species continue blooming without infestation and its subsequent damage. This result held even when weevils were introduced purposefully onto the plants and suggests that ornamental populations would be better selected from those individuals that were able to bloom successfully, rather than from a random or uncontrolled group of plants.

It has always been recommended that an agave not be planted in the hole of an agave that died of weevil damage, on the theory that you could not be sure that all larvae were dead. But it might be better advice to be sure to avoid planting the offset or bulbil of an agave that died of weevil damage, and instead try to find one that came from a blooming, therefore possibly resistant, parent.

There is another way to look at the demise of an agave from weevil infestation. Unless you are determined to see the plant bloom or need the resulting seed, you could consider that the garden benefited for many years by the extraordinary vegetative beauty of the plant. The plant will die from the bloom, and while you did not see the bloom, it might have served the garden just as well, now opening a place for another wonderful agave to take its place.

Other diseases can infect agaves from time to time. The plants may be infected with one of several specific viral diseases. Control is difficult, as with all virus attacks, but the incidence is most serious in plants that are in poor cultural condition or have been severely damaged.

A puzzling series of symptoms shows up in the late summer in some years on agaves in the low desert. Leaves turn yellow from the base and a patch of dead tissue forms a corky, hard edge near the base of the plant. This irregularly formed scar moves up the leaf as it grows. Thrips and a mite have been designated as causes of this situation. Possibly a fungal infection is coincident with or vectored by the insects. Use of a good fungicide drench has helped, but severely infested plants should be destroyed or isolated from other agaves.

Other fungal infections can occur in agaves, again usually as the result of overwatering, crowns that are set too low in the soil, or the collection of too much litter in the leaves. All fungal infections respond to a good drench of fungicide if they are noticed early.

Agaves are susceptible to a condition known as water spotting. It is mechanical damage to the leaf, often caused by vigorous overhead watering. Why such a leaf would be so susceptible to this damage is puzzling, but it is very common in certain species. It shows up as spots or lesions that turn from a tan to orange discoloration to become a hard, well-defined roundish black spot. Heavily damaged leaves are unsightly, but there is no direct danger to the plant. The only risk is secondary infection.

Some cold-sensitive agaves, such as *Agave attenuata, A. celsii,* or *A. desmettiana,* have a cold response that looks like a disease. Leaves become pale, often with pale lines or tracks. In some the paleness becomes a general loss of vigor and color on the leaf, often with black spots that seem to have no origin throughout the leaf. This phenomenon is a cold response that disappears when warm weather returns.

A similar yellowing occurs in many *Agave* species when the weather is extremely hot. In the low desert this common phenomenon is alarming, but always temporary. Plants that yellow in the heat need to be watered very well during the hot spell, but watering alone does not reverse the coloration—it just keeps the plant healthy and vigorous until the temperature turns down. With the return of more moderate temperatures, most leaves will return to color, but some will dry for all or a part of their length.

Yuccas are relatively free from insect pests. Scale insects have been reported, and treatment for these sucking insects is, as for many other plants, the use of specific scale insecticides, insecticidal soaps, or horticultural oils. Occasionally stem-boring insects can infest yuccas, and these should be treated with a general-purpose insecticide designed for boring insects. Agave snout weevils also have been known to infect *Yucca recurvifolia.* Growing yuccas in humid climates can pose cultural problems particularly for some species. When soils stay too damp during the winter, the lack of aeration in the root zone begins to break down root tissue, allowing the introduction of bacteria and fungi that can destroy the roots and ultimately kill the plant. Choosing plants that have a greater tolerance to cool, wet soils prevents problems, as will keeping less well-adapted plants in raised beds or extremely well drained soils.

The plants of the Nolinaceae appear to be relatively free of pests and diseases. Because of their xerophytic habits, it is safe to assume that excessive watering and soils saturated for long periods of time are detrimental to the plants and eventually lead to root rot and death as in *Agave* and *Yucca*. This sensitivity would probably be most pronounced in *Beaucarnea* and *Calibanus*, which both have expanded woody bases at the soil level. Occasionally we have noticed rotted crowns of trunked species of *Nolina*, particularly *N. matapensis*, in ornamental settings. The cause is not known, but possibly overwatering or crown watering allows the introduction of bacteria and fungi. Other species of *Nolina*, as well as species of *Beaucarnea* and *Calibanus*, would meet with similar fates should the crowns of the plants be kept too moist.

CHAPTER 4

Species Profiles

It was a difficult task to pick the individual species that are contained in these species profiles. In general, species were chosen because they were in horticulture, at least regionally, or we believed that they were handsome, desirable, or so interesting that their use should be encouraged. And still some were left out, some that are really beautiful. It was hard to leave out *Agave shrevei*, *A. sebastiana*, numerous *Manfreda* species, other fascinating yuccas, and dasylirions. But these plants and many like them are so difficult to obtain that we chose to leave them as a footnote, rather than a profile. In many instances they are mentioned within the profile of another species. Finally, only the most well-known or well-used synonyms are listed, in chronological order.

Agave albomarginata Gentry

SIZE: *Agave albomarginata* sets many offsets of few-leaved rosettes with distinctive long, thin leaves. Plants have a very short stem and are 3.2 ft. (1 m) tall.

LEAVES: The thin leaves are 1 in. (2.5 cm) wide and 3–4 ft. (1–1.2 m) long. They are blue-gray, flat, and wider at the base. The margin is straight and covered with a white, horny border that can detach. It has teeth only in the lower two-thirds of the leaf. The teeth are white, especially in the middle of the leaf, and spaced 1.25–2 in. (3.2–5 cm) apart. The terminal spine is short, gray with a dark tip, and thinly decurrent.

BLOOM: The inflorescence is a spike 13–20 ft. (4–6 m) tall. The flowers are greenish yellow.

DISTRIBUTION: *Agave albomarginata* was described from plants in the collection at the Huntington Botanical Garden, San Marino, California. Nothing more is known at present about its natural distribution, but there is speculation it may be a part of the greater *A. lechuguilla* complex, which is centered in northeastern Mexico.

PROPAGATION: Propagation is by removal of the offsets or by seed.

CULTURAL REQUIREMENTS: *Agave albomarginata* has been cultivated in California and in Phoenix for some time and has shown no special difficulties of cultivation. Although its exact cold tolerance is unknown, it has survived temperatures well below 25°F (–4°C) without damage. It likely could tolerate much colder temperatures.

SIMILAR OR RELATED SPECIES: No other species combines the long, linear blue-gray leaf and a white margin with distant teeth.

USES: Hardly common in cultivation, *Agave albomarginata* is a remarkable-looking agave that could be useful in any succulent or other dry garden. Its striking form and features make it a fine specimen or focal plant as well as a container plant.

Agave americana Linnaeus   PLATES 2, 3

SYNONYMS: *Agave complicata* Trelease ex Ocheterana, *Agave gracilispina* Engelmann, *Agave melliflua* Trelease, *Agave zonata* Trelease, *Agave felina* Trelease, *Agave rasconensis* Trelease, *Agave subzonata* Trelease

COMMON NAMES: Century plant, Maguey

SIZE: *Agave americana* is a commanding species to 6–10 ft. (1.8–3 m) tall and 13 ft. (4 m) wide. It is the image of *Agave* for much of the world and fittingly was the species that Linnaeus used in 1753 to describe the genus. It is the most cosmopolitan of agaves with the longest ornamental history. Although highly variable, it is always large, often with numerous offsets.

LEAVES: The leaves are 6–10 in. (15–25 cm) wide and 3–6.5 ft. (1–2 m) long. They are very smooth and hard, nearly rigid, with a deep gutter that often causes them to recurve dramatically at the tip. Each rosette has 20–40 leaves. The most frequently seen color form in horticulture has gray to gray-blue leaves with significant amounts of horizontal stripes on the back. There also are dark green and many variegated color forms. The margin is undulate with dark brown teeth that turn gray with age. The teeth are downcurved, variable in length, usually less than 0.5 in. (1.3 cm) long, and spaced 0.75–2 in. (2–5 cm) apart. The stout, conical terminal spine is 1–2 in. (2.5–5 cm) long with a definite groove on the upper surface. It is decurrent 4–6 in. (10–15 cm) down the margin. Among the countless forms of the species, three are seen widely. *Agave americana* var. *expansa* (Jacobi) Gentry (synonym *A. expansa* Jacobi) is among the largest forms. Its leaves are 7–9.5 in. (18–24 cm) wide and 4–5 ft. (1.2–1.5 m) long with widely spaced teeth and broad crossbanding. *Agave americana* var. *oaxacensis* Gentry is a very white glaucous form known only from cultivation in the Mexican states of Oaxaca and San Luis Potosí. Its leaves are straighter, more outstretched, with small teeth. *Agave americana* subsp. *protoamericana* Gentry was described by Gentry as the only wild population of this species that he could find. It is slightly smaller with leaves 6.5–8.5 in. (17–22 cm) wide and 2.5–4 ft. (0.8–1.2 m) long. The teeth are spaced regularly, and the leaf is flat to guttered. *Agave americana* also has several variegated forms, many of which have a perplexing series of names. *Agave americana* var. *marginata* Trelease has yellow or white stripes on the leaf margin. *Agave americana* var. *marginata* 'Aurea' Trelease is particularly enormous, with plants up to 10 ft. (3 m) tall or more. The falling, arched leaves are yellow variegated, often with pink edges. *Agave americana* var. *medio-picta* Trelease has yellow or white stripes longitudinally through the middle of the leaf. Many of these are much smaller plants than the type. Gentry chose to combine all variegated forms, regardless of color or arrangement, into one taxon he called *A. americana* var. *picta* Gentry. *Agave americana* var. *striata* Trelease has cream or white coloring that is finely striped through the leaf, which usually is a pale glaucous blue-gray.

BLOOM: The inflorescence is a panicle that rises 16–26 ft. (5–8 m) above the plant. It has 15–35 branches with bloom on the upper half to third of the stalk. The flowers are yellow and occur from June to August. Plants usually bloom after about 10 years of growth in the ground particularly in warm climates, up to 35 years or more in cool climates.

DISTRIBUTION: The natural distribution of *Agave americana,* except for subspecies *protoamericana,* is speculative and uncertain. The species is so widely used for fiber and ornamental purposes even in Mexico that it is difficult to ascertain its true natural origins. Subspecies *protoamericana* was documented to occur in scattered populations in the Sierra Madre Oriental of eastern Mexico. The ornamental distribution of this species crosses the globe. The species was long used for fence-rows in Mexico and occurs throughout that country, particularly in the northeastern parts. It is common in the United States as an ornamental in all the warm regions from California to Florida and throughout the warm Mediterranean areas of Europe and northern Africa. The species has become feral in almost all these locations as well as southern Africa, India, and Australia.

PROPAGATION: Propagation is by removal of the offsets, although seed is set in some locations.

CULTURAL REQUIREMENTS: A highly forgiving species, which is probably the reason for its great success, *Agave americana* grows in hot areas of limited rainfall, such as southern Arizona, or in areas of cooler temperatures, such as the Mediterranean coastal climates of Spain, Italy, and California. Often grown in pots, it becomes large but not nearly as massive as plantings in the ground. In southern Arizona it is highly susceptible to infestation by the agave snout weevil. In fact, it is rare to see this species bloom out in Phoenix or Tucson because of the timing of this damage. *Agave americana* tolerates temperatures to 15°F (–9°C) and perhaps lower.

SIMILAR OR RELATED SPECIES: *Agave fourcroydes* has straight leaves that are very narrow. *Agave franzosinii* has a paler, nearly white leaf that contrasts strongly with its chestnut teeth and it lacks the groove in the terminal spine. *Agave weberi* has fleshy, usually much wider leaves with minute teeth that generally are only on the lower half of the leaf.

USES: *Agave americana* has a long history of ornamental use, dating back to the very first European introductions from the New World. It also is an important fiber plant in the tropical parts of its range, although other species with less aggressive teeth and spines have taken over the trade. Ornamentally, it is a wonderful plant in a garden large enough to accommodate it. This plant makes a dramatic addition to a long border or entry, clusters well in a large planting, and mixes with most other succulents. White-variegated forms are particularly lovely and, because they are smaller, mix well with either small succulents or perennials.

Agave angustifolia Haworth   PLATE 4

SYNONYMS: *Agave jacquiniana* Schultes, *Agave ixtli* Karwinsky ex Salm-Dyck, *Agave elongata* Jacobi, *Agave excelsa* Baker, *Agave zapupa* Trelease, *Agave prainiana* Berger, *Agave pacifica* Trelease, *Agave yaquiana* Trelease

SIZE: *Agave angustifolia* is highly variable in size and form. The rosette can be 3–5 ft. (1–1.5 m) tall and 6.5–8 ft. (2–2.4 m) wide. Many variegated forms are much smaller, while some forms from the northern part of the species's range are much larger. Plants set numerous offsets and are rarely solitary.

LEAVES: The linear to lanceolate leaves are numerous and very stiff. They are 1–4 in. (2.5–10 cm) wide and 2–4 ft. (0.6–1.2 m) long, flat on the upper surface, becoming convex toward the tip, narrower toward the stem but with a thick base. They are most often light green to gray-green in color, but there is considerable variation. The teeth are small, curved, and spaced fairly far apart, 0.5–1.5 in. (1.3–3.8 cm), on a straight margin. The terminal spine is short, not decurrent, and stout. Most teeth and spines are dark brown, but in some forms they are a glossy garnet or black. Countless forms and varieties have been named over the years. Gentry recognized the following varieties. *Agave angustifolia* var. *deweyana* (Trelease) Gentry (synonym *A. deweyana* Trelease) has somewhat narrower leaves and more remote teeth than the type. It is found in the Mexican states of Tamaulipas and Veracruz. *Agave angustifolia* var. *letonae* (Taylor) Gentry (synonym *A. letonae* Taylor ex Trelease) is a nearly white-leaved form with a broad trunk. It is a favored plantation form in El Salvador and to a lesser extent in Guatemala. *Agave angustifolia* var. *marginata* Hort. has either white or yellow stripes on the edge of the leaf. Although Gentry gives no varietal status to a var. *variegata,* the name has been long in use and generally refers to the same plants indicated by var. *marginata. Agave angustifolia* var. *nivea* (Trelease) Gentry (synonym *A. nivea* Trelease) has dull blue-gray leaves. It is a locally grown fiber and fence plant in Guatemala. *Agave angustifolia* var. *rubescens* (Salm-Dyck) Gentry (synonym *A. rubescens* Salm-Dyck) has narrow, much less rigid leaves that are 1–1.5 in. (2.5–3.8 cm) wide and 2.5–4.25 ft. (0.8–1.3 m) long, with red-brown teeth and spines. It is the most xeric form of the species and occurs at least from the Mexican states of Sonora to Oaxaca. *Agave angustifolia* var. *sargentii* Trelease has a short trunk and gray-green leaves that are much more oblong than the type, 1–1.25 in. (2.5–3.2 cm) wide and 10–12 in. (25–30 cm) long, with glossy black teeth.

BLOOM: The inflorescence is a panicle 10–16 ft. (3–5 m) tall with 10–20 branches. The green to yellow flowers can occur anytime from November to March and have been reported for some forms in the summer. Bulbils are often formed following flowering.

DISTRIBUTION: *Agave angustifolia* has a wide geographic distribution from the Mexican state of Sonora east to the state of Tamaulipas and south through Costa Rica. It occurs on beaches, in open plains, in foothills, and in open rocky slopes at elevations from sea level to 1500 ft. (460 m).

PROPAGATION: Propagation is by removal of the offsets or bulbils.

CULTURAL REQUIREMENTS: *Agave angustifolia* has been cultivated for a very long time, and it probably was cultivated in the Caribbean at the time of Columbus's first voyage. It still is grown there extensively for fiber. The species tolerates almost any conditions and soils. In the low desert it grows well in full sun if kept regularly watered through the summer. In other areas it grows in full sun with moderate summer watering. It has good cold tolerance with severe leaf damage reported at 16°F (–9°C).

SIMILAR OR RELATED SPECIES: The combination of a short, round, non-decurrent terminal spine, widely spaced teeth, and numerous, stiff, straight, flat leaves usually separates *Agave angustifolia* from all other agaves of similar size and form. *Agave pacifica*, an invalid name, can still be found in the nursery trade. It refers to a form of *A. angustifolia* that is common in the Mexican state of Sonora and has particularly long, narrow leaves, 20–47 in. (51–119 cm) long and 1.5–3 in. (3.8–8 cm) wide. *Agave sisalana* is virtually toothless. *Agave tequilana* has straight, flattened leaves and a long, decurrent spine. *Agave sisalana* and *A. tequilana* are very much larger plants in maturity than most forms of *A. angustifolia*.

USES: *Agave angustifolia* has been grown for its fiber for centuries. In the nineteenth century plants were taken into Florida as a fiber crop and distributed from there throughout the subtropical world. Only in more recent times has *A. sisalana* replaced this species as a fiber crop because of its finer texture. *Agave angustifolia* still can be found through the Caribbean basin and in parts of southern Africa as a crop plant. In the Mexican state of Sonora many local peoples used it for food as well. As a garden plant, it commonly is used anywhere in the warm parts of the world. It was introduced to European gardens early and the plethora of names attached to it attests to its popularity and the striking variation in the species. Its compact form and high degree of symmetry make it a lovely subject for perennial plantings, container culture, or as a focus of a more formalized planting. Its ability to tolerate a wide variety of soil conditions and accept more water than most agaves makes it available to any warm region garden.

Agave attenuata Salm-Dyck PLATE 5

SYNONYMS: *Agave glaucescens* J. Hooker, *Agave cernua* Berger, *Agave pruinosa* Lemaire ex Jacobi
COMMON NAME: Fox-tail agave

SIZE: *Agave attenuata* is a distinctive species with a large rosette of leaves perched on a long, curving stem. The head of leaves ranges from 2 to 4 ft. (0.6–1.2 m) wide, and the stem can be 1.5–5 ft. (0.5–1.5 m) long from the base. The stem often has numerous smaller rosettes arising from the base or along the length, and some plants have branching stems. The stem is smooth and a pale gray color.

LEAVES: The soft and fleshy leaves are usually smooth-margined but occasionally are very finely serrated, and widest in the middle. The tip of the leaf is acute, but very soft. Each rosette has 15–35 leaves. The leaves are 9.5–27.5 in. (24–70 cm) long and 4.5–8 in. (11–20 cm) wide, a pale green to blue-green, flat to slightly concave, and thin. A stunning blue-gray selection sometimes known as *Agave attenuata* 'Nova' comes from a collection at Huntington Botanical Garden, San Marino, California. The inflorescence is straight, rather than sinuous, and the color of the leaf is a powdery, ethereal blue. This extremely handsome selection is not commonly grown outside of California.

BLOOM: The inflorescence is a dense, racemose spike 6.5–12 ft. (2–3.7 m) long. It usually curves downward and rises back up in a distinctive curve. The common name fox-tail agave derives from this feature. The flowers are pale cream to greenish yellow and occur generally in December and January.

DISTRIBUTION: The natural occurrence of *Agave attenuata* has been documented from the state of Mexico to central Jalisco at an elevation of 6000–6500 ft. (1800–1950 m) on high rocky outcrops. The original type was collected in 1834 at some unknown location in central Mexico and was described from individuals in cultivation in Europe. Few localities are known, and the species is considered somewhat rare and local in its natural distribution.

PROPAGATION: Propagation is by seed or by removal of the offsets. Offsets on the stem can be removed with a sharp cut anytime and placed in moist sand or pumice until roots are formed.

CULTURAL REQUIREMENTS: *Agave attenuata* is frost tender and requires protection when nighttime temperatures go below 32°F (0°C). Individuals at the Desert Botanical Garden have died at temperatures of 25°F (–4°C). This species thrives in the coastal areas of California in full sun, but in the low desert needs light shade to help maintain better leaf color and vigor. In the desert it is common to see yellow or nearly translucent leaves from heat stress in the late summer. This condition can be mitigated somewhat with increased watering, and the leaves usually revert back to a more normal leaf color with cooling temperatures. *Agave attenuata* tolerates weekly watering in the low desert and less in cooler temperatures.

SIMILAR OR RELATED SPECIES: *Agave attenuata* can be distinguished from all other soft-leaved agaves by its distinctive pale, naked stem and its large, soft, almost flat leaves. Young single plants could be mistaken for *A. desmettiana*, which has shorter and narrower leaves and a clear terminal spine. Young plants of *A. ellemeetiana* might be confused with *A. attenuata*, but they have widely spaced small teeth on the margin of the leaf. Two known hybrids of *A. attenuata* have been reported: a cross with *A. potatorum*, known as *A. ×guingnardii* Hort., and one with *A. xylonacantha* without a specific name. These old crosses were made probably before the turn of the twentieth century, and current records of them are sparse. A third cross, with *A. shawii*, is more recent and very attractive but not commonly available.

USES: *Agave attenuata* is a widespread ornamental plant that has been cultivated since its first appearance in Europe in the mid-nineteenth century. Its lack of teeth and spines, large graceful rosettes, and unusual arching stem make it a favorite of patio gardens in frost-free zones. It is a suitable poolside or patio plant anywhere if adequate shading and frost protection can be provided. Although it is big, it is an excellent subject for a large container and will grow to full size. Grown in the ground in the low desert, it matures quickly.

Agave avellanidens Trelease PLATE 6

SIZE: A medium-sized plant, *Agave avellanidens* forms a solitary rosette 2–4 ft. (0.6–1.2 m) tall and 3–5 ft. (1–1.5 m) wide. Mature plants may form a noticeable stem up to 1.5 ft. (0.5 m) tall.

LEAVES: The thick, fleshy, green to gray-green leaves are 3.5–5.5 in. (9–14 cm) wide and 12–21 in. (30–53 cm) long with undulate, slightly mammillate or occasionally straight margins. A horny border most frequently marks the margin. The teeth are highly variable, gray or brown, and always prominent. Most are curved and arise from a distinct teat; but others are straight and come directly off a straight margin. Highly exaggerated forms with very large teeth on equally large teats are known. The teeth are 0.25–0.5 in. (0.6–1.3 cm) long and are spaced 0.25–1 in. (0.6–2.5 cm) apart. The terminal spine is strong, conical, 1–1.75 in. (2.5–4 cm) long, and long decurrent.

BLOOM: The inflorescence is a panicle 13–20 ft. (4–6 m) tall with 25–35 short branches in the upper half of the stalk. The flowers are pale yellow but dry to an orange-yellow color and occur in late spring—April and May.

DISTRIBUTION: *Agave avellanidens* is known from the midsection of Baja California, but the full extent of its range is known poorly.

PROPAGATION: Propagation is by seed.

CULTURAL REQUIREMENTS: *Agave avellanidens* is very drought tolerant and in cool climates probably would need to be grown very dry. In the desert regions it does well in full sun on rocky soils. Intermittent summer watering maintains good vigor, but this plant needs minimal winter watering.

SIMILAR OR RELATED SPECIES: *Agave avellanidens* is extremely difficult to distinguish from *A. shawii* subsp. *goldmaniana*. The latter has a larger, wider inflorescence as well as other floral differences. *Agave avellanidens* is separable from the closely related *A. gigantensis* by the concave leaf and much smaller teeth and teats of the former. *Agave zebra* has a very rough leaf and a much longer terminal spine than *A. avellanidens*.

USES: *Agave avellanidens* is an attractive ornamental despite its formidable armature. The contrast of the pale teeth on a green leaf and the plant's bold upright form make it a dramatic specimen plant or addition to a large-scale succulent garden. Its extreme hardiness to drought makes it a fine choice for a very dry garden or a difficult location.

Agave bovicornuta Gentry

PLATE 7

COMMON NAMES: Cow horn agave, Lechuguilla verde

SIZE: *Agave bovicornuta* is a medium-sized and solitary species. At maturity it is 2.5–3 ft. (0.8–1 m) tall and can be 5–6.5 ft. (1.5–2 m) wide. Plants commonly grown in Arizona are rarely this wide, but more often 4 ft. (1.2 m) or less.

LEAVES: The leaves are 5.5–6.5 in. (14–17 cm) wide and 24–31 in. (61–79 cm) long and are much wider at the middle than either end. The margin is highly undulate with prominent teats on which are perched straight or curved teeth that are distinctly dimorphic. Typically, there are interstitial teeth. The teeth vary in size with the largest 0.25–0.5 in. (0.6–1.3 cm) long and spaced 0.75–1.5 in. (2–3.8 cm) apart. The leaves are yellow-green to green, and young leaves have a decidedly satin sheen. The leaves are smooth and strongly bud imprinted. The terminal spine is fairly short, strong, and, like the teeth, a chestnut brown color, often with a red cast.

BLOOM: The inflorescence is a panicle 16–23 ft. (5–7 m) tall with 20–30 branches. The flowers are held in the upper half of the stalk. Blooming generally commences when plants are 12–18 years old, but we have experience with several individuals that bloomed after 5 years in the ground.

DISTRIBUTION: *Agave bovicornuta* occurs in local colonies on the west side of the Sierra Madre Occidental in the Mexican states of Sinaloa, Sonora, and Chihuahua. It is found at 3000–6000 ft. (900–1800 m) in rocky outcrops in oak and pine woodlands.

PROPAGATION: Propagation is by seed.

CULTURAL REQUIREMENTS: Despite its woodland habitat, this species does very well in the low desert of the southwestern United States. Like many agaves, it appreciates light shade in the summer where the sun is intense. Shade plus regular summer irrigation prevent the summer yellowing that is common in this species. *Agave bovicornuta* is slightly frost tender, but tolerates a short, light frost. It should be protected anytime the temperature goes below 25°F (−4°C). Elsewhere it would be a container plant.

SIMILAR OR RELATED SPECIES: *Agave bovicornuta* most closely resembles *A. maximilliana* Baker and *A. wocomahi* Gentry, both of which are offered for sale very rarely. It is distinguished from all other agaves by the highly undulate margin, the smooth yellowish green leaves, various and dimorphic teeth, and solitary habit.

USES: *Agave bovicornuta* is a highly ornamental plant that mingles well with colorful wildflowers and perennials. The satiny sheen of the leaves is particularly handsome and, when the plant is sited where it can be backlit or featured in a landscape, the red-brown teeth and spines add further interest.

Agave bracteosa S. Watson ex Engelmann   PLATE 8

SIZE: *Agave bracteosa* is a small to medium-sized species rarely more than 12 in. (30 cm) tall and wide. It forms new rosettes from the leaf axils or rhizomes and can become a large mound in old age. The entire mound can be 2–2.5 ft. (0.6–0.8 m) wide.

LEAVES: The leaves are 19.5–27.5 in. (49–70 cm) long and 1–2 in. (2.5–5 cm) wide. They arch, curve and recurve gracefully, but are never very numerous, giving the plant an open irregular form. They are pale green with a more or less triangular shape that is wider at the base and narrows to an acute tip without a terminal spine. The margin is smooth.

BLOOM: The inflorescence is a dense spike 4–5.5 ft. (1.2–1.7 m) tall with blooms arising only on the upper third of the spike. The flowers are white to pale yellow and begin to bloom in June and July. A single clump may have numerous individuals in bloom simultaneously. This species is polycarpic and blooms many times in its life, a most unusual trait in agaves. The flowers have no tube and resemble those of *Hesperaloe* by being more open and flattened in appearance.

DISTRIBUTION: *Agave bracteosa* occurs naturally in the northern Sierra Madre Oriental on cliffs at 3000–5000 ft. (900–1500 m). It is endemic to this region of the Mexican states of Coahuila and Nuevo León, and is remarkably uncommon in cultivation considering its light unarmed leaves and polycarpic habit.

PROPAGATION: Propagation is by seed or by removal of the offsets.

CULTURAL REQUIREMENTS: In nature *Agave bracteosa* occurs in areas with 15–20 in. (38–51 cm) of rainfall annually. In the low desert it does best with regular irrigation (every 7–10 days) during the hottest part of the summer. It is particularly susceptible to yellowing as the result of heat stress if it is exposed to full sun in the summer, but quickly recovers if it is kept well watered. Light shade prevents yellowing in the summer. In cooler or Mediterranean climates this species performs extremely well.

SIMILAR OR RELATED SPECIES: *Agave bracteosa* is quite unmistakable with its thin, graceful, succulent, curved leaves, the relatively small size, and lack of discernible terminal spine. Even very small plants exhibit these characteristics. Plants in bloom are equally distinctive with the white to cream flowers.

USES: *Agave bracteosa* is a vastly underutilized agave for small gardens, containers, or succulent gardens. It was used historically in Spanish and other Mediterranean gardens and may still be in many of these gardens. It is frost sensitive for north ern gardens, but its size and gentle leaves make it a superb subject for container culture.

Agave celsii J. Hooker   PLATE 9

SYNONYMS: *Agave botteri* Baker, *Agave bouchei* Jacobi, *Agave haseloffii* Jacobi, *Agave micracantha* Salm-Dyck, *Agave mitis* Monachino ex Salm-Dyck

SIZE: *Agave celsii* is a medium-sized to large species with individual rosettes to 27 in. (69 cm) tall and wide. It produces offsets from axillary branches and forms extensive colonies over time.

LEAVES: The leaves are 3–5 in. (8–13 cm) wide and 12–24 in. (30–61 cm) long, much wider at the middle than the base, flat, and narrowing to form a gutter toward the tip. They are soft, succulent, upcurved, and graceful. The leaves vary in color from a bright apple green to a glaucous gray. The margin is straight or slightly undulate with tiny, closely spaced teeth that are white to reddish brown. The teeth often are bicuspid, some with small crests or tufts at the end. The terminal spine is weak, gray, 0.25–0.75 in. (0.6–2 cm) long, and long decurrent. *Agave celsii* var. *albicans* (Jacobi) Gentry, formerly considered a separate species, has glaucous gray leaves that are nearly white and very large tepals.

BLOOM: The inflorescence is a spike with the flowers held on the upper half to third of the spike. The flowers, which often are lax with age, are a greenish color with tinges of red, purple, or lavender on the interior, and commence in May.

DISTRIBUTION: *Agave celsii* occurs in eastern Mexico from the states of Nuevo León and Tamaulipas to San Luis Potosí and Hidalgo. It is uncommon in cultivation, especially in the United States.

PROPAGATION: Propagation is by seed or by removal of the offsets.

CULTURAL REQUIREMENTS: Because *Agave celsii* is not grown extensively, there is little information on its cold tolerance. It is considered frost tender but has withstood temperatures to 25°F (–4°C) in Phoenix and has survived temperatures to 12°F (–11°C) in eastern Texas. It certainly benefits from overhead protection during frost. It needs light to full shade in the low desert full sun, but in coastal or milder conditions can be planted in light shade to full sun. Clumps can be kept in bounds by removing pups as they form. Frequent irrigation is necessary in the summer in the hottest regions.

SIMILAR OR RELATED SPECIES: *Agave celsii* is similar to *A. chiapensis* in leaf shape and size, but the latter has large brown or gray teeth and a strong terminal spine. Certain clones of *A. guiengola* resemble *A. celsii* var. *albicans*, but the latter has much smaller, finer, and more regularly spaced teeth.

USES: *Agave celsii* is a beautiful agave for a shady spot or interplanted with soft, low succulents. When grown out of the low desert, particularly, it needs plenty of room so that the large clumps can form over time. It does not seem to clump quite as readily in the hot, dry climate of the low desert.

Agave cerulata Trelease   PLATE 10

SIZE: *Agave cerulata* is a medium-sized species that grows 10–20 in. (25–51 cm) tall. It produces extensive offsets, often forming vast colonies of plants.

LEAVES: The leaves are 1.5–3 in. (3.8–8 cm) wide and 10–20 in. (25–51 cm) long, lanceolate, tapering gradually to the tip, and somewhat wider at the base. They vary in color from yellow-green to gray-green and blue-green. The margin is straight or very slightly undulate, with small teeth on low teats along its length. The teeth are quite variable in size, shape, and spacing with the larger ones toward the tip. It is common for the plant to lack teeth on significant portions of the leaf. The teeth are weak, break off easily, and are surrounded at the base by a distinctive dark ring. The terminal spine is 1–2 in. (2.5–5 cm) long, fine, gray, and decurrent at least to the teeth. Three subspecies are recognized. *Agave cerulata* subsp. *dentiens* (Trelease) Gentry (synonym *A. dentiens* Trelease) has an open, few-leaved rosette with leaves 1.5–3 in. (3.8–8 cm) wide and 16–27.5 in. (40–70 cm) long. The leaves are glaucous light gray, often with noticeable crossbanding. The teeth are very small or absent. *Agave cerulata* subsp. *nelsonii* (Trelease) Gentry (synonym *A. nelsonii* Trelease) is smaller and more compact than the type. The glaucous green leaves measure 2–3 in. (5–8 cm) wide and 8–14 in. (20–36 cm) long. *Agave cerulata* subsp. *subcerulata* Gentry is another few-leaved form with an open rosette. The leaves tend to arch upward, are fleshy, and are guttered. They are glaucous white to green with very prominent teats and teeth.

BLOOM: The inflorescence is a panicle 6.5–11.5 ft. (2–3.5 m) tall with 6–12 lateral branches. The flowers are held in umbels. The flower buds are coated with a waxy, white blush but open to a pale yellow color.

DISTRIBUTION: *Agave cerulata* is the most numerous agave in western Mexico. It is found throughout the midsection of Baja California, usually below 2950 ft. (900 m) in elevation and often in vast colonies.

PROPAGATION: Propagation is by seed or by removal of the offsets.

107

CULTURAL REQUIREMENTS: *Agave cerulata* is extremely forgiving of very harsh conditions. We have seen numerous individuals at the Desert Botanical Garden that have lived on the perimeter of the garden for more than 20 years where they are unirrigated and untended yet thriving. In cooler climates it would be wise to grow this species very dry. Wetter conditions, even in nature, tend to produce plants with wider leaves and a more open rosette.

SIMILAR OR RELATED SPECIES: *Agave cerulata* is a variable and complicated complex of plants. Many forms can be confused with other species, particularly with *A. deserti*. In general, *A. cerulata* is more yellow than gray, has leaves that are from five to twelve times longer than they are wide (as opposed to *A. deserti* where the ratio is four to seven times longer than wide), and has the distinctive ring around the teeth and a white waxy blush on the buds.

USES: *Agave cerulata* was a significant source of food in historic times for the Seri Indians of the Baja peninsula. As an ornamental plant, it is an outstanding choice for very arid, hot sites or locales, but is not used as much as it should be. The species complex varies enormously, lending yet more interest for the gardener. Subspecies *dentiens* has particular ornamental value owing to its blue-gray coloring and lack of teeth.

Agave chiapensis Jacobi   PLATE 11

SIZE: *Agave chiapensis* is a medium-sized species that rises on a short stem and is solitary or forms clusters of offsets. The rosette is open and spreading.

LEAVES: The ovate leaves vary in size from 3 to 6 in. (8–15 cm) wide and from 14 to 20 in. (36–51 cm) long. They are thick, smooth, shiny green or gray-green, and flat to slightly guttered. The margin is slightly undulate and punctuated by tiny dark brown teeth arranged closely along the edge. The terminal spine is sturdy, straight, 0.75–1.25 in. (2–3.2 cm) long, red-brown, and decurrent to nearly the middle of the leaf.

BLOOM: The inflorescence is a spike up to 6.5 ft. (2 m) tall and often curves at maturity. The flowers are yellow to green tinged with red or purple.

DISTRIBUTION: *Agave chiapensis* is known from the Mexican state of Chiapas where it occurs on the face of limestone cliffs and outcrops.

PROPAGATION: Propagation is by seed or by removal of the offsets.

CULTURAL REQUIREMENTS: Little used outside of frost-free areas, *Agave chiapensis* enjoys the reputation of being very cold tender, undoubtedly because of its nearly tropical natural distribution. Its hardiness, however, has rarely has been tested. Plants in Phoenix, Arizona, with overhead protection have survived significant cold nights, lower than 25°F (−4°C), with little damage. In the low desert, overhead protection for shading and for frost protection is advised. In frost-free coastal areas plants could be grown in full sun.

SIMILAR OR RELATED SPECIES: *Agave chiapensis* resembles the slightly more common *A. celsii* but can be distinguished by its firmer, thicker leaves with brown or gray teeth (as opposed to the white or red teeth of *A. celsii*), and its strong, pungent spine (as opposed to the very weak spine of *A. celsii*).

USES: *Agave chiapensis* is an extremely handsome plant for containers or for large plantings where the clonal colonies could be grown unhindered. It makes a beautiful mass planting but is seldom used or seen. The plant has a strong tropical appearance and makes an excellent addition to gardens where other tropicals or bold-foliaged plants are used.

Agave chrysantha Peebles PLATE 12

SYNONYMS: *Agave palmeri* var. *chrysantha* (Peebles) Little ex Benson, *Agave repanda* Trelease

SIZE: *Agave chrysantha* grows as a single rosette, rarely with offsets. Plants vary from 20 to 39 in. (51–100 cm) tall and from 31 to 71 in. (79–180 cm) wide.

LEAVES: The leaves are narrow relative to the length, 3–4 in. (8–10 cm) wide and 16–30 in. (40–76 cm) long, and a glaucous blue-gray to yellow-green with a deep gutter. The margin generally is straight, but can be undulate with small teeth, which are 0.25–0.5 in. (0.6–1.3 cm) long, spaced 0.5–1 in. (1.3–2.5 cm) apart, and straight to flexed. The terminal spine is slender but strong, 1–1.75 in. (2.5–4.4 cm) long, brown to chestnut, and decurrent to the first set of teeth.

BLOOM: The inflorescence is a panicle 13–23 ft. (4–7 m) tall with 8–18 ascending branches. The flowers are held on extremely crowded umbels, with reports of 300 or more flowers in a single umbel. The flowers are a distinctive golden-yellow, rarely with any red tinge, and occur from June to August. They produce copious amounts of nectar and, with sufficient numbers of plants in bloom, a strong odor, sometimes equated with coconut, is noticeable.

DISTRIBUTION: *Agave chrysantha* is endemic to the central Arizona chaparral at elevations of 3000–6000 ft. (900–1800 m). Found chiefly in the Santa Catalina, Pinal, and Mazatzal mountains of Maricopa, Pima, and Pinal counties, it also has known populations west and east of this range.

PROPAGATION: Propagation is by seed, by removal of the offsets, or by rare bulbils.

CULTURAL REQUIREMENTS: *Agave chrysantha* is easy to grow. It does well in full sun in the low desert and requires full sun elsewhere. Good drainage is essential. Although specific cold tolerance is undocumented, the species could be hardy to 15°F (–9°C) or lower given its natural range. Cultivated plants are susceptible to infestations by the agave snout weevil.

SIMILAR OR RELATED SPECIES: *Agave chrysantha* is extremely similar to *A. palmeri*, and for some time botanists considered it a variety of that species. Without flowers it can be very difficult to tell one species from another as individual variation is high in both species, and depending on where the plant originated, the differences can be noteworthy or negligible. *Agave chrysantha* has longer leaves that are somewhat more narrow relative to the length, a more glaucous appearance to the leaf, larger teeth that are spaced further apart, and a heavier terminal spine. In bloom the red-tinged flowers of *A. palmeri* and the extreme congestion of the flowers in *A. chrysantha* separate the two species. *Agave chrysantha* would also be confused with certain individuals of *A. parryi*, but it usually is separable by its longer and narrower leaves. *Agave murpheyi* can be separated from *A. chrysantha* by its longer, much narrower leaves with smaller teeth and small terminal spine.

USES: Although occurring in an area of great pre-historic settlement, *Agave chrysantha* has few documented uses. Ornamentally, it is a beautiful plant for desert gardens. It is big and, therefore, should be sited carefully. It provides excellent contrast and interest for a wildflower planting, native garden, or perennial planting. In the low desert it also is prized for its ability to withstand full sun conditions, although in this area it looks best if the plants receive watering every two weeks in the summer. The cold tolerance of this species allows it to be grown in areas that are dry and cold.

Agave colorata Gentry   PLATE 13

SIZE: *Agave colorata* is a small species that usually is single or with a few offsets. In maturity it forms a short stem.

LEAVES: The leaves are 5–7 in. (13–18 cm) wide and 10–23 in. (25–58 cm) long. They are ovate ending in a sharp tip, although one population has long, lanceolate leaves. The leaves are a glaucous blue-gray and quite rough to the touch. The margin is fanciful with strong undulations and large prominent teats of various sizes and shapes. A very strong bud imprint marks the leaves, which usually are crossbanded, often with a pink cast, and end in a brown spine 1–2 in. (2.5–5 cm) long.

BLOOM: The inflorescence is a panicle 6–10 ft. (1.8–3 m) tall with 15–20 branches on the upper half of the stalk. It commonly is weak and leans as it emerges. The buds and bracts are reddish, but the flower opens bright yellow. Bloom begins early in Phoenix, often late February or March, but can begin as late as June. It is thought to take 15 years for a plant to bloom.

DISTRIBUTION: *Agave colorata* is a plant of the coastal zones of the Mexican state of Sonora with one population reported in higher elevations in the state of Sinaloa. In all areas of its natural distribution it is uncommon. It is a relatively uncommon species in cultivation, although there has been a surge of interest in it in the 1990s in the desert regions of Arizona.

PROPAGATION: Propagation is by seed or by removal of the offsets.

CULTURAL REQUIREMENTS: This very forgiving ornamental species can grow in almost any soil as long as there is adequate sharp drainage. In the low desert it tolerates full sun to partial shade, but in coastal areas full sun is best. In the low desert it is winter hardy, but has been little grown outside the region so the full cold tolerance is unknown.

SIMILAR OR RELATED SPECIES: Most plants of *Agave colorata* offered are similar to those from the type locality and are entirely distinctive, having the combination of few ovate leaves, short size, extraordinary crenations on the leaf, and blue-gray leaves that are crossbanded markedly. Plants from the long-leaf populations are rare, but could be difficult to distinguish from *A. shrevei* var. *matapensis* Gentry, which has no banding and generally a narrower leaf, and *A. palmeri*, which has little or no undulation on the leaf margin. *Agave guadalajarana* has much narrower leaves and the leaves are much more numerous. Countless hybrids with this species and many other species frequently are offered for sale. They exhibit a confusing array of characteristics. Most are rough, have some crossbanding even if it is faint, and show some undulation or crenation on the leaf.

USES: Historically, *Agave colorata* was roasted and eaten, used as the basis for wine, and even reduced for sugar. The species is becoming very popular in the low desert of Arizona as an ornamental plant, particularly in naturalistic gardens. It is a beautiful specimen or accent plant. Its small size makes it a fine container plant where the dramatic bud imprints and leaf crenations can be most easily admired.

Agave datylio Simon ex Weber

COMMON NAME: Datilillo

SIZE: *Agave datylio* is a stemless species with rosettes from 24 to 39 in. (61–100 cm) tall and 3.25–5 ft. (1–1.5 m) wide. It makes offsets freely.

LEAVES: The leaves are linear or lanceolate, rigid, deeply guttered, and 1–1.5 in. (2.5–3.8 cm) wide and 20–31 in. (51–79 cm) long. They are green to yellow-green and glaucous, with a straight margin and small, flat, dark teeth spread far apart on the leaf. The dark terminal spine is large, 1–1.5 in. (2.5–3.8 cm) long, conical, and slightly decurrent.

BLOOM: The inflorescence is a panicle 10–16 ft. (3–5 m) tall with 8–15 branches. The flowers are green-yellow and occur from September through December.

DISTRIBUTION: *Agave datylio* is known only from the Cape Region of Baja California, Mexico.

PROPAGATION: Propagation is by seed or by removal of the offsets. There are no records of bulbil formation, but a plant of *Agave datylio* var. *vexans* (Trelease) I. M. Johnston (synonym *A. vexans* Trelease) set a few bulbils after bloom at the Desert Botanical Garden in Phoenix.

CULTURAL REQUIREMENTS: *Agave datylio* is extremely drought tolerant, especially var. *vexans*, but has limited cold tolerance. It should be grown with excellent drainage, in full sun, even in the low desert, and on the dry side. There are few records of the cold tolerance of this species, although it has remained unharmed at 25°F (–4°C) in Phoenix.

SIMILAR OR RELATED SPECIES: The combination of yellowish green leaves that are deeply channeled and the leaf size distinguishes *Agave datylio*. *Agave subsimplex* has narrow, deeply channeled leaves, but they are much shorter, 8–14 in. (20–36 cm), and wider. *Agave decipiens* has leaves that are twice as long and wide, firm and fleshy, with a very short terminal spine. *Agave angustifolia* is, likewise, a much larger plant; the leaves are thin and fibrous, and the terminal spine is not decurrent.

USES: *Agave datylio* is not a common ornamental species but could be used much more in extremely hot or arid conditions, or in dry coastal locations.

Agave decipiens Baker

SYNONYM: *Agave laxiflora* Baker
SIZE: *Agave decipiens* is an arborescent species with a large

rosette placed atop a 3–10 ft. (1–3 m) tall stem. Usually at least a few offsets are at the base of the plant.

LEAVES: The bright green leaves are 3–4 in. (8–10 cm) wide and 29–39 in. (75–100 cm) long, fleshy, rigid and channeled. Each rosette has 20–30 leaves, which are held rigidly and which spread from the center. The margin is wavy with teeth held on low prominences, as well as small interstitial teeth. The leaves narrow toward the base, and the base is very thick and clasping around the trunk. The terminal spine is 0.25–0.75 in. (0.6–2 cm) long, conical, dark brown, and not decurrent to the margin.

BLOOM: The inflorescence is a large, thick panicle 10–16 ft. (3–5 m) tall with 10–12 branches. The flowers are green to yellow.

DISTRIBUTION: *Agave decipiens* is known from the Mexican state of Yucatán, but those individuals are probably from cultivated stock. Plants in Florida are considered the only known indigenous populations.

PROPAGATION: Propagation is by bulbils, which are prolific after flowering.

CULTURAL REQUIREMENTS: This plant requires excellent drainage and ample water in dry, hot summer regions. In the low desert, plants in some shade get larger and have a deep green color, although individuals in greater sun have thrived as well. This species thrives in the warm, humid climate of southern Florida.

SIMILAR OR RELATED SPECIES: Only *Agave karwinskii* Zuccarini, which is very uncommon in cultivation, approaches the size of a mature specimen of *A. decipiens*, but it lacks the interstitial teeth. Younger plants of *A. decipiens* are recognized by the combination of thick, fleshy leaves with fairly widely spaced teeth on short prominences, interstitial teeth, and lack of decurrence.

USES: In a large garden nothing can beat the drama and presence of such a wonderful specimen as *Agave decipiens*. It is attractive when young and without a trunk, but it is best to consider placement carefully to allow for the full massive size of a mature individual. In nearly frost-free areas the species can be used similarly to a yucca.

Agave deserti Engelmann   PLATE 14

SYNONYMS: *Agave consociata* Trelease, *Agave pringlei* Engelmann ex Baker

COMMON NAME: Desert agave

SIZE: *Agave desert* is a medium-sized species with rosettes that range from 12 to 19 in. (30–49 cm) tall and 16–24 in. (40–61) cm wide. It can be solitary, have few offsets, or form extensive clonal colonies.

LEAVES: The leaves are 2–3 in. (5–8 cm) wide and 6–16 in. (15–40 cm) long, but vary considerably in the width-to-length ratio. They are gray, blue-gray, or green, glaucous, and frequently have a banded appearance. The leaves are thick, rigid, markedly concave to guttered on the top with regularly spaced small teeth. While the margin of most forms is straight, the teeth can arise from flat, fleshy teats. The teeth generally are spaced 0.25–0.75 in. (0.6–2 cm) apart and are no more than 0.5 in. (1.3 cm) long, but there is considerable variation. The teeth are weak and easily broken off. The terminal spine is strong, dark brown aging to gray, 0.75–1.5 in. (2–3.8 cm) long, and decurrent. The two identified subspecies intergrade and can be extremely difficult to separate on leaf habit alone. *Agave deserti* subsp. *pringlei* (Engelmann ex Baker) Gentry is much greener than the type. It has longer leaves, up to 27 in. (69 cm) long, and a strong spine that is decurrent to the middle of the leaf. *Agave deserti* subsp. *simplex* Gentry is solitary in habit.

BLOOM: The inflorescence is a panicle 8–13 ft. (2.4–4 m) tall with 6–15 branches. The flowers are held on umbels in the upper fourth of the stalk. They are bright yellow and occur from May to July. Individuals may take a very long time to bloom in nature, but exact figures are known poorly.

DISTRIBUTION: *Agave deserti* is distributed widely in the arid plains and rocky ranges of southern California, southern and western Arizona, northern Sonora in Mexico, and the northern half of the Baja peninsula. It ranges from 300 to 5000 ft. (90–1500 m) in elevation, giving it one of the most extensive elevation ranges in the genus.

PROPAGATION: Propagation is by seed or by removal of the

offsets. In nature, vegetative reproduction appears to be the most significant strategy, and the drier the area, the more plants rely on this type of reproduction. In nature, seed germination is erratic and apparently dependent on a sequence of rain events throughout the seedlings' first year. In cultivation, seed germinates readily and grows steadily.

CULTURAL REQUIREMENTS: *Agave deserti* requires outstanding drainage and looks best in a full sun location. Mature plants are cold tolerant to 5°F (–15°C) and smaller plants or seedlings to 17°F (–8°C). In cooler climates this species should be grown very dry and with as much sun and heat as possible.

SIMILAR OR RELATED SPECIES: *Agave deserti* is a confusing array of forms, many of which are understood poorly. *Agave mckelveyana* is a smaller plant, with small, narrow leaves. In bloom or in nature these species are not as difficult to distinguish, but small plants or certain individuals can look remarkably similar. Differences and distinctions between this species complex and the equally variable complex of *A. cerulata*, which occurs just south of this group, are discussed under *A. cerulata*. *Agave utahensis* has leaves that are more rigid and a ring around the base of the teeth that is lacking in *A. deserti*. *Agave subsimplex* has much narrower leaves than *A. deserti*.

USES: *Agave deserti* was used extensively by all peoples within its range for food. Some groups roasted the plant in pits, while others roasted it above ground. Animals use it extensively for food and shelter. This species also has a long history as a fiber source. Ornamentally, it is among the loveliest agaves for a very hot and dry spot. Certain individuals, particularly subsp. *simplex*, are striking with regular, large teeth and a blue to gray cast. The species works well in a mixed succulent or desert shrub planting.

Agave desmettiana Jacobi   PLATES 15, 16; FIGURE 3-4

SYNONYMS: *Agave regeliana* Jacobi, *Agave miradorensis* Jacobi

SIZE: *Agave desmettiana* is a small to medium-sized species with a distinctive upright, urn-shaped rosette in most individuals. The rosette is from 27 to 35 in. (69–89 cm) tall.

LEAVES: The turgid but brittle leaves are fleshy and narrow to a thick base. They are openly ascending to urn-shaped, guttered on the top, and range from pale greenish yellow to dark blue-green. The leaves are 3–8 in. (8–20 cm) wide and 20–31 in. (51–79 cm) long. Most plants lack teeth on the leaf margin, or have very fine teeth near the leaf base. Forms with yellow margins exist in cultivation. The terminal spine is 0.75–1 in. (2–2.5 cm) and dark brown.

BLOOM: The inflorescence is a panicle 8–10 ft. (2.4–3 m) tall with 20–25 branches. The flowers are a pale yellow. Blooms occur after plants have been in the ground 8–10 years. The plants set bulbils prolifically in some individuals.

DISTRIBUTION: No natural populations of *Agave desmettiana* are known. The species is cultivated widely in Mexico, in Europe, and in the western United States. It reportedly was described from a plant brought to Europe from El Mirador, Sartorius's garden in Veracruz, Mexico, but could have come to him from anywhere. This species was described formally as *A. desmettiana* in 1866. Given the plant's lovely association with Sartorius's garden, it is too bad the rules of nomenclature dictate that the old name, *A. miradorensis*, must be retired.

PROPAGATION: Propagation is easy by seed, by removal of the offsets, or by bulbils.

CULTURAL REQUIREMENTS: This agave does best with some shade in the low desert, but can tolerate nearly total shade with excellent results. In cooler climates it may be grown in partial shade or full sun, especially on a Mediterranean coast. Plants grow steadily with minimal supplemental irrigation, or can accept regular irrigation without an adverse impact. Offsets are set early in the life of a plant, growing to nearly the size of the original by the time it blooms, which is generally 8–10 years. This species is somewhat cold tender with damage occurring below 25°F (−4°C).

SIMILAR OR RELATED SPECIES: Only *Agave weberi* has the combination of long, fleshy leaves with little or no marginal teeth and a stout terminal spine. *Agave desmettiana* is separable by its more guttered leaf, smaller size, and leaves that are a dark blue-green. Mature plants of *A. weberi* have a large open rosette, while mature plants of *A. desmettiana* have a more tightly held rosette at least half the size of *A. weberi*.

USES: *Agave desmettiana* is an extraordinarily attractive agave with a beautiful form. It is equally attractive in the ground or in a large container. Although it grows best in some shade in the low desert, in cooler or milder climates it should be grown in the full sun. The species has limited cold tolerance, although our experience suggests that its cold limits may have been exaggerated. Many bulbils once survived overnight temperatures of 25°F (−4°C) with limited damage. Plants in the ground with overhead protection have survived even lower temperatures undamaged.

Agave ellemeetiana Jacobi

SIZE: *Agave ellemeetiana* is a stemless, medium-sized species 12–20 in. (30–51 cm) tall and 27–39 in. (69–100 cm) wide. It forms an open rosette of 20–35 leaves and produces a few offsets.

LEAVES: The succulent, smooth, ovate to oblong leaves are bright green and 5–8 in. (13–20 cm) wide and 20–27 in. (51–69 cm) long. The margin is unarmed and red-brown, but can have fine serration near the tip. The margin is detachable. The leaves are fairly flat above and round below, ending in a short, barely callused tip. They are held upright or recurved when young, but downcurve as they mature.

BLOOM: The inflorescence is a tight spike 10–15 ft. (3–4.6 m) tall. The flowers are bell-shaped and pale green-yellow. Blooming begins close to the base and continues to the end of the spike.

DISTRIBUTION: The natural distribution of *Agave ellemeetiana* is subject to speculation, but it is thought to be somewhere near Jalapa in the Mexican state of Veracruz. It is considered a fairly rare and local endemic. Horticulturally, the species has been known in European gardens since at least 1864. La Mortola, a garden on the Italian Riviera, had plants in the nineteenth century and so did the Royal Botanic Gardens, Kew, although the plants at La Mortola are thought to have died out.

PROPAGATION: Propagation is by seed or by removal of the offsets.

CULTURAL REQUIREMENTS: *Agave ellemeetiana* was cultivated since the mid-nineteenth century in European gardens, chiefly in pots, and thrived under these conditions. Specific details of its culture are difficult to ascertain, but like *A. guiengola*, it prefers light shade and protection from hard frosts.

SIMILAR OR RELATED SPECIES: *Agave ellemeetiana* is separable from *A. guiengola*, a close relative, by the bright green leaf color and the reddish, unarmed margin. *Agave guiengola* has blue-gray leaves with a dark brown margin punctuated by coarse teeth. Some authors consider *A. pruinosa* Lemaire a synonym of *A. ellemeetiana*, but Gentry (1982) rejects that notion and considers *A. pruinosa* conspecific with *A. attenuata*. This position raises many questions concerning *A. ellemeetiana* and *A. attenuata*, and it would be reasonable to expect hybrids from the European collections to be unknowingly called by either name.

USES: Ornamentally, *Agave ellemeetiana* is an extremely handsome species, although often difficult to locate. The combination of the bright green leaves, accented by the reddish margin, and of an open, soft appearance makes it a handsome garden choice and an elegant container plant.

Agave felgeri Gentry

COMMON NAME: Mescalito

SIZE: A small plant, *Agave felgeri* is characterized by having a few narrow leaves in a loose rosette. Offsets form dense, clonal colonies.

LEAVES: The narrow, linear leaves are 0.25–0.5 in. (0.6–1.3 cm) wide and 10–12 in. (25–30 cm) long. They are light green to yellow-green, often with a pale median stripe. The margin is narrow and brown with sparse filaments. The terminal spine is weak, gray, and less than 0.5 in. (1.3 cm) long.

BLOOM: The inflorescence is a spike 1.5–8 ft. (0.5–2.4 m) tall with the flowers held on the upper fourth of the stalk. Plants bloom erratically and irregularly in May through August and again in October.

DISTRIBUTION: *Agave felgeri* is a rare and scattered species of the coastal areas and plains of the Mexican state of Sonora. It is found in extremely rocky, xeric locales. Occasionally it is cultivated in the southwestern United States.

PROPAGATION: Propagation is by seed, by offsets, or by separating clones from the colony.

CULTURAL REQUIREMENTS: This extremely rugged plant grows in full-sun rocky locations in the low desert and requires only intermittent summer watering to remain healthy. In containers it is susceptible to overwatering, so care should be given to keep it in a very sunny, hot location.

SIMILAR OR RELATED SPECIES: *Agave felgeri* appears extremely similar to *A. schottii,* although in nature their ranges do not overlap. The leaf of *A. felgeri* has a rough, scabrous surface, while that of *A. schottii* is generally smooth. Both species have weak, sparse filaments, but those of *A. schottii* usually are somewhat coarser.

USES: No ethnobotanical uses are reported for *Agave felgeri.* Ornamentally, it is useful for low desert gardeners with rocky, rugged locations. It spreads and offers some green relief for xeric hillsides or road scars.

Agave filifera Salm-Dyck   FIGURE 2-3

SYNONYMS: *Agave filamentosa* Salm-Dyck, *Agave filamentosa* var. *filamentosa* Baker

SIZE: *Agave filifera* is a small to medium-sized species that grows as a caespitose clump of many dense rosettes to 20 in. (51 cm) tall and 26 in. (66 cm) wide.

LEAVES: The numerous leaves are dark green marked by a white bud imprint. The margin is smooth but has abundant fine, recurved filaments. The leaves measure 0.75–1.5 in. (2–3.8 cm) wide and 6–12 in. (15–30 cm) long and are straight with the widest point at the middle of the leaf. The slightly grooved, but generally flattened, terminal spine is gray and 0.25 in. (0.6 cm) long.

BLOOM: The inflorescence is a spike 6.5–8 ft. (2–2.4 m) tall.

The flowers are greenish with a red to purple blush and purple stamens. They cover the upper half of the stalk, and each bloom is held on a short pedicel.

DISTRIBUTION: The natural distribution of *Agave filifera* is not well known or documented, although records exist from the Mexican states of Hidalgo and San Luis Potosí. The species was described from cultivated specimens in European gardens, and subsequent verification in the field has been slight.

PROPAGATION: Propagation is by seed or by removal of the offsets.

CULTURAL REQUIREMENTS: This agave has been cultivated for nearly 200 years and does extremely well in either containers or the ground. In coastal or cooler areas it grows well in full sun, but it should be provided ample room because the numerous offsets occur rapidly and increase the size of the overall plant dramatically. In the low desert, light shade and light frost protection help keep the plant looking its best.

SIMILAR OR RELATED SPECIES: *Agave filifera* and *A. schidigera* are so similar that many authors suggest they represent one quite variable taxon. Considering how readily they hybridize, how similar the hybrids look to the "species," and how variable the entire group is, the chance of these two being one species is good. Generally the name *A. filifera* is used for plants with numerous offsets and whiter, more numerous filaments. *Agave schidigera* typically is solitary or with a small number of offsets. Numerous horticultural plants and hybrids involve *A. filifera*. Some of the more commonly encountered are mentioned here. *Agave* ×*romanii* Hort. is a hybrid with *A. xalapensis* Roezl ex Jacobi, and *A.* ×*villarum* Hort. is a hybrid with *A. xylonacantha* Salm-Dyck. A name still encountered in the trade, *A.* ×*leopoldii* Hort. (synonym *A.* ×*leopoldii* II Hort.), is a hybrid with *A. schidigera*; it has leaves that tend to spread and white stripes on both sides of the leaves.

USES: Ornamentally a beautiful plant, *Agave filifera* complements a variety of styles and plantings. The strong green leaves in a tight rosette, with the filaments and contrasting white markings, make *A. filifera* a good accent or focal plant either in the ground or in containers.

Agave fourcroydes Lemaire

SYNONYM: *Agave sullivani* Trelease

COMMON NAME: Henequen

SIZE: *Agave fourcroydes* is a large species that can develop a 3–5.5 ft. (1–1.7 m) tall trunk under optimal conditions. The species produces offsets that can result in very large clumps.

LEAVES: The thin, narrow, lanceolate leaves are 3–5 in. (8–13 cm) wide and 4–6 ft. (1.2–1.8 m) long. They are gray-green with a straight margin and no horny edge. The slender, dark teeth are spaced widely along the margin. The terminal spine is stout and round, 0.75–1 in. (2–2.5 cm) long, dark brown, and not decurrent. The leaves are very thick at the base, nearly round, with the leaf guttered along the length. In some individuals the teeth appear to rise on a very small mammillate margin.

BLOOM: The inflorescence is a panicle 16–20 ft. (5–6 m) tall with 10–18 branches. The flowers are green to yellow and sterile, but set prodigious numbers of bulbils after flowering.

DISTRIBUTION: *Agave fourcroydes* is a sterile hybrid that has long been cultivated for fiber throughout eastern Mexico. It is most common in the states of Yucatán, Veracruz, and Tamaulipas, but is found either ornamentally or agriculturally throughout warm regions worldwide.

PROPAGATION: Propagation is by removal of the offsets or bulbils.

CULTURAL REQUIREMENTS: *Agave fourcroydes* is very frost tender and even in the low desert needs frost protection. Temperatures at or below 28°F (−2°C) cause serious leaf damage. The plants accept full sun in any region and grow best with regular summer irrigation in hot summer areas.

SIMILAR OR RELATED SPECIES: *Agave fourcroydes* can be distinguished from other large agaves by its fairly tall stem, narrow but long, guttered gray-green leaves, and small, slender teeth on a straight margin. This species can be difficult to separate from selected clones of *A. angustifolia*, but it usually is larger and the leaves are guttered distinctly as opposed to the rigid, flat leaves of *A. angustifolia*. *Agave decipiens* has leaves that are thick and fleshy, and the margin is undulate with the teeth held on teats. *Agave sisalana* has no or minute teeth on the margin.

Uses: *Agave fourcroydes* is grown commonly for its tough, strong fiber that reportedly is resistant to seawater. Ornamentally, it is a handsome agave for a larger garden in a warm, frost-free area, where its gray-green leaves add strong textural interest and color contrast.

Agave franzosinii Baker   PLATE 17

Size: *Agave franzosinii* is a very large, striking species 6.5–10 ft. (2–3 m) tall and to 15 ft. (4.6 m) wide. Rarely solitary, the plants usually are surrounded by offsets of varying sizes.

Leaves: The leaves are glaucous light gray-blue to gray-green and, in some individuals, nearly white. The leaves are 9–14 in. (23–36 cm) wide and 6–7 ft. (1.8–2.1 m) long, rough, lanceolate, and widening significantly toward the tip. They are open, spreading, and flat, becoming guttered toward the tip. In most individuals the final few inches of the leaf roll inward sharply to the spine, causing the leaf to recurve gracefully. Each rosette has about 50 leaves. The teeth arise from a wide base, are 1–3 in. (2.5–8 cm) long, recurved, and chestnut-brown. The terminal spine is 1–2 in. (2.5–5 cm) long, often sinuous, and decurrent down the inrolled tip to the first teeth.

Bloom: The inflorescence is an enormous panicle 26–37 ft. (8–11 m) tall. The flowers are yellow and occur from July to September.

Distribution: No record exists of a natural distribution of *Agave franzosinii*. It has been known ornamentally for more than 100 years, particularly in European gardens. Whether it is an unusual form of *A. americana*, with which it clearly is related closely, or a one-time hybrid remains open to further work.

Propagation: Propagation is usually by removal of the offsets, although seed is formed.

Cultural requirements: *Agave franzosinii* performs well in full sun or partial shade. In the low desert it requires regular summer irrigation to look its best. In cooler or coastal climates it can be grown with moderate supplemental water. While it can be grown in pots, the enormous size makes that difficult and unrewarding.

SIMILAR OR RELATED SPECIES: Few other plants are as large and light blue-gray to white, as is *Agave franzosinii*. Young plants could be confused with the closely related *A. americana*, but even the palest forms of the latter are rarely so bright as this species. *Agave franzosinii* can be distinguished from *A. americana* by the combination of a wider leaf, highly contrasting teeth and spine color, a flatter leaf surface over the entire length of the blade, rough leaf surface, and the lack of a groove on the top of the terminal spine.

USES: *Agave franzosinii* can be used to insert a bright spot in a dark corner or to create a focal point unexpectedly from a curve or turn. It needs plenty of space to look its best. It looks outstanding with a dense, dark green background to further exaggerate its brilliant leaf color. While somewhat similar to *A. americana*, this species is much less common, particularly in the United States, but with its outstanding ornamental characteristics it should be more frequently considered.

Agave geminiflora (Tagliabue) Ker-Gawler   PLATE 18

SYNONYMS: *Littaea geminiflora* Tagliabue, *Agave angustissima* Engelmann

SIZE: Typically solitary, the rosette of *Agave geminiflora* reaches 2–3 ft. (0.6–1 m) tall. The mature plant rises on a short stem with a very dense rosette of 100–200 leaves.

LEAVES: The leaves are linear and very narrow, 0.25–0.5 in. (0.6–1.3 cm) wide and 18–24 in. (46–61 cm) long. The margin is smooth with very fine filaments along the edge. The number of filaments varies, with some individuals having no filaments. The leaves are a dark green color and flexible. The flat, gray terminal spine is less than 0.25 in. (0.6 cm) long. *Agave geminiflora* var. *atricha* Trelease (synonym *A. geminiflora* var. *knightiana* Drummond) has stiffer, shorter leaves, and no filaments. Plants of this variety are 11–14 in. (28–36 cm) wide.

BLOOM: The inflorescence is a narrow spike 9–12 ft. (2.7–3.7

m) tall. The flowers are held in pairs and occur on the upper two-thirds of the stalk. They are yellow with a flush of red or purple at the base.

DISTRIBUTION: *Agave geminiflora* was described originally from cultivated plants in Europe but was found in 1951 near Ocotillo in the Mexican state of Nayarit. There it grows in oak woodlands at 3000–4000 ft. (900–1200 m) elevation.

PROPAGATION: Propagation is by seed. *Agave geminiflora* does not make offsets or bulbils, although plants in crowded containers may produce some multiheaded individuals and occasional offsets.

CULTURAL REQUIREMENTS: *Agave geminiflora* is somewhat cold tender and should be protected from harsh cold even in the low desert. It tolerates considerable shade in the low to mid desert regions and benefits from ample summer watering. Plants in containers grow well and quickly, but can become decrepit if not kept amply watered and given ample room. In mild coastal areas plants should be grown in full sun to achieve the best form.

SIMILAR OR RELATED SPECIES: All other species of this size with numerous filaments, such as *Agave filifera, A. multifilifera,* or *A. schidigera,* have leaves that are much flatter and wider than those of *A. geminiflora. Agave stricta* has very narrow leaves and no filaments. *Agave striata* has rounded, sometimes keeled, thin leaves without filaments and many fewer leaves than the 100 or more common in *A. geminiflora.* The leaves of *A. schottii* and *A. felgeri* are thin with filaments, fewer in number, and flat on the top. *Agave geminiflora* has been cultivated for more than 100 years, and named hybrids and varieties are known. *Agave ×taylori* Hort., a hybrid with *A. filifera,* is distinguished by having very thin leaves that are well marked with white and are highly filamentous. A second hybrid with *A. filifera* was known as *A. ×wrightii* Drummond.

USES: The numerous leaves so symmetrically arranged make *Agave geminiflora* a unique landscape plant. It is an excellent choice to accent perennial or other color plantings, or to use in a fairly tight mass planting. It is a particularly effective container plant near a patio or pool. Although not very large, it should be sited carefully so that the tight rosette can mature without interference.

Agave ghiesbreghtii Lemaire ex Jacobi

SYNONYMS: *Agave roezliana* Baker, *Agave purpusorum* Berger, *Agave huehueteca* Standley & Steyerman

SIZE: *Agave ghiesbreghtii* is a medium-sized species with extensive sets of offsets. The rosette is 19.5–27.5 in. (49–70 cm) wide. This graceful plant has slightly incurved leaves and striking color contrasts.

LEAVES: The leaves are 2.75–4 in. (7–10 cm) wide and 11.75–15.75 in. (29.5–40 cm) long, slightly wider at the middle of the leaf, dark green, sometimes lighter, with a thin brown to gray horny edge. The leaves generally are few, typically 30–40 on the plant, and flat to very slightly guttered above and convex below. The teeth are straight, brown, and typically occur only on the lower two-thirds of the leaf. The slightly decurved terminal spine is only 0.5 in. (1.3 cm) long. There are two recognized varieties. *Agave ghiesbreghtii* var. *leguayana* Baker has longer leaves than the type and very small, closely spaced teeth. *Agave ghiesbreghtii* var. *rohanii* Baker is quite compact with concave blue-green leaves.

BLOOM: The inflorescence is a spike 8.25–13 ft. (2.5–4 m) tall. The flowers are a greenish brown, often to purple, and begin to bloom from March through May.

DISTRIBUTION: *Agave ghiesbreghtii* is found in the state of Mexico south to Guatemala.

PROPAGATION: Propagation is by seed or by removal of the offsets.

CULTURAL REQUIREMENTS: Cold tolerance is not well known in *Agave ghiesbreghtii*. In Phoenix the plant has shown no damage to 25°F (−4°C), but may be able to tolerate lower temperatures. Plants in the low desert do best with moderate to steady summer watering if grown in the full sun. This species does well in an enriched garden soil. In more moderate climates it should be grown in strong sun with moderate summer watering.

SIMILAR OR RELATED SPECIES: *Agave ghiesbreghtii* is distinguished from *A. lophantha* and *A. lechuguilla* by its leaves that are slightly wider at the middle of the leaf and slightly curved, a thin brown border with very small, straight teeth, and a uniform, not striated, leaf surface. It can be separated from *A. schidigera* by its lack of filaments, by having teeth only on the upper two-thirds of the leaf, and by its wider, less numerous leaves. Owing to its long history of cultivation, this species has produced countless hybrids.

USES: *Agave ghiesbreghtii* is a wonderful garden plant. It contrasts extremely well with lush perennial plantings, offers good color and contrast with the leaf and the margin, and is graceful as an accent or other focal planting. It grows well in containers.

Agave gigantensis Gentry

SIZE: *Agave gigantensis* is a solitary stemless species 1.5–3 ft. (0.5–1 m) tall and 2.5–4 ft. (0.8–1.2 m) wide. The rosette has few leaves and is open and spreading.

LEAVES: The strongly lanceolate leaves are 4–6 in. (10–15 cm) wide and 15–29 in. (38–75 cm) long. They are rigid, thick, smooth and light green to gray-green, but can turn red or purple when the plant blooms. The margin is deeply undulate to mammillate with a horny border from the tip to halfway down the leaf in most individuals. The teeth are spaced widely, 2–3 in. (5–8 cm) apart, and fantastic in shape, curling, curved, or straight, sometimes in pairs, and usually on a very broad base that in some individuals forms a continuous border between the teeth. The terminal spine is strong, 1–2 in. (2.5–5 cm) long, either straight or curved, and is decurrent to the middle of the leaf.

BLOOM: The inflorescence is a panicle 13–16 ft. (4–5 m) tall with 15–25 umbels in the upper third of the stalk. The flowers begin as waxy, white buds but emerge a pale yellow.

DISTRIBUTION: Probably a rare endemic, *Agave gigantensis* is known only from the Sierra de la Giganta of central Baja at elevations from 2000 to 5000 ft. (600–1500 m).

PROPAGATION: Propagation is solely by seed.

CULTURAL REQUIREMENTS: Little is known about the specific cultural requirements of *Agave gigantensis*, but in the Phoenix area it performs equally well in full sun or partial shade with irregular summer irrigation. In cooler climates it would undoubtedly need to be grown dry. There is little information on its cold tolerance, but plants have remained undamaged to 25°F (–4°C) in Phoenix.

SIMILAR OR RELATED SPECIES: Similar to *Agave avellanidens*, which occurs north of it, *A. gigantensis* is separable from the former by its more exaggerated teats and by its larger teeth that are spaced widely. Older specimens of *A. avellanidens* have a visible stem. *Agave zebra* has crossbanded leaves with a rough surface and a very long terminal spine.

USES: *Agave gigantensis* is used locally in the production of mescal and is considered superior for this product. Ornamentally, the moderate size and fantastic teeth and spines of this species make it a stunning specimen in a dry, rocky location.

Agave guadalajarana Trelease

SIZE: *Agave guadalajarana* is a small, compact, tightly formed species that is solitary, rarely with offsets. The rosette ranges from 10 to 13.75 in. (25–35 cm) wide.

LEAVES: The obovate to oblong leaves are 3–4.75 in. (8–12 cm) wide and 8–12 in. (20–30 cm) long. The margin is distinctly to heavily mammillate with small teeth toward the base of the leaf becoming much more prominent toward the tip. The leaves are gray to gray-green, some nearly white. The terminal spine is strong, straight or slightly sinuous, and dark red-brown fading to tan.

BLOOM: The inflorescence is slender and 13–16 ft. (4–5 m) tall with 15–20 branches. The yellow flowers are held in umbels.

DISTRIBUTION: *Agave guadalajarana* has a limited distribution in and around Guadalajara, the capital of the Mexican state of Jalisco, at 5000 ft. (1500 m) elevation.

PROPAGATION: Propagation is by seed or by removal of offsets.

CULTURAL REQUIREMENTS: *Agave guadalajarana* is cultivated widely, but is fairly cold tender, even in the low desert. It appreciates very sharp drainage and in the low desert requires partial shade.

SIMILAR OR RELATED SPECIES: *Agave guadalajarana* is similar to *A. colorata*, but can be separated by its numerous leaves that generally are much narrower than those of *A. colorata*. Older plants of *A. colorata* often have a short stem, while those of *A. guadalajarana* are entirely stemless. Many individual collections of this species were referred to *A. megalacantha* Bourgeau, but no evidence shows that the latter name is valid or even synonymous with *A. guadalajarana*.

USES: *Agave guadalajarana* is a lovely, small blue-gray plant that complements smaller succulent or perennials. It is an excellent container plant.

Agave guiengola Gentry   PLATE 19

SIZE: *Agave guiengola* is a medium-sized species that is mostly solitary, occasionally with offsets. The rosette is 30–40 in. (76–102 cm) wide.

LEAVES: The glaucous blue-gray leaves are up to 22 in. (57 cm) long and 5–6 in. (13–15 cm) wide. They are thick and succulent, widening dramatically near the midpoint and tapering sharply to the tip to form a wide gutter. The margin is straight with small brown to maroon teeth that appear like serrations on the leaf. The teeth typically alternate by size, with one tooth twice the size of the next, although some irregularity can occur. The terminal spine is strong, brown to maroon, shortly decurrent, and occasionally not at all. There are relatively few leaves on a plant, and the plant looks open and slightly flat.

BLOOM: The inflorescence is a spike 5–6 ft. (1.5–1.8 m) tall with flowers growing near the base. The flowers are pale yellow to yellow-white and occur in February and March.

DISTRIBUTION: *Agave guiengola* is an endemic occurring on a limestone formation of the same name on the Isthmus of Tehuantepec in the Mexican state of Oaxaca. It is found between 300 and 3000 ft. (90–900 m) elevation.

PROPAGATION: Propagation is by seed or by the removal of

the occasional offset. Plants in crowded containers tend to set many more offsets than plants in the ground.

CULTURAL REQUIREMENTS: *Agave guiengola* tolerates more shade than most agaves without any noticeable etiolation of the leaves. In fact, it is advisable to grow it in at least partial shade in the low desert. It is reported to be cold sensitive, but individuals with overhead protection have withstood air temperatures of at least 25°F (–4°C) in Phoenix. Regular summer irrigation is important in the low desert to keep the plants in good condition. In milder climates plants can be grown in partial shade or full sun with only moderate summer irrigation.

SIMILAR OR RELATED SPECIES: *Agave guiengola* is distinguished from *A. ellemeetiana* by regular marginal teeth and a strong terminal spine. In addition, *A. ellemeetiana* is polycarpic while *A. guiengola* is monocarpic. *Agave guiengola* can be separated from *A. celsii* var. *albicans* by the larger, wider leaves and larger teeth.

USES: *Agave guiengola* reportedly is used in the Mexican state of Oaxaca for mucilage and indeed the cut leaf is extremely mucilaginous. The plant is a stunning ornamental with pale, nearly white leaves accented by dark teeth and spines and with a large, open habit. Its form lends itself well to container culture, although one may want to reduce the number of offsets from time to time. This agave tolerates more water in the summer than some, but drainage must be excellent. In the low desert it is a striking choice for a dry, shady location.

Agave havardiana Trelease   PLATE 20

SIZE: *Agave havardiana* is a medium-sized species 16–24 in. (40–61 cm) tall and 20–31 in. (51–79 cm) wide with tightly held, fairly numerous leaves in a very symmetrical rosette. It is usually solitary or with very few offsets.

LEAVES: The leaves are a glaucous gray to dull green, occasionally yellowish, very thick at the base, rigid, and wide at the middle of the leaf, tapering to a sharp tip. They are 6–8 in. (15–20 cm) wide and 12–24 in. (30–61 cm) long. The upper surface is concave and the lower surface is convex. The margin is straight or slightly undulate. The teeth are spaced 1–2 in. (2.5–5 cm) apart. At the upper end of the leaf, the teeth tend to be straight and larger, while at the lower end the teeth are reflexed and smaller. The terminal spine is stout, dark brown aging to gray, 1–2 in. (2.5–5 cm) long, and decurrent sometimes as a continuous border.

BLOOM: The inflorescence is a panicle 6.5–16 ft. (2–5 m) tall. The flowers are held in umbels, are green-yellow tinged with red-purple, and occur in June and July.

DISTRIBUTION: *Agave havardiana* occurs in western Texas, southeastern New Mexico, into the Mexican states of Coahuila and Chihuahua at elevations from 4000 to 6500 ft. (1200–1950 m). It sometimes is seen as an ornamental in Texas and New Mexico.

PROPAGATION: Propagation is by seed or by the occasional offset.

CULTURAL REQUIREMENTS: *Agave havardiana* does well in a wide variety of garden conditions. In Phoenix and other low desert locations it grows well with light shade and intermittent summer watering. In milder areas it should be grown in full sun. Because of its native range, it has good cold tolerance and can grow in much higher, or in cold, dry locations. It is reported to tolerate cold well below 0°F (−18°C).

SIMILAR OR RELATED SPECIES: *Agave havardiana* can be distinguished from the closely related *A. neomexicana* by its wider, often longer gray to gray-green leaves. *Agave parryi* usually has straighter teeth, and is narrower at the base of the leaf with a flatter leaf.

USES: Apache Indians used this agave extensively as a wild collected food, roasting the heart of a plant just about to bloom in a open pit. As an ornamental, this handsome plant is compact and regular in its habit. Like many of its near relatives, it is a superb plant when seen from above if the garden has such a spot. It blends well with small-scale perennials, wildflowers, or other succulents.

Agave lechuguilla Torrey

PLATE 21

SYNONYMS: *Agave poselgeri* Salm-Dyck, *Agave multilineata* Baker, *Agave heteracantha* Hort.

COMMON NAMES: Shin dagger, Lechuguilla

SIZE: *Agave lechuguilla* is a medium-sized species that sets offsets freely. The rosette has few l aves and is 10–18 in. (25–46 cm) tall and 16–27 in. (40–69 cm) wide.

LEAVES: The leaves are straight, ascending or curved toward the center, with a concave top and convex below. They are 1–1.5 in. (2.5–3.8 cm) wide and 10–19.5 in. (25–49 cm) long. Usually a rosette has 20 leaves, but there can be as few as 8 or as many as 60. The leaves are a light green, occasionally yellowish green, and strongly striated. The striations typically are much paler than the leaf color. The leaf margin is straight with a thin, gray horny border that is detachable. The widely spaced, irregular, down-curved brown teeth age to gray. The terminal spine is conical, straight, and 0.5–1.5 in. (1.3–3.8 cm) long, beginning brown but fading to gray with age. Old texts and some European collections recognize a variety of *Agave lechuguilla* called *A. nigrescens* Hort. It has dark blue-green leaves that are frequently undulate. A form, *A. nigrescens* f. *inermis* Hort., is colored similarly but has no teeth. While neither name is valid today, these two forms can be found occasionally.

BLOOM: The inflorescence is spikelike and rises 8–16 ft. (2.4–5 m) above the plant. The flowers are yellow with red or purple shading and occur from May through July. Some authors report bloom when plants are as young as 3–4 years old, but other plants are 20 years old before they bloom.

DISTRIBUTION: *Agave lechuguilla* is extremely common and widespread, ranging from southern New Mexico through west Texas and south into Mexico through the states of Chihuahua, Tamaulipas, Zacatecas, and San Luis Potosí to Hidalgo. It occurs from 3000 to 7000 ft. (900–2100 m) elevation, on limestone soils or outcrops, and often is in extensive dense colonies. Gentry (1982) reports from another author a count of 21,000 plants per acre (52,500 per hectare) and colonies of many dozens of square feet have been reported.

PROPAGATION: Propagation is by seed or by removal of the offsets. This species reportedly self-pollinates in nature.

CULTURAL REQUIREMENTS: *Agave lechuguilla* is a resilient species capable of growing and thriving in a wide variety of cultural conditions. It tolerates extreme heat and looks its best in full sun regardless of the region. It naturally occurs in areas that receive 12–20 in. (30–51 cm) of rain annually, but it endures and often thrives on much less rainfall, particularly in cooler areas. In the low desert it is best to water this species well once or twice a month during the summer to prevent yellowing. It has good cold tolerance and is able to withstand temperatures down to 0°F (–18°C).

SIMILAR OR RELATED SPECIES: *Agave lechuguilla* is confused easily with its close relative *A. lophantha* but can be distinguished by the concave or nearly round aspect of the leaf, a straight margin, and more irregular teeth. Countless hybrids exist between these two species. Because the two intergrade freely in vast portions of their respective ranges, differences between certain individuals can become subtle and unreliable. A form in some Texas populations has an irregular compound inflorescence.

USES: Despite the name (*lechuguilla* means "little lettuce" in Spanish), the species has no history of being eaten by people. Historically, it was an extremely important plant for soap production in its range. Although poisonous to cows, it has been a secondary browse for deer and javelina. It has a highly fibrous leaf, and twine and rope production have long been important throughout the range of the species. It is the source of the fiber known as *ixtle* or *istle*. Ornamentally, *A. lechuguilla* is a handsome plant but must be given some room since it forms extensive colonies rather quickly. Occasional individuals do not produce offsets and are lovely in pots or close quarters where the graceful leaf striation can be best enjoyed. It is a good ornamental choice for very dry climates, especially in the colder regions, or where care is minimal.

Agave lophantha Schiede   PLATE 22

SYNONYMS: *Agave univittata* Haworth, *Agave heteracantha* Zuccarini, *Agave vittata* Regel, *Agave mezortillo* Hort.

SIZE: *Agave lophantha* is a medium-sized species that is solitary or with offsets around the base. The rosette is 20–40 in. (51–102 cm) tall and 12–24 in. (30–61 cm) wide. The plant has an open, somewhat spreading appearance, with 30–80 leaves in the rosette.

LEAVES: The leaves vary in color from a dark deep green to a pale yellow-green. Some plants have a light midstripe that is prominent in some leaves and missing in others. The leaves are 1–2 in. (2.5–5 cm) wide and 12–27 in. (30–69 cm) long, rigid, straight with a slight widening at the middle of the leaf, and flat. They are lined with fine teeth, occasionally doubled, which can be straight or curved and which rise from broad teats. A thin, horny gray border marks the edges of the leaves. The terminal spine is brown to gray, 0.5–0.75 in. (1.3–2 cm) long, thin, and pliant. Several varieties are in the literature, some of which, though not listed below, have distinctions so fine as to be wondrous. Many of these plants may be the result of hybridization with the closely related *Agave xylonacantha* and *A. ghiesbreghtii*. Plants formerly known as *A.* ×*perbella* Hort. are hybrids between *A. lophantha* and *A. xylonacantha*, and plants known as *A. pulcherrima* Hort. may be from the same parents. *Agave lophantha* var. *angustifolia* Berger has variegated leaves. *Agave lophantha* var. *brevifolia* Jacobi has short leaves 12 in. (30 cm) long, and a blunt tip. *Agave lophantha* var. *coerulescens* (Salm-Dyck) Jacobi (synonym *A. coerulescens* Salm-Dyck) has light blue-gray leaves. *Agave lophantha* var. *subcanescens* Jacobi has a leaf margin and spine that are almost white.

BLOOM: The inflorescence is a spike 11.5–13 ft. (3.5–4 m) tall. The flowers are light green to yellow and occur in June.

DISTRIBUTION: *Agave lophantha* is found in the Rio Grande Valley of Texas in Starr and Zapata counties where it is a rare local species on sandy hills. The range continues into Mexico to the state of Veracruz at elevations of 100–5000 ft. (30–1500 m) on limestone formations.

PROPAGATION: Propagation is by seed or by removal of the offsets.

CULTURAL REQUIREMENTS: *Agave lophantha* has demonstrated cold tolerance to 20°F (−7°C) and probably could tolerate more if the freeze was short and the plant was kept very dry. It looks best in the low desert with some light shade, but tolerates full sun if given ample water in the summer.

SIMILAR OR RELATED SPECIES: Often confused with *Agave lechuguilla* with which it hybridizes and intergrades freely, *A. lophantha* can be distinguished by the broader leaf, little or no striation on a flat leaf, and a weak terminal spine. It still is common to see plants sold as *A. univittata,* an invalid name.

USES: Perhaps because of its more limited range and numbers, no record of the ethnobotanical uses of *Agave lophantha,* either historically or in the present day, is available. Ornamentally, the species is stunning in either a garden planting or in a container. Individual plants can have striking contrasts between the leaf color, the gray margin, and the teeth. In many individuals the median stripe is quite pronounced and very attractive. In the Phoenix area this species is becoming more common in cultivation, although many plants sold by this name undoubtedly are hybrids.

Agave macroacantha Zuccarini   PLATE 23

SIZE: *Agave macroacantha* is a small to medium-sized species with a rosette from 10 to 16 in. (25–40 cm) tall and about as wide. It has a very short stem and forms offsets from the stem at the base of the plant.

LEAVES: The leaves are linear, flat above, and rigid with strong radial symmetry. They are about 1 in. (2.5 cm) wide and 10–14 in. (25–36 cm) long. The leaves are a dusky blue-gray to green with a straight margin and dark brown teeth. The teeth are small and spaced 0.25–1 in. (0.6–2.5 cm) apart. The straight terminal spine is 1–1.5 in. (2.5–3.8 cm) long and is not decurrent. It, too, is dark brown, nearly black.

BLOOM: The inflorescence is a slender stalk rising to 6.5 ft. (2 m) with 10–14 branches in the upper half of the stalk. The flowers are green with a purple tinge and often have a fuzzy exterior. Plants frequently set at least some bulbils.

DISTRIBUTION: *Agave macroacantha* is restricted to areas of the Mexican state of Oaxaca and around Tehuacán in the Mexican state of Puebla.

PROPAGATION: Propagation is by seed, by removal of the offsets, or by bulbils.

CULTURAL REQUIREMENTS: In the low desert this species requires some shade or an eastern exposure to look its best. In the summer, watering every two weeks is sufficient, and we know of plants that receive much less and still look outstanding. With overhead protection the plant rarely shows frost damage in the Phoenix area, but it is reported to be too tender to grow in Tucson. On the coast of California or any other Mediterranean climate, it is an excellent plant for locations with full sun to light shade. In cooler climates this plant is best grown on the dry side.

SIMILAR OR RELATED SPECIES: All other blue-gray-leaved agaves with dark contrasting teeth and spine are much larger and have much wider leaves. The size; contrast between the leaf, teeth, and spine; and leaf color make *Agave macroacantha* a most distinctive agave.

USES: *Agave macroacantha* is highly ornamental in either a pot or in the garden. Its modest size, even including the offsets, makes it ideal for smaller gardens or patios. It can be used with perennials, other succulents, or a wildflower planting to create interest and contrast, and for its beautiful form.

Agave marmorata Roezl

SYNONYM: *Agave todaroi* Baker

SIZE: *Agave marmorata* is a medium-sized species 4 ft. (1.2 m) tall and 6.5 ft. (2 m) wide. It is stemless and solitary with 30 or fewer leaves in a rosette.

LEAVES: The leaves are glaucous blue-gray with crossbanding and a rough surface. They are flat with a highly mammillate margin and are 8–12 in. (20–30 cm) wide and 1.25–4.5 ft. (0.4–1.4 m) long. The teeth are large, rusty brown, set up on large teats spaced 0.75–1 in. (2–2.5 cm) apart. The terminal spine is short, 0.5–1 in. (1.3–2.5 cm) long, conical, and rarely decurrent.

BLOOM: The inflorescence is a panicle 10–16 ft. (3–5 m) tall. The flowers are a golden-yellow and occur in May or June.

DISTRIBUTION: *Agave marmorata* is found only around Tehuacán in the Mexican state of Puebla.

PROPAGATION: Propagation is solely by seed.

CULTURAL REQUIREMENTS: This lovely agave is somewhat frost tender. It has been killed at temperatures of 20–25°F (–7 to (4°C). It requires regular summer irrigation in the low desert, some light shade, and protection from frost.

SIMILAR OR RELATED SPECIES: *Agave marmorata* resembles the closely related A. *zebra*, but is distinguished from the latter by its much shorter terminal spine that is not decurrent and the flat surface of the leaf. The combination of a mammillate margin with strong teeth, rough gray leaves with crossbanding, size, and lanceolate leaves separates it from most other gray-leaved agaves. *Agave gigantensis* has smooth, much smaller leaves, with a much longer, strongly decurrent terminal spine.

USES: *Agave marmorata* is a very attractive garden plant with a graceful form. Its cold tenderness restricts its use in the ground to nearly frost-free areas, but in sheltered locations or in large containers it does very well. It should do well in any Mediterranean climate as well.

Agave mckelveyana Gentry

SIZE: *Agave mckelveyana* is a small species that is usually single or with few offsets. The rosette is 8–15 in. (20–38 cm) tall and has 30–40 leaves.

LEAVES: The leaves are 1.25–2 in. (3.2–5 cm) wide and 8–14 in. (20–36 cm) long, rigid, and straight. They are glaucous green or yellowish green with a straight or slightly undulate margin. The teeth are few, firm, curved toward the base of the leaf, and gray with a reddish tip. The terminal spine is 0.5–1.5 in. (1.3–3.8 cm) long, chestnut brown, and shortly decurrent with the margin.

BLOOM: The inflorescence is a panicle 6.5–10 ft. (2–3 m) tall with 10–19 branches in the upper half of the stalk. The flowers are yellow and open from May to July.

DISTRIBUTION: *Agave mckelveyana* is found in western Arizona in the chaparral-juniper associations at 3000–6000 ft. (900–1800 m). It often is the only agave found in these areas.

PROPAGATION: Propagation is by seed or by removal of the offsets.

CULTURAL REQUIREMENTS: *Agave mckelveyana* rarely is used ornamentally, but plants in collections present few problems of cultivation. The species undoubtedly has good cold tolerance owing to its natural distribution and should be able to tolerate temperatures to 0°F (–18°C) or more. In the low desert and other arid regions, it does best with regular summer irrigation.

SIMILAR OR RELATED SPECIES: *Agave mckelveyana* is distinguished from the very similar *A. deserti* subsp. *simplex* by its downcurved, firmly attached teeth and by floral characteristics. Selected individuals could be extremely difficult to distinguish without flowers. The leaves of *A. mckelveyana* generally are thinner than those of most forms of *A. deserti*. *Agave mckelveyana* is distinguished from *A. utahensis* by the lack of a ring around the base of the teeth.

USES: No ethnobotanical uses are recorded for *Agave mckelveyana*. Ornamentally, it is a good subject for containers or small areas because of its size, but it is just as handsome a plant in the ground. Its presumed cold tolerance makes it a good garden plant for cold, dry areas, and perhaps for well-drained locations in the southeastern United States.

Agave multifilifera Gentry   PLATE 24

COMMON NAME: Chahuiqui

SIZE: *Agave multifilifera* is a medium-sized species that grows as a single rosette of numerous leaves, usually 200 or more. The plant has a noticeable trunk at maturity and can be 3 ft. (1 m) tall and 5 ft. (1.5 m) wide.

LEAVES: The linear-lanceolate leaves are flat on the top and slightly convex below with abundant, long, widely spaced filaments. The margin is smooth but the leaf ends in a firm, but pliant green spine that is 0.5 in. (1.3 cm) long. Individual leaves are 0.25–1.25 in. (0.6–3.2 cm) wide and 20–31 in. (51–79 cm) long and downcurved in age.

BLOOM: The inflorescence is a spike to 16 ft. (5 m) tall on which flowers are dense and begin near the end of the leaves. The flowers are green with pink on the edges and occur in May or June.

DISTRIBUTION: *Agave multifilifera* occurs in the mountainous regions of the Mexican states of Chihuahua, Durango, and Sinaloa at elevations of 4500–6500 ft. (1350–1950 m).

PROPAGATION: Propagation is by seed.

CULTURAL REQUIREMENTS: *Agave multifilifera* is fairly recent in the trade and some of its tolerance for heat and cold are not well documented. Plants, however, have been known to tolerate cold to 25°F (–4°C) without damage. Considering its native range, this species could be expected to show even greater cold tolerance. With steady summer watering, it performs well in the low desert. In cooler climates it should do well with only occasional supplemental watering in summer.

SIMILAR OR RELATED SPECIES: Mature individuals of *Agave multifilifera* are very distinctive with the combination of a trunk, numerous leaves, and heavy filamentation. Younger plants could be mistaken for *A. filifera* but have many more and much longer leaves, and filaments up to three times as long and more numerous. *Agave multifilifera* differs from the much rarer *A. schottii* var. *treleasii* in having over four times the number of leaves, many more filaments, and a much shorter terminal spine. Certain individuals of *A. schidigera* could be mistaken for *A. multifilifera*, but the former have half as many leaves, smaller leaves that are much more rigid, and fewer, coarser filaments. While the numerous leaves and dense filamentation of *A. multifilifera* would suggest *Yucca elata*, the two species are readily distinguished: *A. multifilifera* has a strong terminal spine, while *Y. elata* has a small and very weak spine.

USES: No ethnobotanical uses are recorded for *Agave multifilifera*. Ornamentally, this species should enjoy a wider audience. The numerous long, loosely flowing leaves with their complement of dense white filaments are extremely attractive in either a large container or in the ground. This agave complements larger perennial plantings or sets off a corner or focal point extremely well.

Agave murpheyi Gibson PLATES 25, 26

SIZE: A medium-sized species, *Agave murpheyi* is 3 ft. (1 m) tall and 24–31 in. (61–79 cm) wide. It is solitary usually or with very few offsets.

LEAVES: The lanceolate leaves measure 2.5–3 in. (6–8 cm) wide and 20–25.5 in. (51–65 cm) long and vary in color from light gray to dark glaucous blue-green or yellow-green. A yellow variegated form is known. The leaves show a light crossbanding and can have a clear bud imprint. They are flat at the base, but become more concave toward the tip. Small brown teeth occur at regular intervals along the margin, and the terminal spine is short, 0.5–0.75 in. (1.3–2 cm) long.

BLOOM: The inflorescence is a panicle 10–13 ft. (3–4 m) tall. The flowers are waxy green to yellow with purple tips and occur in March and April, although winter flowering is common in the low desert. Plants may set all or a portion of the spike in the late fall or early winter, appear to stop during the coldest weeks, then resume flowering once the weather warms in March. Plants set profuse numbers of bulbils.

DISTRIBUTION: *Agave murpheyi* is endemic to central Arizona along the rocky slopes at elevations from 1500 to 3000 ft. (460–900 m). It can be locally common, but is never extensive in its distribution. It is cultivated in the Mexican state of Sonora and becoming increasingly common as an ornamental species in southern Arizona.

PROPAGATION: Propagation is by removal of the bulbils or offsets. The bulbils are persistent on the plant for a long time, allowing them to achieve a vigorous size. The species rarely sets seed.

CULTURAL REQUIREMENTS: *Agave murpheyi* grows well in the low desert with bi-weekly summer watering and very good drainage. It can grow equally well in full sun or shade, but in areas outside the hottest deserts would demand full sun. It has no serious pest or disease problems. Its cold tolerance is not well documented, although cultivated plants have withstood temperatures of 25°F (–4°C). Given its distribution in Arizona, however, it could be expected to tolerate temperatures considerably lower than that.

SIMILAR OR RELATED SPECIES: *Agave murpheyi* could be mistaken, especially when young, with *A. chrysantha*. It is distinguished from the latter, however, by its straight, grayish somewhat crossbanded leaf with small teeth and small terminal spine.

USES: *Agave murpheyi* in its natural distribution is associated closely with historic human settlements and is thought to have been a very important food source. The evidence is strong that this species was cultivated behind rock dams and terrace gardens and that the plants we see are just feral populations of those old cultivations. The origin of the species is in some doubt; it possibly has been cultivated a very long time and the wild origins are lost or so much changed as to be unrecognizable. Certainly it shares with other known long-cultivated agaves a short life span, large size, and the formation of bulbils. As an ornamental plant, it is tough and handsome, making an excellent addition to dry gardens. It can be used to accent perennials, wildflowers, or as an addition to a succulent garden.

Agave neomexicana Wooten & Standley   PLATE 27

COMMON NAME: Mescal

SIZE: *Agave neomexicana* is a small to medium-sized species with rosettes averaging 10–16 in. (25–40 cm) tall and 12–27 in. (30–69 cm) wide. Plants form numerous offsets, making very compact rosettes.

LEAVES: The leaves are slender, lanceolate, concave above, and convex below. They measure 2–5 in. (5–13 cm) wide and 8–18 in. (20–46 cm) long and are a light glaucous blue-green to gray. Strong teeth occur along the margin, and the horny margin commonly is discontinuous. The terminal spine is 1–1.25

in. (2.5–3.2 cm) long, rounded, and decurrent to the one or more teeth.

BLOOM: The inflorescence is a panicle 8–11 ft. (2.4–3.4 m) tall with 10–17 branches on the upper half of the stalk. The flowers are red in bud and yellow when open. They occur in June and July.

DISTRIBUTION: *Agave neomexicana* is restricted to the mountains of southeastern New Mexico and western Texas. It is used as an ornamental in both those states.

PROPAGATION: Propagation is by seed or by removal of the offsets.

CULTURAL REQUIREMENTS: *Agave neomexicana* requires good open drainage and regular summer watering in the low desert to thrive and look its best. It has very good cold tolerance down to –20°F (–29°C) or more. In the low desert, partial shade is recommended, but anywhere else the plant thrives in full sun.

SIMILAR OR RELATED SPECIES: Closely related to *Agave parryi*, *A. neomexicana* differs by its much narrower, straight, lanceolate leaves, with at least some horny margin. *Agave parryi* has a generally flatter leaf as well. *Agave havardiana* has wider, frequently longer leaves that are gray to gray-green.

USES: Like many of its near relatives, *Agave neomexicana* figured prominently in the diet and ceremonies of the Indian peoples who occupied the region before the Spanish conquest. In some areas this species still is collected and roasted for ceremonial occasions. As an ornamental, it is a lovely agave in any garden setting. Its moderate size and extremely regular form make it a good contrast for more leafy plantings of perennials and wildflowers. Its cold tolerance gives it a very wide potential range of use.

Agave ocahui Gentry PLATE 28

COMMON NAMES: Ocahui, Ojahui, Amolillo

SIZE: *Agave ocahui* grows as a single, symmetrical rosette 12–20 in. (30–51 cm) tall and 20–39 in. (51–100 cm) wide. *Agave ocahui* var. *longifolia* Gentry has much longer leaves, 23.5–35 in. (60–89 cm) long and 0.75–1 in. (2–2.5 cm) wide, and the resulting rosette is, therefore, much larger.

LEAVES: The numerous, straight, dark green leaves are widest at the base and can reach 10–20 in. (25–51 cm) long and 0.5–1 in. (1.3–2.5 cm) wide. They are stiff and flattened on the top. The margin is straight, smooth, and lined with a narrow reddish brown border that detaches from old leaves. The terminal spine is sharp but fairly flexible and weak.

BLOOM: The inflorescence is a delicate spike 10 ft. (3 m) tall. The flowers are a bright yellow. Some authors report that plants take about 20 years to bloom. There are records at the Desert Botanical Garden for five individuals that bloomed at 5–18 years of age.

DISTRIBUTION: *Agave ocahui* is known only from the northeastern part of the Mexican state of Sonora at elevations between 1500 and 4500 ft. (460–1350 m). Variety *longifolia* is scattered widely in east central Sonora.

PROPAGATION: Propagation is by seed. The plant is not known to make either bulbils or offsets.

CULTURAL REQUIREMENTS: *Agave ocahui* tolerates a wide range of conditions from full sun to partial shade and thrives in any well-drained soil. It forms a more compact form in full sun even in the low desert, where moderate summer watering is necessary to keep it from becoming yellowed and to maintain vigor. This species has exhibited cold tolerance to 15°F (–9°C) and is thought by some to be able to tolerate 5°F (–15°C). It is a fine container plant requiring minimal care.

SIMILAR OR RELATED SPECIES: Out of bloom, young plants of *Agave ocahui* and *A. pelona* are difficult to distinguish, but in bloom the flowers of *A. pelona* are a remarkable red-wine color that is unusual in agaves. Without the flower, *A. pelona* can be distinguished by its leaves, which have a fine narrow edge that is light, sometimes white, as opposed to the brown to reddish brown edge of *A. ocahui*. Furthermore, the leaves of *A. pelona* are a dark shiny green with a slightly more exaggerated flat top and curved underside. All other straight-leaved, dark green, solitary agaves of this size have marginal teeth and more pungent terminal spines.

USES: *Agave ocahui* is used in the Mexican state of Sonora for its strong, long fibers, and the name *ocahui* is a Mexican Indian word for "cord" or "fiber." Leaves also contain significant amounts of the compound smilagenin and are crushed in the manner described for *A. vilmoriniana* and used as a cleansing brush. Ornamentally, this beautiful specimen agave tolerates almost any exposure and any soil. Its great cold tolerance gives it a potential ornamental range throughout much of the arid Southwest. The solitary habit and relatively small size make it an ideal container plant. Some individuals are extremely attractive for the vivid distinction between the green leaf and the dark margin. *Agave ocahui* with its tight, regular form makes a fine addition to lush plantings of desert perennials or wildflowers.

Agave palmeri Engelmann   PLATE 29

COMMON NAME: Palmer's agave

SIZE: *Agave palmeri* is a medium-sized species 3.25–4 ft. (1–1.2 m) tall and 20–47 in. (51–119 cm) wide. It is typically solitary or forms few offsets.

LEAVES: The leaves are lanceolate, rigid, and guttered for the entire length. They are 3–4 in. (8–10 cm) wide and 14–29 in. (36–75 cm) long, but there is considerable variation in different parts of the range. The leaves are pale green to a glaucous light green or gray-green with a straight margin, occasionally undulate, and small, regular teeth, with even smaller teeth between them. The terminal spine is needlelike, slightly flexible, 1–2 in. (2.5–5 cm) long, and decurrent to the first teeth.

BLOOM: The inflorescence is a panicle 10–16 ft. (3–5 m) tall with 8–12 branches. The flowers are pale yellow to green-yellow with dark red tips. The tip color is prominent especially when the plant is in bud.

DISTRIBUTION: *Agave palmeri* occurs widely in the United States in southeastern Arizona and southwestern New Mexico and in the Mexican states of Sonora and Chihuahua. It is found at elevations from 3000 to 6000 ft. (900–1800 m), usually on limestone soils, and often in very large stands.

Plate 1. Garden at Boyce Thompson Southwestern Arboretum, Superior, Arizona

Plate 2. *Agave americana*

Plate 3. *Agave americana* showing symptoms of agave snout weevil infestation. Photo by Mary Irish

Plate 4. *Agave angustifolia* var. *marginata*

Plate 5. Flowering *Agave attenuata* at Huntington Botanical Gardens, San Marino, California

Plate 6. *Agave avellanidens*

Plate 7. *Agave bovicornuta*

Plate 8. *Agave bracteosa*

Plate 9. *Agave celsii*

Plate 10. *Agave cerulata*

Plate 11. *Agave chiapensis*

Plate 12. *Agave chrysantha*

Plate 13. *Agave colorata*

Plate 14. *Agave deserti*

Plate 15. *Agave desmettiana*

Plate 16. Flowers of *Agave desmettiana*

Plate 17. *Agave franzosinii*

Plate 18. *Agave geminiflora*

Plate 19. *Agave guiengola*

Plate 20. *Agave havardiana.* Photo by Mary Irish

Plate 21. *Agave lechuguilla*

Plate 22. *Agave lophantha*

Plate 23. *Agave macroacantha*

Plate 24. *Agave multifilifera*

Plate 25. *Agave murpheyi*

Plate 26. *Agave murpheyi* planted in rock dam display at the Desert Botanical Garden, Phoenix, Arizona

Plate 27. *Agave neomexicana*

Plate 28. *Agave ocahui*

Plate 29. *Agave palmeri*

Plate 30. *Agave parryi*

Plate 31. *Agave parryi* var. *huachucensis*

Plate 32.
Agave parryi
var. *truncata*

Plate 33. *Agave parviflora*

Plate 34. *Agave pygmae*

Plate 35. *Agave salmiana* var. *crassispina*

Plate 36.
Agave scabra

Plate 37. *Agave schidigera.* Photo by Greg Starr

Plate 38. *Agave schottii*

Plate 39. *Agave shawii*

Plate 40. *Agave sisalana*

Plate 41. *Agave striata* subsp. *falcata*

Plate 42. *Agave stricta*

Plate 43. *Agave tequilana*, variegated form

Plate 44. *Agave titanota*

Plate 45. *Agave toumeyana*

Plate 46. *Agave utahensis* var. *nevadensis*

Plate 47. *Agave victoriae-reginae*

Plate 48. Mass planting of *Agave victoriae-reginae*, Lotusland, Montecito, California

Plate 49. *Agave vilmoriniana*

Plate 50. *Agave weberi*

Plate 51. *Agave xylonacantha*

Plate 52. *Agave zebra*. Photo by Jane Schlosberg

PROPAGATION: Propagation is by seed or by removal of the offsets. Much has been written about the interrelationship of this species and the lesser long-nosed bat. It has been surmised by many that the bats were so important to this agave's pollination success that a decline in the bat signaled a decline in the species. Research in southeastern Arizona has shed new light on the pollination dynamics of this species and suggests that, while bats can certainly pollinate this species, a host of other agents are at work, and all of them are successful.

CULTURAL REQUIREMENTS: *Agave palmeri* grows best on rocky, basic soils. It has been documented to tolerate cold temperatures down to 14°F (–10°C). In the low desert it requires regular summer irrigation to maintain vigor and prevent the common summer yellowing of many agaves.

SIMILAR OR RELATED SPECIES: *Agave palmeri* and *A. chrysantha* are related closely and share several similarities. The latter has much larger, more widely spaced teeth, a grayer cast to the foliage, a larger, wider leaf, and a heavier terminal spine. *Agave palmeri*, however, is a highly variable species, particularly with respect to leaf characteristics, and hybrids of this species and *A. chrysantha* are known in the wild and in cultivation, creating further confusion.

USES: *Agave palmeri* has been used for the production of mescal in northeastern Mexico for hundreds of years. Besides being useful as a beverage, it is useful as food when the emerging bud is roasted, and the leaves make excellent fiber. As a garden plant, this species would have many of the same uses as its closer relatives: as a foil for wildflower or perennial displays, and as a contrast in succulent gardens. The strong regular shape of the rosettes makes the species a good focal or specimen plant on patios or other more formal settings.

Agave parrasana Berger

SYNONYM: *Agave wislizenii* Engelmann

SIZE: One of the smaller species, *Agave parrasana* grows as a solitary plant 2.5–3 ft. (0.8–1 m) wide.

LEAVES: The leaves are obovate, nearly round, ending in a

sharp and abrupt tip. They are 4–8 in. (10–20 cm) wide and 8–12 in. (20–30 cm) long, and are gray to blue-gray. Gray-brown teeth are found along the margin mainly near the tip of the leaves. The thin terminal spine is 0.75–1 in. (2–2.5 cm) long and decurrent. The leaves are held tightly, almost like a bud, giving the plant a very distinctive form.

BLOOM: The inflorescence is a panicle that rises 10–13 ft. (3–4 m) above the plant and has 12–15 branches. The flower buds are enclosed in a large reddish-purple bract but open a bright yellow ringed with red or purple. The flowers develop in June and July.

DISTRIBUTION: *Agave parrasana* is known from limited locales in southeastern Coahuila, Mexico, at elevations from 4500 to 8000 ft. (1350–2400 m). It is uncommon in cultivation.

PROPAGATION: Propagation is by seed.

CULTURAL REQUIREMENTS: *Agave parrasana* does well in the low desert in the shade of large trees or shrubs that provide a broken shade pattern. In coastal areas or at higher elevations it should grow in full sun. The species is cold hardy in the Phoenix area, but there is little information outside of this region. Given its natural range, it should tolerate dry cold to at least 22°F (–6°C).

SIMILAR OR RELATED SPECIES: The tight form of *Agave parrasana* with short, nearly round, blue-gray leaves, a short terminal spine, and teeth only at the end of the leaf separates this species from all other small blue-gray agaves. Young plants of *A. parrasana* and *A. parryi* var. *truncata* could be difficult to distinguish, but mature plants are very different in size.

USES: *Agave parrasana* is among the most ornamental agaves, vying with *A. victoriae-reginae* in the exquisite regularity of its form. If possible, this plant should be viewed from above to appreciate its amazing symmetry. It makes a good focal point and is excellent in pot culture.

Agave parryi Engelmann   PLATES 30, 31, 32

SYNONYMS: *Agave chihuahuana* Trelease, *Agave patonii* Trelease

Size: *Agave parryi* forms a tight, nearly round rosette with 100–160 leaves closely held to each other. It can be solitary or form extensive colonies of offsets. The rosette is 12–20 in. (30–51 cm) tall and 20–29 in. (51–75 cm) wide.

Leaves: The leaves vary in size, but generally range from 3 to 5 in. (8–13 cm) wide and from 10 to 16 in. (25–40 cm) long. They are broadly linear to ovate, coming to a sharp tip. In all forms the leaves are smooth, thick, rigid and flat to barely concave on the top surface. They are light gray to light blue-green and have a straight or very slightly undulate margin from which arise variably sized red-brown teeth. The largest and most prominent teeth are towards the tip. The terminal spine is stout, flat, brown, 0.75–1 in. (2–2.5 cm) long, and long decurrent. There are three very distinct varieties of this species. *Agave parryi* var. *couesii* (Engelmann ex Trelease) Kearney & Peebles (synonym *A. couesii* Engelmann ex Trelease) is much smaller than the type with a leaf shape somewhat between the more lanceolate form of var. *huachucensis* and the extremely obovate form of var. *truncata*. It is found in small local populations in central Arizona, and in older literature was recognized as a separate species. *Agave parryi* var. *huachucensis* (Baker) Little ex Benson (synonym *A. huachucensis* Baker), often considered a separate species in old literature, is the largest and most robust variety with leaves up to 25 in. (64 cm) long that are more lanceolate than the type. It occurs in southeastern Arizona and into the Mexican state of Chihuahua. *Agave parryi* var. *truncata* Gentry is a particularly handsome form known for years as *A. patonii*. As the name suggests, the leaves are obovate to ovate. They also are 3–5 in. (8–13 cm) wide and 4–12 in. (10–30 cm) long and a bright glaucous blue-gray color with a reddish-brown margin, teeth, and terminal spine. This variety has copious numbers of offsets and occurs only in the Mexican state of Durango.

Bloom: The inflorescence is robust and rises 11–20 ft. (3.4–6 m) with 18–30 stout branches. The flowers are held on large umbels in the upper half of the stalk. They are a bright lemon yellow with tints of red or pink when in bud and occur from June through August.

DISTRIBUTION: *Agave parryi* ranges from central and southeastern Arizona to southwestern New Mexico, into the Mexican states of Chihuahua and Durango at elevations from 1500 to 8000 ft. (460–2400 m). In the low desert of Arizona this species and particularly its var. *huachucensis* are the most common ornamental agaves available other than *A. americana*. It is not nearly as common elsewhere.

PROPAGATION: Propagation is by seed or by removal of the offsets.

CULTURAL REQUIREMENTS: Because of its extensive range, *Agave parryi* can tolerate an equally large range of cultural conditions. It is among the most cold hardy agaves, and the most northern populations are unmarked at temperatures of (–20°F (–29°C). Variety *couesii* is cold tolerant down to 0°F (–18°C), but var. *huachucensis* and var. *truncata* are much less cold tolerant (see Table 3-1). In the low desert *A. parryi* does well in full sun with ample summer water, but thrives in partial shade. It has few soil requirements, even for an agave, but does best with good drainage.

SIMILAR OR RELATED SPECIES: It can be difficult to distinguish some individuals of *Agave parryi* from the closely related *A. havardiana* and *A. neomexicana*. Both of the latter species have a more concave leaf above and convex below, giving them a triangular cross section, whereas the leaf of *A. parryi* is generally flat on the top surface or only slightly concave. Some botanists question whether the populations listed for many years in the Guadalupe Mountains of western Texas belong to this species or to the very closely related *A. neomexicana*. Selected individuals and populations can be very difficult to distinguish. *Agave parryi* differs from all other blue-gray agaves by the combination of a straight margin, variable teeth, numerous leaves, and size.

USES: Long used as a good source of mescal, *Agave parryi* still is used infrequently for making that beverage. Ornamentally, it is among the most common species in cultivation in the low desert owing to its cold hardiness, excellent form, and quick and easy propagation. It looks lovely planted among perennials and wildflowers, and sets off a naturalistic planting very well. Although these plants rarely are seen in mass, they are extremely picturesque in groupings and could be considered more often. The smaller forms make very good container plants, and all forms are excellent accent plants and foundations for a succulent garden.

Agave parviflora Torrey PLATE 33

SIZE: *Agave parviflora* is a very small, compact species usually between 4 and 6 in. (10–15 cm) tall and 6–8 in. (15–20 cm) wide. It may be single or have caespitose offsets, which occur at the base of the plant but rarely are numerous.

LEAVES: The leaves are less than 0.5 in. (1.3 cm) wide and 2–4 in. (5–10 m) long. They are dark green, linear to oblong, and marked with a white bud imprint. The margin is straight with short, coarse, white filaments along the edge. The leaves have tiny teeth at the base and a short, 0.5 in. (1.3 cm) long, weak terminal spine.

BLOOM: The inflorescence is a spike 3–6 ft. (1–1.8 m) tall. The flowers are pale yellow and develop in June or July. Although monocarpic and sure to die after flowering, plants remain green and attractive for up to 2 years following flowering.

DISTRIBUTION: *Agave parviflora* occurs in extreme southern Arizona in the United States and in northern Sonora, Mexico, near the border with Chihuahua, on rocky, dry hills. It is uncommon in cultivation, although its popularity increased in the 1990s.

PROPAGATION: Propagation is by seed or by removal of the offsets.

CULTURAL REQUIREMENTS: To retain the charming compact habit, it is necessary to water *Agave parviflora* with a spare hand. Overgrown plants have larger than average leaves and tend to spread out more. The plant grows well in full sun in most areas; however, in the low desert, light shade helps maintain the best form and health of the plant.

SIMILAR OR RELATED SPECIES: The only species similar to *Agave parviflora* in size and appearance is *A. polianthiflora*. The two are impossible to distinguish without their flowers and are often mistaken one for another. In *A. polianthiflora,* the spike and the flowers are a soft, rosy pink. While the stalk in *A. parviflora* can be pink, the flowers are yellow. *Agave toumeyana* subsp. *bella* is quite similar as well, but differs by its numerous offsets and a brown border on the leaf margin.

Uses: Because of its size, *Agave parviflora* is an exquisite pot plant and blends well with other succulents in dish gardens. It is a charming addition to smaller-scale perennial or wildflower plantings or in a rock garden. It grows well in full sun in the low desert and demands strong light in other regions.

Agave pelona Gentry   FIGURE 1-1

Common name: Mescal pelón

Size: *Agave pelona* is a solitary, medium-sized species characterized by long, stiff leaves in an open rosette. The entire plant is 16–24 in. (40–61 cm) tall and 24–31 in. (61–79 cm) wide.

Leaves: The leaves are linear, shiny, and dark green with a reddish to purple tint that is exaggerated by drought or old age. They are 1–2 in. (2.5–5 cm) wide and 14–20 in. (36–51 cm) long with a strong terminal spine 1.5–3 in. (3.8–8 cm) long. The leaves are flat and stiff with a smooth whitish border that detaches when it dries.

Bloom: The inflorescence is a raceme that rises 6.5–10 ft. (2–3 m) above the plant. The flowers occur only in the upper half of the stalk. They are a striking wine-red color and are bell-like in their form. Bloom begins from April to June.

Distribution: *Agave pelona* is endemic to northwestern Sonora, Mexico.

Propagation: Propagation is by seed.

Cultural requirements: *Agave pelona* has demonstrated cold tolerance to at least 21°F (–6°C). It grows well in full sun or partial shade, even in the low desert. The leaves can yellow in the extreme heat of the low desert summer, but recover if kept well watered once the temperature moderates.

Similar or related species: *Agave pelona* is very distinctive with a strong tip, dark green leaves with a reddish cast, and a white margin. *Agave ocahui* has a much weaker, more flexible terminal spine, dark green leaves with no red cast, and a brown margin. The unique wine-red flower color clearly separates *A. pelona* from *A. ocahui*, which has a yellow bloom.

USES: *Agave pelona* is used by indigenous people for fiber and in past times was roasted and the heart eaten. It very occasionally is used for the making of mescal, particularly for home consumption. This species is a spectacular ornamental plant. The solitary habit makes it equally suitable for containers or as a garden plant to complement perennials or other succulents. The dark shiny leaves are particularly well suited to plantings of wildflowers and other small colorful plants.

Agave polianthiflora Gentry

SIZE: *Agave polianthiflora* is a small species with either a single rosette or a few offsets. The rosette is 4–8 in. (10–20 cm) tall and 8–11.75 in. (20–29.5 cm) wide.

LEAVES: The linear leaves are widest in the middle and are 0.25–0.5 in. (0.6–1.3 cm) wide and 4–8 in. (10–20 cm) long. White bud imprints mark the leaves above and below. The margin has white, widely spaced filaments in the upper half with minute teeth on the lower half.

BLOOM: The inflorescence is a spike 4–6 ft. (1.2–1.8 m) tall. The flowers are rose-red and occur above the middle of the stalk. The stamens are not exserted in this species, a characteristic which is unusual in *Agave* but very common in *Polianthes* and from which the species derived its name.

DISTRIBUTION: *Agave polianthiflora* occurs irregularly on rocky outcrops on both sides of the Sonora-Chihuahua border in Mexico and east toward Ciudad Chihuahua at elevations between 4000 and 6000 ft. (1200–1800 m). This species is not common in horticulture, but it often is mistaken for *A. parviflora*.

PROPAGATION: Propagation is by seed or by removal of the offsets.

CULTURAL REQUIREMENTS: *Agave polianthiflora* is best grown in full sun, even in the low desert, to maintain good form. Plants grown with too much shade become leggy and soft. They do best on a very lean amount of water, even in very hot

151

climates. Overwatered plants get large, and the leaves spread out, resulting in a floppy, fallen appearance.

SIMILAR OR RELATED SPECIES: *Agave polianthiflora* is virtually identical to *A. parviflora* vegetatively. The two species can be distinguished reliably only by their bloom, which is pink-red in this species and yellow in *A. parviflora. Agave toumeyana* subsp. *bella* has many, even numerous offsets and a brown border on the leaf margin.

USES: The Warihio Indians reportedly have used this species as food and consider it an exceptionally sweet agave when roasted. The old inflorescence stalks were used for arrow shafts. Ornamentally, *Agave polianthiflora* is excellent for container culture, mixed with small-scale succulents, wildflowers, or perennials, or in a small rock bed.

Agave potatorum Zuccarini

SYNONYMS: *Agave scolymus* Karwinsky, *Agave saundersii* J. Hooker, *Agave verschaffeltii* Lemaire, *Agave potatorum* var. *verschaffeltii* (Lemaire) Berger

SIZE: *Agave potatorum* is a small species that usually is solitary and stemless. The form described here is the most common one encountered in horticulture, but old references list as many as 33 varieties of this species based on leaf characteristics alone. The rosette is open, spreading, and symmetrical with 50–80 leaves.

LEAVES: The leaves are ovate, oblong, or short lanceolate, but vary considerably in shape, size, and color. They are mostly 3.5–7 in. (9–18 cm) wide and 10–15.75 in. (25–40 cm) long and a glaucous gray-green to white. The margin is mammillate, often dramatically so, with distinct teats. The rusty-colored teeth are 0.25–0.5 in. (0.6–1.3 cm) long and are spaced 0.5–1 in. (1.3–2.5 cm) apart. The light brown terminal spine is sharp, 1–1.75 in. (2.5–4.4 cm) long, often sinuous or twisted and decurrent.

BLOOM: The inflorescence may be either a raceme or a panicle 10–20 ft. (3–6 m) tall. The flowers are a light green-yellow with red tinges surrounded by red bracts and occur from September to December.

DISTRIBUTION: *Agave potatorum* is a subtropical species that occurs in the semi-arid highlands of the Mexican states of Puebla and Oaxaca at elevations of 4500–7500 ft. (1350–2250 m).

PROPAGATION: Propagation is by seed.

CULTURAL REQUIREMENTS: *Agave potatorum* requires some frost protection, although the overhead protection of a tree or awning is sufficient in the low desert of Phoenix. Ample summer watering in the warmest regions is required. Arid coastal conditions would be ideal for this species.

SIMILAR OR RELATED SPECIES: *Agave titanota* has much longer, more linear leaves with larger more variable teeth held on an undulate, but not mammillate margin. *Agave parryi* var. *truncata* has generally smaller leaves that are oblong, short, and truncate at the tip with a margin that rarely is mammillate. Young plants of *A. potatorum* can be mistaken for *A. colorata;* however, the latter is very scabrous, with few leaves, and the teeth are greatly reduced in size, or missing altogether, near the base of the leaf.

USES: *Agave potatorum* makes an outstanding container plant because of its smaller size and regular proportions. Seen from above it is a masterpiece of symmetry and color, and in the low desert is particularly effective in light shade, where the light-colored foliage serves to light up a dark area. In more moderate climates it can be grown in full sun mixed with small perennials or other succulents.

Agave pygmae Gentry   PLATE 34

SIZE: *Agave pygmae* is a diminutive species with few to many offsets. It usually is less than 12 in. (30 cm) tall and wide.

LEAVES: The ovate, truncate leaves are 3–5 in. (8–13 cm) wide and 5–11 in. (13–28 cm) long. They are fleshy, firm, and gray-green to blue-gray. The margin is very mammillate with downcurved teeth on variably sized teats. The teeth are small, less than 0.25 in. (0.6 cm) long, and are spaced 0.5 in. (1.3 cm) apart. The terminal spine is grooved, short-decurrent, and only 0.5–0.75 in. (1.3–2 cm) long.

BLOOM: The inflorescence is a panicle 6.5–10 ft. (2–3 m) tall with 8–12 open umbels. The flowers are yellow.

DISTRIBUTION: *Agave pygmae* was described from a plant found on the Mexico-Guatemala border at an elevation of 3000 ft. (900 m). Further distributions are not known.

PROPAGATION: Propagation is by seed or by removal of the offsets.

CULTURAL REQUIREMENTS: *Agave pygmae* tolerates very high heat if given adequate shade and moisture during the summer. In less rigorous heat it would undoubtedly do fine in full sun to partial shade. Although the species's cold tolerance is not documented, its known distribution suggests that frost protection should be provided. Plants in Phoenix have remained unharmed at 25°F (–4°C).

SIMILAR OR RELATED SPECIES: Morphologically similar to its close relative *Agave seemanniana*, *A. pygmae* is distinguished readily by its tiny size. While Gentry (1982) considered the plant might be a depauperate form because of the limestone on which it grew, plants long cultivated in Phoenix, Arizona, have achieved very little size beyond what is described.

USES: No ethnobotanical uses for this plant are documented. As a garden plant, *Agave pygmae* is very attractive and its small size makes it useful for any size garden. It is a superb container plant and, in a container, can be easily moved to provide adequate frost protection.

Agave salmiana Otto ex Salm-Dyck   PLATE 35

SYNONYMS: *Agave cochlearis* Jacobi, *Agave lehmanni* Jacobi, *Agave mitriformis* Jacobi, *Agave atrovirens* var. *sigmatophyla* Berger

COMMON NAME: Maguey de pulque

SIZE: *Agave salmiana* is a very large plant with huge leaves. It produces at least a few offsets and is 5–6.5 ft. (1.5–1.8 m) tall and 10–13 ft. (3–4 m) wide. The rosette has 20–30 leaves.

LEAVES: The leaves are 10–14 in. (25–36 cm) wide and 3.25–6.5 ft. (1–2 m) long and range from dark green to a glaucous gray-green. They are thick, hard, smooth or slightly rough, and fleshy with a very heavy, swollen leaf base. The leaf is guttered along its length and is folded deeply at the tip, exaggerating the dramatic recurve of the terminal spine. The margin is wavy or mammillate with 0.5 in. (1.3 cm) long teeth spaced 1–2 in. (2.5–5 cm) apart. The teeth are flat, curved with a flattened base, and chestnut brown aging to gray. The terminal spine is long, 2–4 in. (5–10 cm), stout, brown aging to gray, and very long decurrent, often to the middle of the leaf. Countless forms and varieties are mentioned in the literature, particularly older horticultural texts. Some of the most widely recognized are listed here. *Agave salmiana* var. *angustifolia* Berger has long linear leaves that are nearly white. It is known from Mediterranean cultivation. *Agave salmiana* var. *crassispina* (Trelease) Gentry (synonym *A. crassispina* Trelease) has fewer and smaller leaves than the type, 6.5–10 in. (17–25 cm) wide and 24–35.5 in. (61–90 cm) long. It is the common wild form in the Mexican states of San Luis Potosí, Puebla, and Oaxaca. *Agave salmiana* var. *ferox* (Koch) Gentry (synonym *A. ferox* Koch) is a very large plant that is often urn-shaped and dramatically recurved, 9–12 in. (23–30 cm) wide and 27–35.5 in. (69–90 cm) long. The teeth and terminal spine are large and heavy. This variety is the most common form in European gardens.

BLOOM: The inflorescence is a stout panicle 23–26 ft. (7–8 m) tall with 15–20 branches. The flowers are yellow tinged with red when in bud.

DISTRIBUTION: *Agave salmiana* is known in wild and cultivated forms from the Mexican states of San Luis Potosí, Hidalgo, and Puebla, west through Guanajuato and Michoacán, and south through Mexico and Querétaro.

PROPAGATION: Propagation is by seed or by removal of the offsets.

CULTURAL REQUIREMENTS: The many forms of this species suggest that there is a plant for every garden situation. Some forms are very cold tender; others have been documented to withstand temperatures down to –4°F (–20°C) without damage. A plant, possibly a hybrid, in eastern Texas has sustained 5°F (–15°C) with minimal damage. The greatest glory of this species is in the Mediterranean climates of Europe and California, where it reaches its full size and remains unmarked by cold. In the low desert, weekly watering in the hottest part of the summer and light shade are required; elsewhere watering can be less frequent and the plant can tolerate full sun. Variety *ferox* is the least cold hardy form and is best grown at temperatures above 25°F (−4°C).

SIMILAR OR RELATED SPECIES: The great size of the leaves with a large, fleshy, mammillate margin and a long, decurrent terminal spine distinguishes *Agave salmiana* from most other agaves. The less common *A. mapisaga* Trelease is related closely and can become equivalent in size but is distinguished by longer linear leaves with very small spines on a straighter margin. Forms of *A. scabra* could be confused, especially when young, but they always are extremely rough to the touch. *Agave marmorata* in some forms could be confused with *A. salmiana*, but the former has a highly exaggerated mammillate margin, and the terminal spine is not decurrent.

USES: *Agave salmiana* is the principle species used in the production of pulque in Mexico, where it provides more than three-fourths of the pulque production in the region. Despite its size, it is an outstanding ornamental agave. The recurved leaves are graceful, lending a delicate touch to so massive a plant. It can be used in a large succulent planting, as the focal point in a large garden, or within a perennial planting for contrast.

Agave scabra Salm-Dyck   PLATE 36; FIGURES 1-1, 4-1

SYNONYMS: *Agave asperrima* Jacobi, *Agave caeciliana* Berger

SIZE: *Agave scabra* is a moderately large species 2–3 ft. (0.6–1 m) tall and 5–6.5 ft. (1.5–1.8 m) wide. The strongly curved leaves with heavy teeth and a long terminal spine make it a distinctive and graceful plant, although the leaves are relatively few, 30–40. This species does not normally have a visible stem but produces offsets freely.

LEAVES: The leaves are 5–6 in. (13–15 cm) wide and 2–3.5 ft. (0.6–1.1 m) long. They are rigid, generally lanceolate, broad, and clasping at the base. The teeth are heavy, downcurved, 0.25–0.5

Figure 4-1. Flowers, *Agave scabra*

in. (0.6–1.3 cm) long, and occur from the middle of the leaf to the base, leaving the upper part of the leaf covered with a smooth, horny border. The leaves vary from light green to gray and are very rough to the touch. The terminal spine is long, 1.25–2 in. (3.2–5 cm), sharp, and long decurrent, and is slightly to greatly recurved. Three subspecies are recognized. *Agave scabra* subsp. *maderensis* Gentry is a single plant rising on a short stem with smooth green to yellowish green leaves. *Agave scabra* subsp. *potosiensis* Gentry has an open, spreading rosette with pale nearly white leaves. *Agave scabra* subsp. *zarcensis* Gentry has shorter, thick, rigid leaves and more modest teeth.

BLOOM: The inflorescence is a panicle 13–19 ft. (4–5.8 m) tall with 8–12 branches. The flowers are yellow and occur from April to June. Plants bloom after approximately 18 years.

DISTRIBUTION: Distributed throughout the Chihuahuan desert in northern Mexico to the state of San Luis Potosí and south to the Pacific Ocean, *Agave scabra* occurs on plains and mountains at elevations of 500–6500 ft. (150–1950 m) on limestone outcrops and dry soils. It ranges into Texas with records from Starr, Webb, and Zapata counties. It is moderately common in cultivation.

PROPAGATION: Propagation is by removal of the offsets or by seed.

CULTURAL REQUIREMENTS: *Agave scabra* grows well in very hot, dry conditions. Subject to rot and etiolation in cool, damp conditions, it requires full sun wherever it is grown. In cooler climates it should be grown very dry. In warmer or hot climates it needs excellent drainage and irregular summer irrigation for best performance. This species is very cold hardy and able to withstand temperatures to 10°F (–6°C). Plantings in Denver indicate the species may be even more cold hardy than reported.

SIMILAR OR RELATED SPECIES: *Agave scabra* resembles the much less common *A. marmorata*, which has, as distinguishing characteristics, a flat leaf surface and much smaller teeth and terminal spine. *Agave zebra* could be confused with the gray color form of *A. scabra*, but the latter has an undulate rather than teated margin, no strong crossbanding, and large, heavy teeth fairly wide apart. The rough leaf surface of *A. sca-*

bra further separates it from almost all similar plants. *Agave scabra* strongly intergrades naturally with *A. americana* and *A. victoriae-reginae*, creating some beautiful hybrids. Most of them are unnamed but usually are striking individuals. Hybrids with *A. victoriae-reginae* are particularly lovely and frequently are known by the invalid name *A. ferdinandi-regis*. These hybrids have the short triangular leaf shape of *A. victoriae-reginae*, the rough surface and somewhat larger size of *A. scabra*, and a dusky color.

USES: *Agave scabra* is an outstanding ornamental species, especially where its deep color and graceful recurved leaves can be fully appreciated. Sometimes grown in pots, it achieves its best form in the ground where it can develop fully. It is an excellent agave for native gardens or areas that receive minimal care. The teeth and spine are very sharp, so it is wise to place plants away from pathways or patios.

Agave schidigera Lemaire   PLATE 37

SYNONYMS: *Agave vestita* S. Watson, *Agave disceptata* Drummond, *Agave ×wrightii* Drummond

SIZE: *Agave schidigera* grows as a single rosette with many leaves. Mature plants can be 27 in. (69 cm) wide and rise from a short stem.

LEAVES: The linear leaves are widest at the middle and 0.5–1.5 in. (1.3–3.8 cm) wide and 12–20 in. (30–51 cm) long. They are dark green, shiny, with a smooth margin from which brown or white coarse filaments arise. The brown-gray terminal spine is 0.25–0.75 in. (0.6–2 cm) long. Usually a strong white bud imprint marks the leaves, and occasionally the leaves have a purple tint.

BLOOM: The inflorescence is a raceme 11.5 ft. (3.5 m) tall. The flowers are green-yellow with a purplish tint and occur on the upper two-thirds of the stalk usually in late summer.

DISTRIBUTION: *Agave schidigera* occurs in Mexico, from northwestern Chihuahua south to Michoacán and east to San Luis Potosí, Zacatecas, and Durango.

PROPAGATION: Propagation is by seed or by removal of the rare offset.

CULTURAL REQUIREMENTS: *Agave schidigera* is a good ornamental that requires light frost and sun protection in the low desert, as well as regular summer irrigation. In coastal or cooler climates it needs water moderately through the summer and minimally in the winter. In these cooler climates it is best planted in the full sun to maintain a tight, well-formed rosette.

SIMILAR OR RELATED SPECIES: Many authors, including Gentry (1982), speculate that *Agave schidigera* and the closely related *A. filifera* are conspecific. Indeed, when looking at the similarities and the homogeneity of hybrids, it is easy to see how such a case could be made, although field work is needed to support these observations. *Agave filifera* has a strong tendency to offset and generally is slightly larger than *A. schidigera*, which has coarser filaments and leaves that in general are thinner and more pliable than those of *A. filifera*. Several named hybrids and forms have been in the trade a long time, including *A.* ×*ortiesiana* Hort., a dwarf form; *A.* ×*leopoldii* (synonym *A.* ×*leopoldii* II), a hybrid with *A. filifera* (see description under *A. filifera*), and *A. schidigera* var. *taylori* Jacobson, an invalid name once applied to a form with wider leaves.

USES: A highly ornamental species, *Agave schidigera* is easy to use with most leafy perennials or as a colorful addition to a succulent garden. Because it is solitary, it makes an excellent potted plant or a focal specimen in a smaller garden. The terminal spines are sharp, so the plant should be sited with care.

Agave schottii Engelmann   PLATE 38

COMMON NAMES: Shin dagger, Amole, Amolillo

SIZE: *Agave schottii* is a small plant rarely more than 12 in. (30 cm) wide. It forms caespitose clumps, some of which reportedly are up to 39 in. (100 cm) wide. It has relatively few leaves, 20–40.

LEAVES: The linear leaves are 0.25–0.5 in. (0.6–1.3 cm) wide and 10–16 in. (25–40 cm) long. They are a yellow-green with a smooth, brown margin that is punctuated by sparse, coarse filaments. Teeth are absent, and the terminal spine is fine and short, 0.25–0.5 in. (0.6–1.3 cm) long. The top of the leaf is plane to slightly concave while the underside is decidedly convex. *Agave schottii* var. *treleasii* (Toumey) Kearney & Peebles (synonym *A. treleasii* Toumey), a much larger version of the species, has leaves much longer and wider than those of the type.

BLOOM: The inflorescence is a spike 5–8 ft. (1.5–2.4 m) tall. The flowers are held on the upper third to half of the stalk. They are a dull yellow and extremely fragrant and occur from April to August.

DISTRIBUTION: *Agave schottii* is distributed widely from southern Arizona through southwestern New Mexico into the Mexican states of Sonora and northwestern Chihuahua at elevations above 3000 ft. (900 m). Found in grasslands and in the edge of oak woodlands, this agave forms extensive colonies on rocky, shallow soils. It is not as common in horticulture as it is in nature. Variety *treleasii* comes from limited areas in southern Arizona

PROPAGATION: Propagation is by seed or by removal of the offsets.

CULTURAL REQUIREMENTS: *Agave schottii* benefits from extra irrigation in the summer in the low desert and has its best color if given some light shade from the afternoon sun. In less intense climates it is best grown in full sun. Considering its natural distribution, it is expected to be very cold hardy, at least to 10°F (−12°C). Plantings in Denver indicate this species may be even more cold hardy than expected.

SIMILAR OR RELATED SPECIES: *Agave schottii* could be easily confused with the more narrow leaved forms of the much less common *A. felgeri*, but can be distinguished by the sparse number of coarse filaments compared to the highly filamentous *A. felgeri*. Some individuals could be confused with *A. toumeyana*, a species with dull green, wider leaves that are quite flat on the top and have at least some white bud imprinting. In addition, *A. toumeyana* has more than twice as many leaves as *A. schottii*. The leaves of *A. schottii* var. *treleasii* are nearly as large as those of *A. toumeyana* but lack the bud imprint of *A. toumeyana*.

USES: A preparation of *Agave schottii* was used in the natural range of the species to wash clothes and hair. Ornamentally, this agave is a fine choice for rocky, shallow soils or to help in soil stabilization on a rocky slope. It should be given ample room to spread into the large colonies that make it so distinctive. Its small size and relatively short inflorescence make the flowers and their intense fragrance easy to enjoy.

Agave seemanniana Jacobi

SYNONYMS: *Agave tortispina* Trelease, *Agave carol-schmidtii* Berger, *Agave guatemalensis* Berger

SIZE: *Agave seemanniana* is a medium-sized, solitary species 2.5–3 ft. (0.8–1 m) wide. The rosette has no more than 20 leaves and is very open and spreading.

LEAVES: The oblong to broadly lanceolate leaves are 5–8 in. (13–20 cm) wide and 12–20 in. (30–51 cm) long. They are flat, thick, and succulent, narrowing toward the base, but vary greatly in size and shape. The leaves are glaucous green to yellow-green and are sometimes lightly crossbanded. The margin is gently or strongly undulate with small, dark brown teeth on low teats. The teeth are widely spaced, 0.5–1.25 in. (1.3–3.2 cm) apart, with a very broad base. The terminal spine is 0.75–1.5 in. (2–3.8 cm) long and decurrent.

BLOOM: The inflorescence is a panicle 10–13 ft. (3–4 m) tall with 18–30 branches.

DISTRIBUTION: *Agave seemanniana* occurs from the Mexican state of Chiapas through Nicaragua at elevations of 1000–5000 ft. (300–1500 m) on limestone outcrops and hillsides.

PROPAGATION: Propagation is by seed.

CULTURAL REQUIREMENTS: *Agave seemanniana* is quite cold tender even in the low desert and needs significant frost protection outside frost-free regions. On the California coast or a Mediterranean climate, it grows in full sun or filtered shade, but in the low desert it requires shade to prevent heat stress and sunburn. In the low desert it thrives with ample summer watering.

SIMILAR OR RELATED SPECIES: The combination of small teeth on broad teats and thick succulent leaves in an open rosette makes *Agave seemanniana* very distinctive.

USES: As an ornamental, *Agave seemanniana* is very attractive, either in the ground or in a pot, for its fleshy, soft but well-spined leaves. It is an excellent choice for a dry, shady frost-free location.

Agave shawii Engelmann PLATE 39

SYNONYMS: *Agave orcuttiana* Trelease, *Agave pachyacantha* Trelease

SIZE: *Agave shawii* is solitary or has numerous offsets with stems to 6.5 ft. (2 m) tall. This species forms extensive colonies, and stems are frequently prostrate and visible.

LEAVES: The glossy dark or light green leaves are 3–4 in. (8–10 cm) wide and 8–20 in. (20–51 cm) long and slightly rough. They are thick, fleshy, and rigid, and flat to slightly guttered on top. The margin is undulate to mammillate and may be smooth or bordered by a thick horny edge. The teeth are generally of a uniform width for the entire length, widening only slightly at the base. They are often straight, but may be hooked or recurved; they arise from a wide teat and are a dark red-brown that contrasts dramatically with the leaf. The terminal spine is the same rich color, 0.75–1.5 in. (2–3.8 cm) long, and long decurrent up to 4 in. (10 cm) down the leaf. *Agave shawii* subsp. *goldmaniana* (Trelease) Gentry (synonym *A. goldmaniana* Trelease) has larger more lanceolate leaves 4–7 in. (10–18 cm) wide and 15–27 in. (38–69 cm) long.

BLOOM: The inflorescence is a stout panicle 6.5–13 ft. (2–4 m) tall with 8–14 branches. The flowers are greenish with purple bracts, making the buds appear purple.

DISTRIBUTION: *Agave shawii* occurs in the maritime parts of northwestern Baja. It is rare in southern California.

PROPAGATION: Propagation is by removal of the offsets or by seed.

CULTURAL REQUIREMENTS: *Agave shawii* requires some relief from the low desert heat, so that light shade of tall mesquites or other open trees is ideal. Subspecies *goldmaniana* is much more heat tolerant. This species has limited frost tolerance and for cultivation in the ground is suited to the low desert, Mediterranean climates, or along the coast of California. In the desert it needs summer irrigation.

SIMILAR OR RELATED SPECIES: The combination of dark glossy green leaves, numerous caespitose offsets, and strong spine and teeth distinguishes *Agave shawii* from most other agaves. Subspecies *goldmaniana* is nearly impossible to separate from *A. avellanidens* based on leaf characters alone.

USES: Highly ornamental, *Agave shawii* could be used much more extensively in gardens. It is a handsome plant that blends well with cacti and other succulents as well as wildflower or perennial plantings. It is extremely effective along a slope where the stunning rosettes can be viewed at eye level.

Agave sisalana Perrine   PLATE 40

SIZE: *Agave sisalana* is a large species that can develop a short stem 16–39 in. (40–100 cm) tall. With its large leaves, the entire plant can be 5–6.5 ft. (1.5–2 m) tall. It sets a moderate number of rhizomatous offsets.

LEAVES: The sword-shaped, straight, stiff leaves are held upright and usually lack marginal teeth, although some individuals have minute irregularly spaced teeth. The leaves are 3.5–4.75 in. (9–12 cm) wide and 35.5–51 in. (90–130 cm) long, thin and fleshy, fibrous, and light blue-green to yellowish green. The terminal spine is 0.75–1 in. (2–2.5 cm) long, conical, and dark brown; it is not decurrent.

BLOOM: The inflorescence is a panicle 16–20 ft. (5–6 m) tall with 10–15 branches on the upper half of the stalk. The plant sets numerous bulbils after flowering.

DISTRIBUTION: There is no known natural distribution of *Agave sisalana*. It is considered a sterile hybrid of cultivated origin.

PROPAGATION: Propagation is by removal of the offsets or the bulbils.

CULTURAL REQUIREMENTS: *Agave sisalana* tolerates a wide range of conditions and soils, but is somewhat frost tender, sustaining considerable damage below 25°F (−4°C). With ample water, plants grow very quickly, but can be grown in arid regions on moderate summer irrigation. Plants do well in either full sun or partial shade even in the low desert. They tolerate a modest amount of summer irrigation in mild summer areas.

SIMILAR OR RELATED SPECIES: *Agave sisalana* can be distinguished from *A. weberi* by its narrow, straight leaves without marginal teeth, from *A. desmettiana* by the straight, upright leaves, and from *A. fourcroydes* by the lack of marginal teeth and by the flatter leaf.

USES: *Agave sisalana* is part of the complex of sterile agave hybrids grown for fiber. It is thought to have derived from plants near the city of Sisal in the Mexican state of Yucatán, hence the species name. It undoubtedly has been in cultivation a very long time for its excellent, very fine fiber. Plants from Mexico were introduced into cultivation in Florida in the early nineteenth century and from there were distributed throughout the West Indies and ultimately to Africa where this agave became one of the principle fiber crop agaves. It has since been reintroduced to Mexico as a crop plant and is once again an important fiber crop species. The fibers are strong and very fine. Many of the most delicate agave products are made from this fiber. As an ornamental, *A. sisalana* is a striking choice. The straight, upright leaves and the plant's high tolerance to a wide range of conditions, except long or severe cold, make it easy to use. It forms a dramatic mass or linear planting, serves as a bold backdrop for perennials, and is a lovely part of a large succulent garden.

Agave sobria T. Brandegee

SYNONYMS: *Agave affinis* Trelease, *Agave carminis* Trelease, *Agave slevinii* I. M. Johnston

SIZE: *Agave sobria* is a small to medium-sized species with few to several offsets. It is 19–59 in. (48–150 cm) wide and generally stemless.

LEAVES: The leaves are linear to lanceolate and vary in color from a glaucous gray or blue-gray to yellow-green. They are 2–4 in. (5–10 cm) wide and 18–31 in. (46–79 cm) long and often are strongly crossbanded and slightly rough to the touch. The margin is undulate or mammillate with small, flattened teeth on wide bases. The teeth are gray with a reddish tip and spaced 1–1.5 in. (2.5–3.8 cm) apart. They can be turned, curled, twisted, and flexed in a variety of shapes. The terminal spine is 1–2 in. (2.5–5 cm) long and decurrent. Two subspecies represent quite distinct forms. *Agave sobria* subsp. *roseana* (Trelease) Gentry (synonym *A. roseana* Trelease) has fewer leaves that are narrow and shorter than the type and usually much wider above the midpoint than below. The very large, contorted, even fantastic teeth are on extremely exaggerated flattened teats that are quite distant on the leaf. These teeth can be 0.5–1 in. (1.3–2.5 cm) long and 0.5 in. (1.3 cm) wide. *Agave sobria* subsp. *frailensis* Gentry has more leaves in a compact rosette. The leaves tend to be blue-gray with smaller teeth that are closer together.

BLOOM: The inflorescence is a panicle 8–13 ft. (2.4–4 m) tall with 8–20 branches. The flowers are pale yellow and can occur from March to November.

DISTRIBUTION: *Agave sobria* is found from sea level to 3500 ft. (1000 m) on the western edge of the Mexican state of Sonora. While it grows in a wide range of rainfall regimes, it is most vigorous in areas with higher rainfall or in north-facing canyons.

PROPAGATION: Propagation is by seed or by the removal of the offsets.

CULTURAL REQUIREMENTS: *Agave sobria* is fairly easy to cultivate and has a demonstrated cold hardiness to at least 25°F (–4°C).

SIMILAR OR RELATED SPECIES: *Agave sobria* could be confused with *A. cerulata,* but the former lacks the brown ring around the base of the teeth. Subspecies *roseana* in particular could be difficult to distinguish from *A. gigantensis;* however, the latter lacks crossbanding and has wider leaves with a long horny border from the spine to the middle of the leaf. *Agave zebra* has very wide, thick leaves and very large teeth.

USES: *Agave sobria* was an important food source in historic times in its range and still is used in the making of mescal. Ornamentally, this species is stunning, particularly some individuals of subspecies *roseana*. In small gardens or where there is a lot of traffic, however, it should be sited far in the background to accommodate its grandiose armature.

Agave striata Zuccarini

PLATE 41

SYNONYMS: *Agave recurva* Zuccarini, *Agave echinoides* Jacobi

COMMON NAMES: Espadin, Espadillo, Guapilla, Soyate, Sotolito

SIZE: *Agave striata* forms dense, extensive colonies with numerous plants arising from axillary branches. It has a short stem. The rosette is 20–39 in. (51–100 cm) tall and 20–47 in. (51–119 cm) wide.

LEAVES: The leaves are very narrow, about 0.25 in. (0.6 cm) wide, and 10–24 in. (25–61 cm) long, with some even longer. They are convex strongly above and below. From a distance individual leaves appear round, but they are rhomboid when seen in cross section. The leaves are a glaucous green color with a minute, serrated yellow margin, and end in a strong, sharp terminal spine that is 0.5–2 in. (1.3–5 cm) long. The leaves often have a red or purple tint. *Agave striata* subsp. *falcata* (Engelmann) Gentry (synonym *A. falcata* Engelmann) has leaves that are wider, 0.25–0.75 in. (0.6–2 cm), and as long as for the species. It has fewer leaves per plant, resulting in the open habit that distinguishes the subspecies most readily.

BLOOM: The inflorescence is a spike 5–8 ft. (1.5–2.4 m) tall. The flowers, which are held loosely on the spike, are yellow, occasionally red-purple, and occur from June to September.

DISTRIBUTION: *Agave striata* is found in northeastern Mexico on both sides of the Sierra Madre Oriental from the states of Coahuila and Nuevo León through San Luis Potosí to Hidalgo. All populations occur on dry hills or limestone plateaus with the northern part of the range very xeric.

PROPAGATION: Propagation is by seed or by removal of plants from the clump.

CULTURAL REQUIREMENTS: *Agave striata* requires full sun to maintain its best form, but in the low desert a light, high shade also produces excellent plants. Plants have shown cold tolerance to 15°F (–9°C) in Tucson, and some populations may have even better cold tolerance. All require infrequent summer watering and virtually none in the winter in the low desert. In more coastal or other cooler climates the plant should be grown very dry.

SIMILAR OR RELATED SPECIES: *Agave striata* is extremely difficult to distinguish from the closely related *A. stricta*. Although the two are best separated by floral characteristics, cultivated plants of *A. striata* have fewer leaves and a more open habit than those sold as *A. stricta*. Subspecies *falcata* is even more open than the type, with wider leaves that are wider at the base.

USES: *Agave striata* is an excellent garden plant. It is able to grow well in extremely dry situations, and it has merit for soil holding, rocky slopes, and at the edge of dry gardens. It is a fascinating and distinctive container choice.

Agave stricta Salm-Dyck   PLATE 42

SYNONYMS: *Agave echinoides* Jacobi, *Agave striata* var. *stricta* Baker

COMMON NAME: Rabo de león

SIZE: *Agave stricta* produces a rounded tight rosette of hundreds of leaves that are strongly recurved and give the plant the look of sea urchins randomly placed in the hills. Extensive colonies can develop with plants arising from prostrate stems 3–6.5 ft. (1–2 m) long.

LEAVES: The leaves appear spherical or round, but on close examination actually are rhomboidal with a strongly convex top and bottom surface. They are 0.25–0.5 in. (0.6–1.3 cm) wide and 10–20 in. (25–51 cm) long, usually a deep green, and striated. The margin is thin and yellow without noticeable teeth but often minutely serrulate with a sturdy 0.5–0.75 in. (1.3–2 cm), gray terminal spine.

BLOOM: The inflorescence is a very crooked spike 5–8 ft. (1.5–2.4 m) tall. The flowers are red-purple and open in July and August.

DISTRIBUTION: *Agave stricta* is found in the Mexican state

of Puebla in the Tehuacán Valley and certain locales nearby. It occurs on dry, limestone formations and dry hills.

PROPAGATION: Propagation is by seed or by removal of plants from a colony.

CULTURAL REQUIREMENTS: *Agave stricta* thrives on a version of benign neglect. In the low desert some relief from the intensity of summer afternoon sun helps keep plants from yellowing badly, but in all other areas full sun is recommended. Overwatering ruins the tight, urchinlike form, so it is best to grow this plant very much on the dry side, particularly in cool or overcast conditions.

SIMILAR OR RELATED SPECIES: *Agave stricta* can be very difficult to separate from some individuals of *A. striata*. Its growth form best distinguishes it: *A. stricta* tends to have many more leaves, which are held very tightly, and are recurved strongly to the center of the plant and dense. Minor floral differences separate the two species as well.

USES: A good plant for rugged rocky areas, *Agave stricta* makes a stunning contrast to softer wildflowers, perennials, or other leafy plantings. It is striking in a pot and can be maintained as a single specimen by removing any new plants that arise.

Agave subsimplex Trelease

SIZE: *Agave subsimplex* is a small species that may be solitary or produce offsets. The rosette is 8–13 in. (20–33 cm) tall and 20–27 in. (51–69 cm) wide.

LEAVES: The leaves vary in size, but usually are 1–2 in. (2.5–5 cm) wide and 5–14 in. (13–36 cm) long. They are a glaucous gray to yellow-green color, lanceolate to ovate, strong and rigid, guttered, smooth, and wider at the base. The margin may be nearly straight or very mammillate. The teeth are variable, but the largest are less than 0.5 in. (1.3 cm) long. They are yellow-gray or brown and are missing or much smaller along the lower half of the leaf. Most teeth are straight, but they can be curved or hooked with the upper leaf teeth hooked toward the tip, and the lower ones hooked toward the base. The terminal spine is

0.75–1.5 in. (2–3.8 cm) long with little or no decurrence. It is often sinuous.

BLOOM: The inflorescence is a slender panicle 6–11 ft. (1.8–3.4 m) tall with 5–8 branches. The flowers are yellow but sometimes pink and open from May to July.

DISTRIBUTION: *Agave subsimplex* has a narrow distribution along the Sonoran coast in Mexico and on some islands in and around the island of Tiburón. It typically is found below 800 ft. (240 m) in elevation. It is not common in cultivation.

PROPAGATION: Propagation is by seed or by removal of the offsets.

CULTURAL REQUIREMENTS: *Agave subsimplex* has been seen occasionally in cultivation in the Tucson and Phoenix areas. Tucson growers report it as frost sensitive, but in Phoenix it is quite hardy, indicating that the plant is damaged below about 25°F (–4°C). This very drought tolerant species grows best in full sun, even in the low desert, on rocky, well-drained soils. In cooler or moister climates it needs to be grown very dry in a hot location.

SIMILAR OR RELATED SPECIES: *Agave subsimplex* strongly resembles *A. deserti* and *A. cerulata,* but in nature is distinguished by its distribution: *A. deserti* is more common north of *A. subsimplex,* and *A. cerulata* generally south of it. In containers it is more difficult to distinguish these three. Generally, *A. deserti* has longer and wider leaves, and *A. cerulata* has even larger leaves, well beyond the range of *A. subsimplex* described here. *Agave subsimplex* lacks the brown ring at the base of the teeth that is characteristic of *A. cerulata. Agave deserti* usually exhibits decurrence of the terminal spine to the first few teeth; *A. subsimplex* is rarely or very shortly decurrent. The pink flowers of *A. subsimplex* are unique, but rarely a practical identification characteristic.

USES: Historically, the Seri Indians of northwestern Mexico used *Agave subsimplex* regularly for food and beverage. Stems were roasted and eaten directly or dried to a cake that could be reconstituted as a beverage. Seeds and flower buds were used to create necklaces. The species is a good ornamental plant for very hot and dry climates.

Agave tequilana Weber   PLATE 43

SYNONYMS: *Agave palmaris* Trelease, *Agave pedrosana* Trelease, *Agave pres-mulae* Trelease, *Agave pseudotequilana* Trelease, *Agave subtilis* Trelease

SIZE: *Agave tequilana* is a large species 4–6 ft. (1.2–1.8 m) tall with rosettes held on a short stem. The long leaves are held rigidly upright. Plants make offsets, particularly as they age.

LEAVES: The lanceolate, very fibrous, rigid leaves are held nearly upright on the plant. They are 3–5 in. (8–13 cm) wide and 35–47 in. (89–119 cm) long, blue-gray to gray-green, occasionally with crossbanding. The small, regularly spaced teeth occur 0.5–0.75 in. (1.3–2 cm) apart along a straight or slightly undulate margin. The terminal spine is short, less than 0.25 in. (0.6 cm) long, broad at the base, dark brown, and decurrent to the first tooth. Among the several variegated forms, one unnamed form is particularly striking with a blue-green midleaf and a creamy yellow margin tinged with pink.

BLOOM: The inflorescence is a panicle 16–20 ft. (5–6 m) tall with 20–25 dense branches. The flowers are green with rosy stamens.

DISTRIBUTION: *Agave tequilana* is known only from near Tequila in the Mexican state of Jalisco. It is grown as an ornamental plant throughout the world.

PROPAGATION: Propagation is by removal of the offsets.

CULTURAL REQUIREMENTS: *Agave tequilana* is somewhat frost-tender and sun-tender in the low desert and should be given overhead protection or light shade. In frost-free locations and milder climates it can be grown in full sun.

SIMILAR OR RELATED SPECIES: *Agave tequilana* is so closely related to *A. angustifolia* that separation, especially of young plants or certain individuals, can be difficult. *Agave tequilana* generally has longer more fibrous (less fleshy) leaves, is bluer rather than green, and has a decurrent terminal spine.

USES: *Agave tequilana* is used to make the alcoholic beverage tequila. In fact, the name tequila is restricted to the distilled product from selected clones grown in and around Tequila, Jalisco. Ornamentally, the species has been known throughout the Mediterranean region of Europe and the warmer parts of the United States, particularly California, for more than 100 years. It is a large plant, but some forms are quite lovely and accent a large succulent planting or a large perennial planting very well.

Agave titanota Gentry   PLATE 44

SIZE: *Agave titanota* is a medium-sized but distinctive species that is solitary or with few offsets. The rosette spreads widely, displaying the extremely light colored leaves.

LEAVES: The rigid leaves are 5–5.5 in. (13–14 cm) wide and 13.75–21.75 in. (35–55 cm) long. They are a glaucous white with a gently undulate horny border. The teeth are variable but are fairly long, up to 0.5 in. (1.3 cm), although the leaf frequently is toothless toward the spine. The spine is hard, conic, deeply grooved, 1–1.5 in. (2.5–3.8 cm) long, and dark brown aging to gray.

BLOOM: The inflorescence is a spike that can rise to 10 ft. (3 m) tall. The yellow flowers are often tinged with lavender and are held on the upper half of the stalk.

DISTRIBUTION: Known only as a very local endemic from the Mexican state of Oaxaca, *Agave titanota* occurs on limestone faces and rocky hills. It is not common in cultivation.

PROPAGATION: Propagation is by seed or by removal of the offsets.

CULTURAL REQUIREMENTS: *Agave titanota* has demonstrated no serious cultural problems in the Phoenix area. Some sun protection in the summer and generous summer watering help keep it looking fit in the low desert, but it would surely be a full sun plant elsewhere. Unlikely to be hardy to extreme cold, the species has remained undamaged in Phoenix where winter lows rarely go below 25°F (–4°C).

SIMILAR OR RELATED SPECIES: The only other nearly white-leaved agaves are *Agave potatorum, A. franzosinii,* or the extremely uncommon *A. angustifolia* var. *letonae. Agave titanota* can be distinguished from *A. potatorum* by its longer, more linear leaves and its much larger and more variable teeth.

Agave potatorum has an extremely mammillate leaf margin. *Agave titanota* can be distinguished from *A. angustifolia* var. *letonae* by its shorter leaves, which are half the length and width of *A. angustifolia* var. *letonae*. *Agave franzosinii* is more than three times the size of *A. titanota*.

USES: Although not widely cultivated, *Agave titanota* deserves greater use because of its extraordinary coloring. As a landscape plant it is exceptionally beautiful with dark or dense foliage for contrast and interest. It is equally dramatic in a pot as long as the pot is large enough to allow the plant to grow and spread to its full size.

Agave toumeyana Trelease

PLATE 45

SIZE: *Agave toumeyana* is a fairly small species, 12 in. (30 cm) wide, but forms large, dense, caespitose colonies. These colonies can be distinctive when old as the oldest plants in the middle die out, leaving a ring of live plants around a vacant middle.

LEAVES: The leaves are linear lanceolate, 0.5–0.75 in. (1.3–2 cm) wide and 8–12 in. (20–30 cm) long, straight, and incurved, giving the rosette an urnlike shape. The leaves are green with a white bud imprint on the upper side and on the underside. The margin is brown, smooth, sometimes with minute teeth at the base, and is covered with thin, white filaments. The brown-gray terminal spine is 0.25–0.75 in. (0.6–2 cm) long. *Agave toumeyana* subsp. *bella* (Breitung) Gentry is distinguished from the species by its very small size, individual leaves that are half as long as those of the type, and its great number of leaves, up to 100 per plant, versus the 40–70 of *A. toumeyana*.

BLOOM: The inflorescence is a spike 5–8 ft. (1.5–2.4 m) tall. The flowers, which are held in the upper third of the stalk, are pale yellow to greenish and occur in June and July. Blooming is very irregular and intermittent.

DISTRIBUTION: A local endemic, *Agave toumeyana* is found in central Arizona in the Pinal, Bradshaw, and New River mountains at elevations of 2000–4500 ft. (600–1350 m). It occurs on limestone and volcanic outcrops.

PROPAGATION: Propagation is by seed, despite erratic bloom sequences, by removal of the offsets, and by bulbils, though the latter are very uncommon.

CULTURAL REQUIREMENTS: *Agave toumeyana* is an easy plant to cultivate in the low desert, requiring full sun to partial shade, rocky soil with excellent drainage, and moderate summer watering. There is no record of its cold tolerance, but given its natural range it certainly should be able to withstand temperatures down to at least 10°F (–12°C) and probably much colder.

SIMILAR OR RELATED SPECIES: Some individuals of *Agave toumeyana* could be confused with *A. schottii*, but their leaves are twice as wide, with more and finer filaments and a prominent white bud imprint. *Agave schottii* var. *treleasii* reaches about the same size as *A. toumeyana*, but again the white imprints and the filaments separate these two species. *Agave toumeyana* subsp. *bella* has a brown leaf margin, while *A. parviflora* has a white leaf margin.

USES: *Agave toumeyana* and *A. toumeyana* subsp. *bella* are exquisite plants when grown as solitary individuals. The combination of leaf imprint and white filaments with the very regular form is striking. Both plants do extremely well in pot culture, but crowding tends to exaggerate their tendency to create root suckers. Overwatering causes the plants to grow elongated leaves that open and lay flatter than normal.

Agave utahensis Engelmann   PLATE 46

SYNONYMS: *Agave newberryi* Engelmann, *Agave haynaldii* var. *utahensis* Terracciano, *Agave scaphoidea* Greenman & Roush, *Agave utahensis* var. *discreta* Jones

COMMON NAME: Yant

SIZE: A fairly small species, *Agave utahensis* is 7–12 in. (18–30 cm) tall and 10–16 in. (25–40 cm) wide, rising on a short stem in older plants. The plant has 70–80 leaves, which are highly variable in form, size, and color. This species often forms large clumps.

LEAVES: The leaves are 0.5–1.25 in. (1.3–3.2 cm) wide and

6–12 in. (15–30 cm) long and usually gray-green. Small easily detached gray teeth are spaced widely on the margin, 0.25–1 in. (0.6–2.5 cm) apart, and have a distinct ring at the base. The terminal spine is 0.75–1.5 in. (2–3.8 cm) long, gray, deeply channeled on the top, and decurrent for a short distance down the leaf. There are two recognized varieties and one subspecies. *Agave utahensis* var. *eborispina* (Hester) Breitung (synonym *A. eborispina* Hester) has a distinctive, elongated, paperlike ivory-colored terminal spine. *Agave utahensis* subsp. *kaibabensis* (McKelvey) Gentry (synonym *A. kaibabensis* McKelvey) is among the handsomest forms of the species with bright green leaves in single rosettes. The teeth are spaced regularly 0.25 in. (0.6 cm) apart and are straight and gray-white. *Agave utahensis* var. *nevadensis* Engelmann is smaller than the type. The rosettes are 6–10 in. (15–25 cm) tall. The leaves are a glaucous blue-gray with much larger teeth and an elongated spine.

BLOOM: The inflorescence is 5–8 ft. (1.5–2.4 m) tall and varies in style often in the same locale. It may be a spike, a raceme, or a panicle. The flowers are a light yellow and open in May and June.

DISTRIBUTION: *Agave utahensis* is the most northern agave in distribution and is found on limestone outcrops and hills in northwestern Arizona, Utah, Nevada, and California. It is uncommon in general cultivation, although some forms have attracted collectors for a long time.

PROPAGATION: Propagation is by seed or by removal of the offsets.

CULTURAL REQUIREMENTS: In containers or in gardens it is advisable to keep *Agave utahensis* very dry when it is cold and to be certain that drainage is exceptional. In the lower desert this plant thrives in a garden, but requires some supplemental watering in the summer. In the low desert, weekly watering in the hottest areas is recommended. This agave tolerates full sun or partial shade, with the best form seen in strong light. It is among the most cold hardy agaves, able to withstand temperatures well below 0°F (−18°C) or more for extended periods of time.

SIMILAR OR RELATED SPECIES: *Agave utahensis* is distinguished from *A. deserti,* which has much wider leaves (twice as wide as those of *A. utahensis*), small teeth that are spaced very widely, and no ring at the base of the teeth. The leaves of *A. subsimplex* are much more guttered, the spine is not decurrent, and there is no ring at the base of the teeth. The leaves of *A. mckelveyana* generally are smaller, very shortly decurrent, and lack the ring at the base of the teeth. *Agave cerulata* is a more robust plant, with leaves more yellow-green or green (as opposed to the gray-green leaves of *A. utahensis*), and has very irregularly formed and spaced teeth.

USES: In historic times *Agave utahensis* played a significant role in the life and diet of many people living near the Grand Canyon. Archaeological evidence abounds that it was roasted and eaten and the fiber was twisted into ropes and other uses. As an ornamental plant, the species and all its forms provide a stunning addition to a garden. The striking color and spine combination of subsp. *kaibabensis,* the remarkable ivory talon of var. *eborispina,* and symmetrical appearance of the type and var. *nevadensis* offer excellent contrast for a perennial or wildflower garden or as a featured plant in a succulent garden or container. Extremely hardy, this plant could be used in any dry, cold region or elsewhere if the drainage is superb and the plant can be kept quite dry in cold weather. In warmer regions it thrives on fairly regular supplemental watering in the summer, in dry winters, and in full sun.

Agave victoriae-reginae Moore   PLATES 47, 48

SYNONYMS: *Agave consideranti* Carrière, *Agave ferdinandi-regis* Berger, *Agave nichelsii* R. Gosselin

SIZE: *Agave victoriae-reginae* is a small to medium-sized species that is immediately recognizable by its extremely dense, tightly regular rosette of hard, triangular leaves marked with white. Plants are from 20 to 27.5 in. (51–70 cm) wide and typically solitary, but occasional individuals may have a few offsets.

LEAVES: The dark green leaves are 1.5–2.5 in. (3.8–6 cm) wide and 6–8 in. (15–20 cm) long with white markings on the surface. The white markings are variable, but are most often thick; they form a triangle on the surface of the leaf, ending a few inches below the terminal spine, and they unite to become a single line up to the terminal spine. The margin is entirely smooth, with a hard, white, horny border. The leaf ends in one to three stiff, black terminal spines that are 0.5–1 in. (1.3–2.5 cm) long, sometimes much shorter. The leaves have a distinctive keel underneath, making them appear triangular, and are very rigid and hard. The white coloration on the leaves is highly variable with some combinations having been named in the past. One, *Agave victoriae-reginae* var. *viridis* Breitung, denotes plants without white markings, while most other names denote patterns of the white markings. Sadly, the names are used rarely in the trade. There is a yellow variegated form.

BLOOM: The inflorescence is a dense spike 10–13 ft. (3–4 m) tall. The flowers are cream colored with a red to purple tinge and occur in the upper half of the stalk.

DISTRIBUTION: *Agave victoriae-reginae* occurs in the Mexican states of Coahuila, Durango, and Nuevo León. Never numerous in its native range, it is now considered a protected and rare species in Mexico where it is given the designation "Danger of Extinction" (*Peligro de extincion*).

PROPAGATION: Propagation is by seed or by removal of the occasional offset.

CULTURAL REQUIREMENTS: Regardless of the location, *Agave victoriae-reginae* achieves its best form in full sun. In the low desert, watering at least twice a month in summer helps prevent yellowing and other heat-related problems. In wet areas or areas with cool summers a full sun position in a raised bed or mound helps the plant achieve its finest form. It is excellent in a shallow container, particularly one with a diameter that closely matches its ultimate size. This species is known to tolerate cold to at least 10°F (–12°C), and plantings in Denver suggest it may be hardy much lower if kept dry.

SIMILAR OR RELATED SPECIES: No agave closely resembles this one; however, some hybrids and forms are known. Near Saltillo, capital of the Mexican state of Coahuila, a hybrid swarm of plants between *Agave victoriae-reginae* and *A. scabra* is known and has been cultivated for a long time. These hybrids often are called erroneously *A. ferdinandi-regis*, a defunct name for this species. Some of these hybrid forms are gorgeous, coupling the smooth edge and hard form of *A. victoriae-reginae* with the dusky colors and size of *A. scabra*.

USES: Ornamentally, *Agave victoriae-reginae* is among the most outstanding and well-loved agaves. It looks wonderful as a single specimen or in a focal spot. Among the most effective plantings we have seen was one where the plant could be viewed from above, such as below a deck. Lotusland, outside of Santa Barbara, California, has a mass planting that creates an imaginative display (Plate 48).

Agave vilmoriniana Berger   PLATE 49

SYNONYMS: *Agave eduardii* Trelease, *Agave houghii* Hort. ex Trelease, *Agave mayoensis* Gentry

COMMON NAMES: Octopus agave, Amole

SIZE: *Agave vilmoriniana* is a large species up to 3 ft. (1 m) tall and 5 ft. (1.5 m) wide. It usually is solitary. The leaves are long, curving and recurving with a graceful deep arch, hence its common name.

LEAVES: The light green, occasionally pale bluish leaves are 3–6 ft. (1–1.8 m) long and 3–4 in. (8–10 cm) wide and few in number. The base of the leaf is very swollen and wide. The leaves taper to a delicate terminal spine that is sharp, but flexible. The leaf margin is smooth with a fine brown border that may resemble a fine serration in some individuals.

BLOOM: The inflorescence is a raceme which can be 10–16 ft. (3–5 m) tall and usually is quite straight. The yellow-white to yellow flowers, which are held tightly on the stalk, are interspersed with numerous bulbils during and after bloom, which occurs from March to May. Cultivated plants bloom 7–10 years after planting on average, although some plants reportedly waited 16 years before blooming.

DISTRIBUTION: Among numerous *Agave* species described in the twentieth century, *A. vilmoriniana* was described by botanists from plants in the garden of Mr. de Vilmorin in Verreves,

France, in 1913. It naturally is distributed in the Mexican states of southern Sonora, Sinaloa, Durango, Jalisco, and Aguascalientes at elevations between 2000 and 5500 ft. (600–1650 m). It is a cliff-dwelling species, and the description of the scene by Gentry (1982) is unrivaled for its vivid depiction of the vertical home of this plant, "In the larger deeper canyons it forms extensive vertical colonies, which when viewed from a distance resemble giant spiders on a wall." This species became extremely popular in the 1990s in southern California and Phoenix, Arizona.

PROPAGATION: Propagation is by removal of the extensive bulbils. Seed set is uncommon and erratic in cultivation.

CULTURAL REQUIREMENTS: *Agave vilmoriniana* is an easy plant to cultivate in the coastal regions of southern California and in the low desert. Elsewhere it probably thrives best as a container plant that should be protected from freezing temperatures. It is frost sensitive and can be damaged below 25°F (–4°C). No hard evidence points to exact cold tolerance, however. In the low desert, light shade improves the color of the leaves and prevents sunburn and yellowing from heat stress. This plant, like many light green or slightly tropical agaves, shows significant yellowing of the leaves during episodes of high heat when grown in the full sun in the low desert. This condition usually is temporary and, if summer watering has been adequate, reverses itself when the weather cools. *Agave vilmoriniana* performs well in pots. Adequate space should be given to the plant because it will grow to nearly full size in a container.

SIMILAR OR RELATED SPECIES: As a young plant *Agave vilmoriniana* could be confused with young *A. desmettiana*, but the latter has a hard terminal spine, darker green color, fine teeth, and a more upright leaf form. The long curving, virtually toothless leaves with their large swollen bases distinguish *A. vilmoriniana* from all other large agaves. A closely related species, *A. chrysoglossa* I. M. Johnston, is not common in cultivation; it has straight, narrow leaves and does not grow bulbils on its inflorescence.

USES: *Agave vilmoriniana* is used widely as a cleanser in the areas in which it occurs naturally. Its common name *amole* is descriptive of this trait and is used for several species, whether in the genus *Agave* or not, that share the trait. Mature leaves, preferably dried, are pounded to fray them into forming an admirable brush. When wetted to release the saponin, the dried leaves produce suds and the leaf brush is used to clean clothes and other goods. The compound smilagenin is present in large concentrations in the old leaves of this species, and some work has been done that suggests possible uses of this chemical in cancer prevention and treatment. As an ornamental, *A. vilmoriniana* has a long history. It was grown in southern France and other parts of the Mediterranean in the early part of the twentieth century. It is a fairly recent entry into American horticulture, but rapidly has become a favorite, chiefly because of its ease of culture, unarmed leaves, attractive form, and fast growth.

Agave weberi Cels ex Poisson   PLATE 50

SYNONYM: *Agave franceschiana* Trelease

SIZE: *Agave weberi* is a medium-sized to large species that is 4–5 ft. (1.2–1.5 m) tall and 6.5–10 ft. (2–3 m) wide. It makes a moderate number of offsets.

LEAVES: The gray-green to shiny green leaves are 5–7 in. (13–18 cm) wide and 3.5–5 ft. (1.1–1.5 m) long. The upper half of the leaf is toothless, but the lower half can have fine teeth along the margin. Rare individuals have more sturdy teeth, and occasional clones have an entirely smooth margin. The margin is straight, and the leaves are guttered on the top with an open, spreading habit. The terminal spine is 1–1.5 in. (2.5–3.8 cm) long with a short groove on the top and is decurrent for 1–2 in. (2.5–5 cm).

BLOOM: The inflorescence is a panicle 23–26 ft. (7–8 m) tall. The flowers are yellow, and some individuals form bulbils.

DISTRIBUTION: A cultivated form of *Agave weberi* is found in the arid parts of Mexico and the southwestern United States. The species is not known to have a wild form.

PROPAGATION: Propagation is by removal of the offsets or bulbils.

CULTURAL REQUIREMENTS: *Agave weberi* can be grown in the low desert in either full sun or partial shade. Plants with too much shade etiolate, forming a floppy, open rosette. Plants in the sun in the low desert need ample irrigation in the summer. The leaves are subject to severe yellowing from heat stress during the hottest summer temperatures, so that extra watering or shade from the sun maintains the plant in good condition. Yellowing from heat disappears, if it was not extreme, when temperatures moderate. This species is moderately hardy, tolerating temperatures to approximately 12°F (–11°C).

SIMILAR OR RELATED SPECIES: *Agave weberi* is related closely to *A. sisalana* from which it can be separated by the fine teeth on the margin, the much wider, fleshier leaf, and the grayer leaf color. *Agave weberi* could be confused with *A. desmettiana*, but is distinguished by its leaves, which are nearly twice as wide and long, with a decurrent spine, and a margin of which at least half is smooth.

USES: *Agave weberi* is large and dominating, but can be extremely attractive in a garden that has room for it. The leaves are soft and pliant, making it easy to mix the plant with softer perennials or shrubs. It is excellent in semi-shade where the color is best shown and complements succulents and cactus gardens very well. It is a bold specimen plant and makes a good choice for matched pairs or large groups of agaves.

Agave xylonacantha Salm-Dyck   PLATE 51

SYNONYMS: *Agave carchariodonta* Pampanini, *Agave kochii* Jacobi

SIZE: *Agave xylonacantha* is a medium-sized species that is 4 ft. (1.2 m) tall and wide. It may be solitary or with numerous offsets. The leaves are spreading and fairly sparse on the plant, rarely more than 20.

LEAVES: The leaves are concave or flat, swordlike or lanceolate, green to yellow-green, often with a light midstripe, and 2.5–4.5 in. (6–11 cm) wide and 14–24 in. (36–61 cm) long. A continuous light brown to gray horny border covers the margin. The teeth are large, flattened, and rise from large teats often with two or more teeth. They are highly variable in size and shape and can be directed forward, backward, or straight. The terminal spine is 1.5–2 in. (3.8–5 cm) long, flexible, and gray. The leaves vary widely, and some forms have been given varietal names by various authors. These are listed below. Many of them could be hybrids as well. *Agave xylonacantha* var. *hybrida* Villars has variegated leaves with the upper side showing a wide, simple (occasionally divided) stripe. *Agave xylonacantha* var. *latifolia* Jacobi has very wide leaves. *Agave xylonacantha* var. *macroacantha* Jacobi is a variegated form with especially large teeth.

BLOOM: The inflorescence is a dense spike 5–6 ft. (1.5–1.8 m) tall. The flowers occur in pairs or trios and are green-yellow.

DISTRIBUTION: Known from the states of Hidalgo and San Luis Potosí in eastern Mexico, *Agave xylonacantha* is long known in cultivation but poorly known in its native range.

PROPAGATION: Propagation is by seed or by removal of the offsets.

CULTURAL REQUIREMENTS: *Agave xylonacantha* is easy to cultivate in a warm area. In the low desert it does best in light shade; elsewhere full sun is required. It needs plenty of room as the resulting clump can be extensive without regular removal of the offsets.

SIMILAR OR RELATED SPECIES: The sinuous margin with the twisting and turning large, flattened teeth held on large teats, and a green lanceolate leaf mark *Agave xylonacantha* as a most distinctive plant. Long in cultivation, the species has been hybridized extensively, principally with *A. lophantha* (to produce hybrids known as *A.* ×*armata* Hort., *A.* ×*aspera* Jacquin, or *A.* ×*hybrida* Verschaffelt), *A. ghiesbreghtii*, and *A. lechuguilla*. Hybrids with *A. attenuata*, *A. filifera* (known as *A.* ×*villarum*, *A.* ×*villae* Pirotta, or *A.* ×*hybrida* Villars), and others also exist.

USES: *Agave xylonacantha* is excellent in a naturalized planting under a tree with a light canopy such as leguminous trees or tall, light shrubs such as creosote (*Larrea tridentata*). It is an effective barrier planting, but can also relieve the tedious greenery of a perennial planting with its interesting, but hard, wavy edges. Some individuals remain without offsets, and they are handsome in containers or located where the odd symmetry of the leaf margin can be appreciated.

Agave zebra Gentry   PLATE 52

SIZE: *Agave zebra* is a medium-sized species that is 1.25–5.25 ft. (0.4–1.6 m) tall and 16–24 in. (40–61 cm) wide. It usually is solitary, but some individuals form a few offsets when young.

LEAVES: The gray leaves have prominent crossbanding and are thick, rigid, rough to the touch, and widely guttered. They are 5–7 in. (13–18 cm) wide and 20–31 in. (51–79 cm) long with a mammillate margin lined with large, downcurved teeth on prominent teats. The leaves are not numerous and as they mature they fold inward, like a folded palm, giving the entire plant a graceful appearance at odds with its rough leaves and aggressive teeth. The terminal spine is up to 3 in. (8 cm) long and is decurrent to the first teeth.

BLOOM: The inflorescence is a panicle 20–26 ft. (6–8 m) tall with 7–14 branches. The flowers, which occur in the upper fourth of the stalk, are yellow and occur from June through August.

DISTRIBUTION: A very local endemic, *Agave zebra* is known from two locales in northern Sonora, Mexico. It occurs on limestone hills at 1500–4500 ft. (460–1350 m) elevation.

PROPAGATION: Propagation is by seed or by removal of the offsets.

CULTURAL REQUIREMENTS: *Agave zebra* is a good plant for very dry gardens as it can tolerate the full sun and arid conditions of the low desert. Plants grown for many years in Phoenix and in southern California have shown no frost damage. When grown with more than infrequent summer watering or occasional winter water, the plant becomes overly large and loses a great deal of its character.

SIMILAR OR RELATED SPECIES: The combination of a mammillate margin and large, curved teeth on crossbanded gray leaves is distinctive and should set off *Agave zebra* from all other gray-leaved agaves. The spine of *A. marmorata* is not decurrent and generally is much larger. *Agave gigantensis* has flat leaves that are smooth, and very widely spaced teeth. *Agave avellanidens* is smoother with a much smaller terminal spine and more upright, straight leaves.

USES: *Agave zebra* reportedly has been used to make mescal. It is certainly among the most beautiful agaves for a desert garden, both in color and in form. It sadly is difficult to find, partly because it makes so few offsets.

Beaucarnea gracilis Lemaire

SYNONYMS: *Beaucarnea oedipus* Rose, *Dasylirion gracilis* (Lemaire) J. F. Macbride

COMMON NAME: Sotolín

SIZE: *Beaucarnea gracilis* is a complex small tree or large shrublike species with many slender, curving, vertical stems that emerge from a large globose woody base. The base is 5–8.25 ft. (1.5–2.5 m) wide and covered with thick gray to brown bark that ages into polygonal or rectangular plates. The thin stems are topped with bristlelike rosettes of small leaves, giving the plant a rather unworldly look.

LEAVES: The small green to blue-green leaves are very straight and rigid, and are arranged in oblong to conical tufts at the ends of the branches. Often the upper half of the rosette consists of living leaves while the lower half has dead leaves or is clean of leaves altogether. The leaves are 9.75–21.75 in. (24–55 cm) long and less than 0.1–0.3 in. (3–8 mm) wide with very fine teeth on the margin.

BLOOM: The ovoid inflorescence is 2–3.25 ft. (0.6–1 m) long and has a stalk 6–7.75 in. (15–20 cm) long. The tiny cream-colored flowers are 0.06–0.1 in. (1.5–3 mm) long. The species is dioecious.

DISTRIBUTION: *Beaucarnea gracilis* occurs in the Mexican states of Puebla and Oaxaca in dry scrub vegetation often with cacti and other succulents. This species is seen rarely in cultivation.

PROPAGATION: Propagation is by seed.

CULTURAL REQUIREMENTS: *Beaucarnea gracilis* should be given a well-drained soil in full sun, although it probably tolerates partial shade in the hottest deserts. Because of its tropical origins, it probably does not tolerate temperatures much below freezing for extended periods of time.

SIMILAR OR RELATED SPECIES: *Beaucarnea gracilis* is somewhat similar to *B. stricta* in that both plants have rigid light green to blue-green leaves. They differ in that the leaves of *B. gracilis* are narrower and generally shorter than those of *B. stricta*. The woody base and stems of the plants also are different. The base in *B. gracilis* is globose and the stems are numerous and narrow, while the base of *B. stricta* is conical and the stems and branches are few and thick.

USES: The drought tolerance and somewhat bizarre appearance of *Beaucarnea gracilis* make it an excellent choice for locations where a tough and very unusual plant is desired. It also works well in large containers if planted in a well-drained medium and located in a mostly sunny position. It makes an excellent contribution to a dry garden of strange and unusually formed plants.

Beaucarnea guatemalensis Rose   PLATE 53

COMMON NAMES: Izote, Izote macho, Izote real

SIZE: *Beaucarnea guatemalensis* is a slender, moderately branched treelike species with vertical branches arising from a swollen cone-shaped base. Plants can reach 19.7–38.8 ft. (6–11.5 m) tall. The base is 3.25–5 ft. (1–1.5 m) wide and covered with thick gray bark that has an irregular pattern of fissures.

LEAVES: The dull green leaves are 1–1.5 in. (2.5–3.8 cm) wide and 2–4 ft. (0.6–1.2 m) long. They are recurved from the central growing point and reflexed about half way along their length. The leaves are thickened and slightly succulent along the midrib, and the margin is either smooth or only slightly toothed.

BLOOM: The broad ovoid inflorescence is 2.25–3.5 ft. (0.7–1.1 m) long and has a pale yellow stalk that is 7–7.75 in. (18–20 cm) long. The cream-colored flowers are very small, about 0.1 in. (ca. 3 mm) or less in length. The species is dioecious.

DISTRIBUTION: *Beaucarnea guatemalensis* naturally is distributed in forests of Guatemala and parts of Honduras. It is relatively rare in horticulture, and little is reported on its distribution or cultural requirements.

PROPAGATION: Propagation is by seed.

CULTURAL REQUIREMENTS: With its tropical origins, *Beaucarnea guatemalensis* should be planted in areas that receive little or no freezing weather. One report mentions that it is tender in central Florida, indicating that a temperature near 25°F (−4°C) would cause damage to the plant. The species probably is limited to areas that receive only occasional and very light freezes. Planting in areas protected from strong wind or the intense sun of the low desert would be recommended. A well-drained but enriched soil is probably best. As a tree of the forests, it should have good tolerance of shady conditions.

SIMILAR OR RELATED SPECIES: *Beaucarnea guatemalensis* is similar to *B. recurvata* and a lesser-known species, *B. pliabilis* (Baker) Rose (synonym *Dasylirion pliabile* Baker), but has wider leaves. Its conical woody base is smaller and of a different shape than the large globose base of *B. recurvata*.

USES: *Beaucarnea guatemalensis* has a softer, more tropical look than most other beaucarneas and is similar in appearance to many tropical dracaenas. It makes a fine specimen plant in partially shaded areas. Its wide and recurving leaves allow it to be grouped with other tropical plants with large or distinct foliage.

Beaucarnea recurvata Lemaire   PLATE 54; FIGURE 2-5

SYNONYMS: *Nolina recurvata* (Lemaire) Hemsley, *Dasylirion recurvatum* (Lemaire) J. F. Macbride, *Dasylirion inerme* S. Watson, *Beaucarnea inermis* (S. Watson) Rose

COMMON NAMES: Ponytail palm, Monja, Palma culona

SIZE: *Beaucarnea recurvata* is a treelike species from 13 to 49 ft. (4–15 m) tall with up to 10 or more vertical or nearly vertical branches arising from a woody globose base. When the plant is mature, the base can be up to 6.5–9.75 ft. (2–2.9 m) wide. It is covered with dark gray to brown-gray bark that displays a quadrangular pattern at least on parts of the base. The stems, which can have one or several branches towards the top, are free generally of leaves or leaf bases except at the ends where they terminate in oblong leaf rosettes.

LEAVES: The leaves are 3.25–5 ft. (1–1.5 m) long and 0.5–1 in. (1.3–2.5 cm) wide. They are recurved, so that the plant looks like a fountain of leaves. The lower parts of the leaves curve and twist as they hang from the rosette center down over the tops of the branches. Older leaves often become reflexed in the middle. The relative amount of leaf curvature and reflexed charactcristics seems to vary significantly within the species, with some individuals being highly recurved or reflexed and others nearly straight with only a slight curvature. The leaves are a dull green color. In some plants the new growth has an attractive maroon coloring that ages to dull green. The margin is finely toothed, almost smooth.

BLOOM: The ovoid inflorescence is 2.25–3.25 ft. (0.7–1 m) long, highly branched, and has a straw yellow to reddish stalk 7.75–11.75 in. (20–29.5 cm) long. The flowers are tiny, 0.06–0.1 in. (1.5–3 mm) or less in length. The species is dioecious.

DISTRIBUTION: *Beaucarnea recurvata* naturally is distributed in the tropical, deciduous forests of the Mexican states of San Luis Potosí, Veracruz, and Tamaulipas. It is the most commonly cultivated *Beaucarnea* species worldwide and is mass produced for sale at garden centers and mail-order businesses. This species is seen planted outdoors wherever frosts are rare and not heavy. It is common in the United States in southern California, and to a lesser extent in extreme southern Texas, the low desert of Arizona, and in central and southern Florida. It also is commonly seen around the Mediterranean basin and Australia.

PROPAGATION: Propagation is by seed.

CULTURAL REQUIREMENTS: *Beaucarnea recurvata* is spectacular as a focal plant for courtyards and as part of a desert or arid garden mixed with cactus and succulents. Its large globose base and vertical stems topped with fountains of long linear leaves give it a most distinct appearance. It does best in well-drained soil or soil that is allowed to dry out between waterings. Plants, particularly young ones, do better with some protection from the most severe desert sun; however, as the plant matures it comes to tolerate very harsh conditions. In coastal or Mediterranean climates full sun is best for the plant. Although the species comes from a tropical climate, it can tolerate light freezing weather. Mature plants have survived freezes down to around 20°F (−7°C). When plants are young they should be protected anytime temperatures fall to near 25°F (−4°C).

SIMILAR OR RELATED SPECIES: *Beaucarnea recurvata* is most similar to *B. guatemalensis* and the lesser-known *B. pliabilis*. The leaves of all three species are somewhat different, although there is some overlap and some confusion concerning the leaf sizes. The leaves of *B. recurvata* reportedly are 0.5–1 in. (1.3–2.5 cm) wide and narrower than those of *B. guatemalensis*, which are greater than 1 in. (2.5 cm) wide. The leaves of *B. pliabilis* are narrow and short, only about 0.5 in. (1.3 cm) wide and less than 3.25 ft. (1 m) long, while those of *B. recurvata* are wider and longer. Other reports have recognized more overlap in the leaf sizes of these species. Another difference can help distinguish them. The leaves of *B. recurvata* are recurved and reflexed, while those of *B. pliabilis* are reportedly recurved but in a more open and rigid form. The base of the trunk of *B. recurvata* differs significantly from those of *B. guatemalensis* and *B. pliabilis*. The trunk of *Beaucarnea recurvata* is globose and large, 6.5–9.75 ft. (2–2.9 m) in diameter, whereas in the other two species the trunk is more conical and less than 5 ft. (1.5 m) in diameter.

USES: With its large globose base and many vertical branches terminating in large rosettes of hanging narrow leaves, *Beaucarnea recurvata* is a dramatic specimen plant wherever it can be grown. It has a variety of good horticultural uses. It can be the focal point of a large courtyard, works well around pools, and fits in well with mass plantings of cacti and other large succulents. It also is an exceptional subject for very large pots.

Beaucarnea stricta Lemaire   PLATE 55

SYNONYMS: *Beaucarnea glauca* Roezl, *Beaucarnea recurvata* var. *stricta* Baker, *Dasylirion strictum* (Lemaire) J. F. Macbride, *Dasylirion laxiflorum* Baker in part

COMMON NAME: Estrellas

SIZE: *Beaucarnea stricta* is a large species with a thick trunk rising from a woody globose to conical base. The base is 2.5–6.5 ft. (0.8–2 m) wide and covered with thick gray to reddish brown bark that develops into an elongate pattern of polygonal plates. The plant is 13–26 ft. (4–8 m) tall and topped with spherical rosettes of leaves. Generally a few thick branches appear toward the top of the trunk on older plants. Younger plants often have a large single trunk with a terminal rosette of leaves.

LEAVES: The leaves have a distinctive blue-green color or are a very pale green and are 0.4–0.5 in. (9–13 mm) wide and 18–29 in. (46–75 cm) long. They are ridged slightly on the underside, and the margin is rough with tiny teeth. The young leaves are stiff, straight, and not recurved as in many other beaucarneas. With age they relax somewhat but they still form a rosette of rather straight leaves.

BLOOM: The branched green to bright yellow inflorescence is 3–4.25 ft. (0.9–1.3 m) long and has a stalk 8–15.75 in. (20–40 cm) tall. The tiny flowers are 0.06–0.14 in. (1.5–3.5 mm) long. The species is dioecious.

DISTRIBUTION: *Beaucarnea stricta* naturally occurs in the tropical deciduous forests of the Mexican state of Oaxaca. Not nearly as common in horticulture as *B. recurvata*, it occasionally is seen growing in Mediterranean climates or desert climates where frosts are uncommon and light. This species is seen sparingly in cultivation in southern California and the warm deserts of Arizona.

PROPAGATION: Propagation is by seed.

CULTURAL REQUIREMENTS: *Beaucarnea stricta* should be planted in full sun in Mediterranean climates near the coast. In hot low or inland deserts it performs best with partial shade. In both areas it requires a well-drained soil that is allowed to dry out between waterings. The cold tolerance of the species is not well known, but plants should probably not be grown where winter temperature drop below 25°F (–4 °C).

SIMILAR OR RELATED SPECIES: *Beaucarnea stricta* is most similar to *B. gracilis*, but relatively easy to differentiate because its leaves are longer and wider. The conical to globose base of *B.*

stricta and its heavy trunk also are different from the more globose trunk of *B. gracilis* from which arise more numerous and
more slender stems. Hybrids between the species appear in nature and, no doubt, in cultivation, which are intermediate in
form. *Beaucarnea stricta* might also be confused with large
blue-green-leaved yuccas or nolinas from a distance. On close
inspection, however, the large swollen base of *B. stricta* should
be evident and sufficient to separate it from those plants.

USES: *Beaucarnea stricta* makes an excellent specimen
plant in situations where a strong structural look can be effective. Its large size and rigid heads of leaves give it a very strong
presence. It also is effective planted with succulents and other
strongly formed plants from arid or semi-arid environments.

Beschorneria yuccoides Koch PLATE 56

COMMON NAMES: Mexican lily, Amole, Sisi

SIZE: *Beschorneria yuccoides* is a medium-sized species
consisting of clumps of soft rosettes to about 6 ft. (1.8 m) tall.
The clump grows new rosettes from the fleshy rhizomatous
roots.

LEAVES: The lanceolate leaves are 15.7–28 in. (40–70 cm)
long and 1.2–3.9 in. (3–10 cm) wide. They are blue-green in
color with very fine, but not sharp teeth along the margin. The
tip of the leaf is soft without a spine. The upper side of the
leaves is smooth and the underside is roughened.

BLOOM: The inflorescence is a reddish panicle that can
reach 4 ft. (1.2 m) tall and has 8–20 branches. The panicle bears
numerous reddish bracts that subtend groups of flowers and are
approximately the same length or longer than the pedicels of
the flowers. The pendulous individual flowers are bright green,
shaped like a narrow funnel, and 1.6–3.3 in. (4–8.5 cm) long.
The species is polycarpic in that the rosettes do not die after
blooming as they do in *Agave* and *Furcraea*.

DISTRIBUTION: *Beschorneria yuccoides* occurs in mountainous areas of central and eastern Mexico at high elevations
from 6000 to 11,500 ft. (1000–3500 m). It occurs in rocky but
rich soils in the pine-oak and other moderately moist to dry

forests or in exposed areas high in the mountains with *Agave* and *Dasylirion* species. It is distributed widely around the world in tropical and Mediterranean gardens and is grown commonly along the Mediterranean basin and Australia. It has even been grown in the mildest climates on the south coast of England and presumably other mild areas in Western Europe. The species also has been grown in California, but is not as common in the United States as in other parts of the world.

PROPAGATION: Propagation is by seed or by removal of the offsets.

CULTURAL REQUIREMENTS: *Beschorneria yuccoides* does best in a rich but well-drained soil that does not experience long periods of drought, although some drying can be tolerated. The species grows best in full sun in coastal Mediterranean climates and moist highland, subtropical or tropical climates. In the low desert or where the sun is intense, it should be given some shade. The species has been know to survive temperatures down to 10°F (−12°C) for short periods. Temperatures much below 5°F (−15°C), however, have been known to kill the plants. A related species, *B. septentrionalis* Garcia-Mendoza, has survived 14°F (−10°C) in North Carolina and can probably tolerate even lower temperatures. Most likely *Beschorneria* species can easily be grown in climates where temperatures do not commonly go below 15–20°F (−9 to −7°C).

SIMILAR OR RELATED SPECIES: Although *Beschorneria yuccoides* is the only species in its genus that is widespread in horticulture, several others have occasionally been grown. *Beschorneria tubiflora* Kunth is similar to *B. yuccoides*, but has narrower, green leaves less than 1.25 in. (3.2 cm) wide and green flowers tinged with brown-purple and subtended by purple bracts. *Beschorneria septentrionalis* has green leaves and red flowers with a green tip borne on a panicle with only four to six branches, as opposed to the more branched panicles of *B. yuccoides*. The pedicels of *B. yuccoides* are equal to or shorter than the flower bracts, while the pedicels of *B. septentrionalis* are longer than the bracts. *Beschorneria albiflora* Matuda is the only species in the genus to develop a recognizable short trunk and to lack small teeth along the leaf margin.

191

Uses: *Beschorneria yuccoides* has been used in Mexico for various economic purposes. The leaves and rhizomes have been used to make a soapy foam for cleaning clothes and household utensils. The flowers have been cooked and eaten with eggs and beans, and the flowering stalks occasionally cooked and eaten like sugar cane or fed to cattle during dry periods. At one time the leaves were used extensively in certain parts of Mexico as a source of fiber, but that use has diminished recently. The species also is used as an ornamental and planted along fields to delimit their extent. Outside of Mexico *B. yuccoides* and several other species are used as ornamentals. They make spectacular medium-sized plants with attractive blue-green sword-shaped leaves and magnificent flowers, particularly when they are used for focal points in gardens and courtyards.

Calibanus hookeri (Lemaire) Trelease   PLATE 57

Synonyms: *Dasylirion hartwegianum* J. Hooker, *Dasylirion hookeri* Lemaire, *Dasylirion caespitosum* Scheidweiler, *Calibanus caespitosus* Rose

Common name: Calibanus

Size: *Calibanus hookeri* is an unusual, low-growing species whose generic name is derived from the monster Caliban in Shakespeare's play, *The Tempest.* The plant is composed of a low hemispherical woody base from which arise tufts of long wiry leaves. The base is 1–3 ft. (0.3–1 m) wide and is covered with a fissured or platelike gray corky bark.

Leaves: The linear, narrow leaves vary in length from 11.75 to 35.5 in. (29.5–90 cm) long and are only 0.08–0.1 in. (2–3 mm) wide. They are blue-green in color and have a roughened margin. They appear on the plant as bundles arising from the upper surface of the woody hemispherical base. As the plant grows and the woody base increases in size, the number of leaf bundles increases. Large, old plants have many leaf bundles, giving the plant the appearance of a head of long, floppy, wiry hair.

Bloom: The inflorescence is a broad, rigid panicle 4–8 in. (10–20 cm) long. It arises from individual tufts of leaves. The tufts die after blooming is completed, but new tufts continue to arise from the top of the plant. The flowers are tiny and purplish. The species is dioecious.

DISTRIBUTION: *Calibanus hookeri* occurs in the dry, mountainous lands of central and northeastern Mexico and has been reported from the states of Hidalgo, San Luis Potosí, and Tamaulipas.

PROPAGATION: Propagation is by seed.

CULTURAL REQUIREMENTS: *Calibanus hookeri* requires a well-drained soil and a sunny position. It does well in full sun in coastal areas, but should be provided some light shade in the hottest desert climates. Little is reported on its cold tolerance, although it easily tolerates temperatures down to at least 25°F (–4°C) and observations in Texas have shown it to be much more tolerant, surviving cold down to 17°F (–8°C).

SIMILAR OR RELATED SPECIES: Few plants look anything like *Calibanus hookeri*, although several nolinas with grasslike leaves could be mistaken for it from a distance. These plants, however, lack the woody base of *Calibanus*.

USES: The leaves of *Calibanus hookeri* have been used for thatching and scouring in the areas of Mexico in which the species is native. The species often is seen today in collections of succulents and unusual xerophytic plants. It is an excellent plant for containers where its interesting woody base can be readily seen. It also is a good plant for dry rock gardens and as a companion for cacti and succulents.

Dasylirion acrotriche (Schiede ex Schultes) Otto

PLATE 58

SYNONYMS: *Dasylirion acrotrichum* Baker, *Dasylirium acrotrichum* J. Hooker, *Dasylirion acrotrichum* Zuccarini, *Yucca acrotricha* Schiede ex Schultes

SIZE: *Dasylirion acrotriche* has a short thick trunk to 5 ft. (1.5 m) tall. It often is covered with dead leaves, which sometimes are removed in ornamental settings. The trunk is solitary, occasionally branched, and is topped with a head of many thin, rigid leaves.

LEAVES: The numerous narrow green leaves have a slight

193

yellow cast and are 0.25–0.5 in. (0.6–1.3 cm) wide at the base. They are 11.75–27.5 in. (29.5–70 cm) long and lined with curved yellow teeth that have a brown tip. The teeth point forward toward the tip of the leaves. The leaves terminate in narrow, 0.75–1.25 in. (2–3.2 cm) long, brushy tips that are white or gray with age. Several varieties exist with different leaf characteristics. *Dasylirion acrotriche* var. *acrotriche* Schiede ex Schultes has leaves 11.75–19.75 in. (29.5–50 cm) long and with a dull surface and coarse brushy leaf tips. *Dasylirion acrotriche* var. *occidentalis* Bogler has smooth-surfaced, longer leaves, 23.75–27.75 in. (60–70 cm) long, that terminate in a fine brushy or almost entire tip. *Dasylirion acrotriche* var. *parryanum* (Trelease) Bogler (synonym *Dasylirion parryanum* Trelease) has a rough whitish green leaf surface with a waxy coating.

BLOOM: The large inflorescence ranges from 6.5 to 13 ft. (2–4 m) tall. The flowers are numerous and tiny, 0.06–0.12 in. (1.5–3 mm) long.

DISTRIBUTION: *Dasylirion acrotriche* is widespread in central Mexico, occurring in the states of Hidalgo, Mexico, Puebla, Querétaro, Aguascalientes, Jalisco, Guanajuato, and Zacatecas. An old species in horticulture, it is grown in several areas throughout the world. It was common in gardens of the Riviera as early as the 1890s. Although not as common as *D. wheeleri*, it can be commonly seen in dry gardens in the warmer parts of California and Arizona.

PROPAGATION: Propagation is by seed.

CULTURAL REQUIREMENTS: *Dasylirion acrotriche* should be grown in full sun and in a well-drained soil. It tolerates high heat and, although its actual cold tolerance is not well known, some reports mention its ability to tolerate temperatures to near 15°F (–9°C).

SIMILAR OR RELATED SPECIES: Somewhat similar to *Dasylirion leiophyllum* and *D. texanum*, two other green-leaved species, *D. acrotriche* differs from both of them in several ways. The teeth of *D. leiophyllum* point toward the leaf bases, whereas those of *D. acrotriche* point toward the leaf tips. The leaves of *D. acrotriche* are narrow, less than 0.5 in. (1.3 cm) wide, and end in a distinctive brushy tip, while the leaves of *D.*

leiophyllum are wider, more than 0.75 in. (2 cm) wide, and do not end in a brushy tip. The brushy leaf tips of *D. acrotriche* help distinguish it from *D. texanum*, as do its thicker trunk and larger number of leaves. Furthermore, its leaves tend to be fairly straight or have only a slight arch, while the older leaves of *D. texanum* tend to be distinctly arched.

USES: *Dasylirion acrotriche* is a good plant for mixed plantings of cacti, yuccas, agaves, and other plants with strong forms. The attractive head of many narrow green leaves and short thick trunks make this a good medium-sized specimen plant. The very brushy leaf tips of *D. acrotriche* var. *acrotriche* are quite different from those of most other rosette-shaped plants and give the plant a very distinctive look in the garden.

Dasylirion leiophyllum Engelmann ex Trelease

SYNONYMS: *Dasylirion stewartii* I. M. Johnston, *Dasylirion heteracanthium* I. M. Johnston

COMMON NAME: Sotol

SIZE: *Dasylirion leiophyllum* is a large and robust species with an erect or reclining trunk up to 5 ft. (1.5 m) tall. The broad trunk, up to 19.75 in. (50 cm) wide at the crown, often is covered with a skirt of dead leaves and is topped by a rosette of long, rigid leaves.

LEAVES: The leaves generally are bright green and have a smooth, shiny surface. They are 0.75–1.5 in. (2–3.8 cm) wide and 35.5–43.25 in. (90–110 cm) long and are lined with stout marginal teeth that are curved downward towards the base. The teeth are 0.12–0.16 in. (3–4 mm) long and turn orange to reddish brown with age. The leaf tips taper to a point and often are bluntly weathered and dry. *Dasylirion leiophyllum* var. *glaucum* (I. M. Johnston) Bogler (synonym *D. stewartii* var. *glaucum* I. M. Johnston) has blue-green leaves with a waxy coating.

BLOOM: The inflorescence is a large tight panicle that varies from 8.25 to 16.5 ft. (2.5–5 m) tall. It is greenish tan in color with occasional red highlights. The individual flowers are tiny, 0.07–0.1 in. (1.8–3 mm) long.

DISTRIBUTION: *Dasylirion leiophyllum* occurs in the grass-

195

lands and desert scrublands of western Texas, southeastern New Mexico, and into the Mexican states of Chihuahua and Coahuila. It is used in horticulture and can be seen as an ornamental primarily in Texas and New Mexico.

PROPAGATION: Propagation is by seed.

CULTURAL REQUIREMENTS: *Dasylirion leiophyllum* is a tough and hardy plant. It requires full sun and well-drained soils, and can tolerate extremes of heat and drought. When first transplanted it should be watered for establishment and then can be given only occasional supplementary water during the driest periods in the summer. The species also is extremely cold hardy, easily tolerating temperatures to 0°F (−18°C). One report indicates that dry and dormant plants can tolerate temperatures down to −20°F (−29°C) for short periods of time.

SIMILAR OR RELATED SPECIES: *Dasylirion leiophyllum* can be distinguished easily from other dasylirions by its leaf margin, which is lined with teeth that predominantly point downward towards the base. This characteristic is most common for teeth on the lower portion of the leaf. No other species has downward-pointing teeth. *Dasylirion leiophyllum* lacks the highly frayed leaf tip of *D. acrotriche*, and its wider leaves help distinguish it from *D. texanum*. In west Texas where the natural ranges of *D. leiophyllum* and *D. texanum* overlap, the two species hybridize, producing plants with intermediate characteristics. In these plants the marginal teeth can point downward, upward, and straight out on the same plants. Many references refer to these hybrids as *D. heteracanthium* I. M. Johnston.

USES: *Dasylirion leiophyllum* is an excellent plant to add a distinctive look to gardens of native and xerophytic plants. The strong shape of the stout trunk and rigid leaves combines well with cacti, yuccas, and other strongly shaped plants. The plant's tolerance of the heat of full sun and of cold allow it to be sited in areas where care cannot be provided constantly.

Dasylirion quadrangulatum S. Watson   PLATE 59

SYNONYM: *Dasylirion longissimum* Lemaire
COMMON NAME: Mexican grass tree

SIZE: *Dasylirion quadrangulatum* is a large species that eventually can have a trunk up to 16.5 ft. (5 m) tall or more and is topped with heads of narrow grasslike leaves. It usually is seen with a much smaller trunk, or as a younger plant with a large sphere of leaves near the ground.

LEAVES: The leaves are unique in the genus for having a margin totally lacking distinct teeth. The margin is either completely smooth or slightly rough. The leaves are 31.5–35.5 in. (80–90 cm) long and very narrow, only about 0.3 in. (8 mm) wide at the base and narrowing to 0.16 in. (4 mm) farther out on the leaf. At first glance the leaves appear to be rounded, but in cross section they actually are angled, consisting of four distinct sides and sometimes a very tiny fifth side. The leaves are held in a rigid but slightly arching manner that is more distinct in some plants than in others.

BLOOM: The narrow, straight inflorescence is 9.75–23 ft. (2.9–7 m) long. The flowers, which are arranged densely on the stalk, are tiny, 0.1 in. (3 mm) long.

DISTRIBUTION: *Dasylirion quadrangulatum* occurs in the dry brushy hillsides and arroyos (small streams that have water intermittently) of northeastern Mexico, specifically in the states of Nuevo León and Tamaulipas.

PROPAGATION: Propagation is by seed.

CULTURAL REQUIREMENTS: *Dasylirion quadrangulatum* can be planted in full sun or partial shade. Some shade in the hottest deserts is advisable. The species reportedly tolerates temperatures down to at least 15°F (–9°C). Supplemental irrigation in the summer during the driest spells particularly in the warmest deserts is recommended. The species could be grown in more humid climates if very good drainage was supplied.

SIMILAR OR RELATED SPECIES: *Dasylirion quadrangulatum* is unlike any other dasylirion in cultivation and could not be confused with any of them. It could possibly be confused with some species of *Nolina*, such as *N. erumpens* or *N. matapensis*, but these plants have flattened leaves, as opposed to the angled leaves of *D. quadrangulatum*. The leaves and overall appearance of *D. quadrangulatum*, however, closely resemble the Australian tree grasses in the genus *Xanthorrhoea*. The flower structure of the Australian plants is very different from that of *Dasylirion.*

Uses: The narrow, delicate, unarmed leaves with their regular arrangement make *Dasylirion quadrangulatum* an exceptional specimen plant for areas near pools or paths where there is considerable human traffic. The plant can be broad, up to 9 ft. (2.7 m) wide, so sufficient space should be allocated to allow its leaves to spread. If given space, it combines well with many other types of plants and its very strong form dominates nearly any location in which it is planted.

Dasylirion texanum Scheele

Common name: Sotol

Size: *Dasylirion texanum* has a short trunk, up to 1.5 ft. (0.5 m) tall, topped by a rosette of rigid to reflexed, arching leaves. The crown of the trunk is medium-sized, 4–7.75 in. (10–20 cm) wide.

Leaves: The smooth, shiny, dark green leaves are 0.25–0.5 in. (0.6–1.3 cm) wide and 27.75–51.25 in. (70–130 cm) long. The margin is lined with small curved teeth that are 0.08 in. (2 mm) long, spaced 0.25–0.50 in. (0.6–1.3 cm) apart, and pointed towards the leaf tips. The teeth are yellow but brown at the tip, which is pointed or bluntly weathered and dry. The leaves emerge from the crown in a rigid fashion, but as they age they often begin to arch downwards toward the ground and they often have a twist towards the tips.

Bloom: The inflorescence is a panicle approximately 8 ft. (2.4 m) tall. It emerges as a greenish color that then fades to tan. It is narrow and slightly club-shaped with a blunt end. The tiny individual flowers are 0.04–0.09 in. (1–2.4 mm) long and arranged densely on the stalk.

Distribution: *Dasylirion texanum* occurs from the Edwards Plateau in central Texas southward into the Mexican state of Coahuila and westward well into western Texas. It often is planted in natural and dry gardens in central and northern Texas.

Propagation: Propagation is by seed or by removal of the offsets in the cool fall or spring months.

CULTURAL REQUIREMENTS: *Dasylirion texanum* should be planted in a well-drained location in either full sun or partial shade. It is heat-tolerant and is cold-tolerant to at least 5°F (−15°C).

SIMILAR OR RELATED SPECIES: *Dasylirion texanum* differs from *D. leiophyllum* in several ways. It is a smaller plant with shorter and narrower trunks. Its leaves are narrower and, unlike *D. acrotriche,* lack frayed tips. Furthermore, its teeth are forward-pointing on the leaf margin, while those of *D. leiophyllum* point backward toward the leaf base.

USES: *Dasylirion texanum* is an excellent plant for dry or native gardens in the southwestern United States. Its size allows it to be planted in areas smaller than those of the larger dasylirions. Although the species tolerates full sun, it also does well in light or dappled shade. Its arching leaves give it a graceful look and allow it to blend effectively with round-leaved shrubs and large native perennials. Because it can tolerate some cold as well as occasionally wet soils, it could probably be used as an ornamental well beyond its natural range.

Dasylirion wheeleri S. Watson ex Rothrock

PLATE 60; FIGURES 2-4, 3-2, 4-2

COMMON NAMES: Desert spoon, Sotol

SIZE: *Dasylirion wheeleri* is a large species with a thick trunk that can reach 5 ft. (1.5 m) tall and is topped by a crown of erect leaves. The trunk can be either erect or reclining and is often covered with a skirt of dead leaves.

LEAVES: The light blue-green to light gray leaves are covered with a waxy coating and are 0.4–1.2 in. (0.9–3 cm) wide and 13.75–43.25 in. (35–110 cm) long. Stout yellow teeth with brown tips line the leaf margin and point forward towards the leaf tips. The upper half of the leaf often is twisted and ends in a fine tip that can often become blunt with age and weathering.

BLOOM: The large, thick inflorescence is 9.8–19.7 ft. (2.9–6 m) tall and 1.25–2 in. (3.2–5 cm) wide at its base. The small flowers are 0.08–0.09 in. (2–2.4 mm) long.

DISTRIBUTION: *Dasylirion wheeleri* occurs in high grass-

Figure 4-2. Flowers, *Dasylirion wheeleri*

lands, shrublands, and open woodlands from 3000 to 6000 ft. (900–1800). It is found in southeastern Arizona and southern New Mexico, ranging southward into the Mexican states of Sonora and Chihuahua. As an ornamental plant, it is common throughout Arizona and southern New Mexico as far north as Albuquerque and is found to a lesser extent in southern California and in Texas.

PROPAGATION: Propagation is by seed.

CULTURAL REQUIREMENTS: *Dasylirion wheeleri* performs well in full sun, but it also grows well in partial shade. It tolerates the high heat of the low desert if given some supplemental summer water to insure good performance. The species is cold hardy to around 0°F (−18°C). Reports of its good performance in North Carolina indicate that it can be adapted to more humid climates if given sun and a well-drained location.

SIMILAR OR RELATED SPECIES: *Dasylirion wheeleri* probably is the most common dasylirion with blue-green leaves in cultivation, although two similar species, *D. glaucophyllum* J. Hooker and *D. cedrosanum* Trelease, are seen occasionally. The leaves of *D. glaucophyllum* are narrower than those of D. *wheeleri*. The leaves of *D. cedrosanum* often, but not always, are slightly wider than those of *D. wheeleri*, but are flat and an ashy white-gray color. *Dasylirion wheeleri* comes into contact in nature with *D. leiophyllum* and *D. cedrosanum*, as well as several other lesser-known species in northern Mexico. Hybrids with intermediate characteristics are known to occur.

USES: *Dasylirion wheeleri* has been used extensively by people who inhabit its natural range. Native people used fibers in the leaves for thatching and to make mats and cordage. They also utilized the plant as food by roasting and eating the young, emerging flower stalks. After European settlers brought cattle to the southwestern United States and Mexico, ranchers split the trunks of plants for cattle feed, particularly in times of drought. In northern Mexico the species was and still is used to some extent today as a raw material in the distilling of a rough liquor known as "sotol." *Dasylirion wheeleri* is used extensively as an ornamental in desert and other dry gardens. Its strong blue-green or gray color provides interest in addition to the strong rosette form and fairly large size. This species is extremely hardy to heat, cold, and very poor soils. It makes an excellent addition to gardens dominated by native plants or gardens that get little care or irrigation. As with the other dasylirions, it is an excellent specimen plant where a strong form is desired.

Furcraea foetida (Linnaeus) Haworth   PLATES 61, 62

SYNONYMS: *Furcraea gigantea* Ventenat, *Furcraea madagascariensis* Haworth, *Agave foetida* Linnaeus

COMMON NAMES: Mauritius hemp, Mediterranean hemp, Green aloe, Malagache aloe

SIZE: *Furcraea foetida* is primarily a trunkless species, although some individuals can have a very small trunk. It produces several offsets from rhizomes and eventually forms clumps of rosettes.

LEAVES: The solid green leaves have a slight dull glossy sheen to their upper side, which is smooth to the touch. The underside is slightly rough and lacks the slightly glossy sheen. The leaf is slightly guttered and the margin is slightly wavy. The margin is smooth or with a few very small teeth scattered along the lower third of the leaf. The leaves vary considerably in length depending on growing conditions, but can reach up to 8 ft. (2.4 m) long. They are 5–8 in. (13–20 cm) wide at their widest points and have a distinct narrowing in their lower third. The leaves terminate in a spineless acute tip. A variegated form, *Furcraea foetida* var. *medio-picta* Trelease, has been grown as an ornamental for many years. Its leaves lack teeth and have heavy cream-colored linear markings throughout. In many clones the cream-colored variegation covers a much larger portion of the leaves than does the green part.

BLOOM: The inflorescence is large and loosely branched, reaching to 25 ft. (7.6 m) tall or higher. The flowers are 1.5 in. (3.8 cm) long, greenish white, and strongly scented. Bulbils are produced on the inflorescence.

DISTRIBUTION: *Furcraea foetida* is native to northern South America and is cultivated widely in frost-free or nearly frost-free climates. It has been commonly planted in southern Florida, southern California, and along the Mediterranean coast. It is naturalized on Mauritius Island and in parts of Madagascar and India.

PROPAGATION: Propagation is by removal of the bulbils or offsets.

CULTURAL REQUIREMENTS: *Furcraea foetida* requires a nearly frost-free climate, with a rich but well-drained soil. Although it tolerates some drought, sufficient water should be applied to the plant during long dry periods. With adequate water the plant can grow rapidly during the warm weather. In coastal climates it performs well in full sun or partial shade. Partial shade is required in hot desert climates to prevent sun burning of the leaves.

SIMILAR OR RELATED SPECIES: *Furcraea foetida* is similar to *F. selloa,* which has brownish teeth lining its leaves. The distinct combination of solid green, slightly glossy leaves, a smooth and often wavy margin, and a soft tip makes *F. foetida* easy to recognize.

USES: An attractive ornamental, *Furcraea foetida* is an excellent specimen plant for a courtyard or a very large pot. Its clumping habit allows it to be used against long walls or on slopes where little care can be given but an attractive and distinctive look might be desired. Because of its deep green color and slightly glossy leaves, it combines well with tropical foliage plants. The variegated variety brightens up shady corners. It also makes a dramatic statement as a specimen plant in a container or in a prominent location in the landscape. One of the plant's common names, Mauritius hemp, is derived from the plant's use as a commercial fiber crop on Mauritius Island in the Indian Ocean.

Furcraea macdougalii Matuda   PLATE 63

SIZE: *Furcraea macdougalii* is a spectacular, large arborescent species with a thick, straight trunk topped with a dramatic head of upward-pointing leaves. The plant can reach 20–23 ft. (6–7 m) tall. The large rosette of leaves often has a light skirt of dead leaves. The trunk is lined with old leaf bases, making it rough in appearance. New rosettes have been known to sprout from along fallen trunks and old trunk bases.

LEAVES: The leaves can be up to 7 ft. (2.1 m) long and 2.75 in. (7 cm) wide with a margin that is folded and lined with curved brownish teeth. The lower part of the leaves is thick and succulent inward, narrowing considerably about half way down the length of the leaf. The leaves are a dull olive green color, somewhat smooth on the upper side, and rough to the touch on the underside. They are held in an upward-pointing rosette and have a slight curve, giving the plant a rigid but graceful appearance.

BLOOM: The massive, loosely branched inflorescence can be 25 ft. (7.6 m) tall. The pendulous flowers are approximately 1 in. (2.5 cm) long and whitish on the outside and a dull green on the inside.

DISTRIBUTION: *Furcraea macdougalii* occurs naturally in a rather limited area in the Mexican state of Oaxaca. It is not common in cultivation but has been planted to a limited extent in southern California, and perhaps elsewhere in nearly frost-free climates.

PROPAGATION: Presumably propagation is by removal of the bulbils. The plant produces suckers from fallen trunks and these also could be used for vegetative propagation.

CULTURAL REQUIREMENTS: *Furcraea macdougalii* should be planted in frost-free or nearly frost-free climates. It appears to have some drought tolerance and would be suitable to rocky or well-drained and dry soils. In the hottest deserts supplemental water should be supplied in the summer, but in coastal or Mediterranean climates it appears to survive well on natural rainfall with only occasional watering during unusually dry periods.

SIMILAR OR RELATED SPECIES: *Furcraea macdougalii* is a very distinct species. Its upward-held but arching, toothed leaves and its arborescent habit tend to separate it from most other furcraeas. It has strongly toothed, green leaves, while the arborescent *F. roezlii* has blue-green leaves with only minute teeth. From a distance *F. macdougalii* may appear as a large yucca, but the hooked teeth along the leaf margin separate it from all yuccas.

USES: A large and imposing plant, *Furcraea macdougalii* makes a dramatic impression in any landscape in which it is used. Its gracefully held leaves attract attention and contribute to its distinctive qualities as a large specimen plant.

Furcraea roezlii André   PLATE 64

SYNONYMS: *Roezlia regia, Roezlia regina, Agave argyrophylla* Hort., *Yucca argyrophylla* Hort., *Yucca parmentieri* Hort., *Yucca tonelliana* Hort., *Beschorneria floribunda* Hort.

SIZE: *Furcraea roezlii* is an impressive, trunked species topped with a single head of strap-shaped leaves. The straight, unbranched trunk can reach 9.75–13 ft. (2.9–4 m) tall and is covered with dead, hanging leaves.

LEAVES: The blue-green leaves are leathery and slightly succulent. Although the leaf generally is flat, the leaf margin curls inward slightly and is lined with very minute teeth. The leaves terminate in a blunt spineless tip and are 3.25–4 ft. (1–1.2 m) long and approximately 3 in. (8 cm) wide. The leaves often have slight curves and twists, giving the rosette a somewhat unkempt look.

BLOOM: The large, branched inflorescences freely produce bulbils. The flowers are 2–2.5 in. (5–6 cm) long and are born on short pedicels mostly in groups of three. They have a whitish color on the inside.

DISTRIBUTION: A native of southern Mexico, *Furcraea roezlii* has been planted as an ornamental along the Mediterranean coast and to a limited extent in southern California.

PROPAGATION: Presumably propagation is by removal of the bulbils.

CULTURAL REQUIREMENTS: Although little is known about the precise requirements of *Furcraea roezlii*, it does well in full sun or partial shade with a well-drained soil in the Mediterranean climate in which it is grown ornamentally. Presumably it is cold sensitive like other furcraeas and requires a nearly frost-free climate.

SIMILAR OR RELATED SPECIES: *Furcraea roezlii* is easy to distinguish from *F. macdougalii*, another large-trunked species, by its blue-green leaves that have only minute teeth; *F. mac-dougalii* has green leaves with brown hooked teeth. From a distance one might confuse *F. roezlii* with a blue-green-leaved yucca such as *Yucca rigida,* but yucca leaves are stiff and terminate in a stiff spine while those of *F. roezlii* are curved slightly, blunt ended, and have no terminal spine. *Yucca rigida* usually has a few branches towards the top of the trunk, resulting in multiple rosettes, while *F. roezlii* is single-trunked and single-headed. *Furcraea roezlii* probably is most similar to *F. bedinghausii* K. Koch, which has smaller leaves, only 2 ft. (0.6 m) long and 2–2.75 in. (5–7 cm) wide, with a short trunk, only to 3 ft. (1 m) tall. Although these plants differ, they may at times be considered and reported as one species, sometimes subsumed under the name *F. bedinghausii.*

USES: *Furcraea roezlii* is an interesting large plant for a prominent location in the landscape. Its leathery, slightly lax leaves give the plant a softer appearance than similar plants such as *Yucca rigida* or *Y. rostrata,* which might also be used in similar situations.

Furcraea selloa K. Koch   PLATE 65

SIZE: *Furcraea selloa* is a medium-sized species with a trunk up to 3–5 ft. (1–1.5 m) tall at maturity and topped with a rosette of long, stiff leaves. Although plants primarily have single trunks, offsets often appear at the base of the main plant and can create a cluster of rosettes.

LEAVES: The dark green leaves are sword-shaped with a defined narrowing toward the base. They are up to 4 ft. (1.2 m) long and 3 in. (8 cm) wide at the widest part. The leaf is slightly guttered, and the margin is undulate. The leaves terminate in a sharp but weak tip. The teeth are brown, hooked, 0.2–0.25 in. (5–6 mm) long, and spaced 1.3–1.6 in. (3.3–4 cm) apart. The most widely planted form of the species is the variegated form, *Furcraea selloa* var. *marginata* Trelease (synonym *F. lindenii* André), the leaves of which have creamy yellow stripes along the margin and sometimes light creamy streaks on the interior.

BLOOM: The large, loosely branched inflorescence can reach

20 ft. (6 m) tall. The flowers are greenish-tinged and 1.5 in. (3.8 cm) long. The plant, like most furcraeas, bears many bulbils on the inflorescence.

DISTRIBUTION: *Furcraea selloa* is a native of Colombia and probably is the most widespread furcraea in cultivation. It is cultivated worldwide where nearly frost-free conditions exist.

PROPAGATION: Propagation is by removal of the bulbils or offsets.

CULTURAL REQUIREMENTS: *Furcraea selloa* performs best in full sun or partial shade. In coastal areas full sun is best, and in the low desert partial shade is preferred. Furcraeas prefer a rich but well-drained soil. They should not, however, be kept moist, but should be left to dry out between waterings.

SIMILAR OR RELATED SPECIES: The small hooked teeth on the leaf margin of *Furcraea selloa* easily separate it from the smooth-margined *F. foetida*. *Furcraea selloa* is similar to several species that have teeth along the leaf margin. Two of these, *F. cabuya* Trelease and *F. hexapetala* (Jacquin) Urban (synonym *Agave hexapetala* Jacquin), might occasionally be seen in cultivation, but lack the small trunk of *F. selloa*.

USES: *Furcraea selloa*, particularly var. *marginata*, is a moderately common ornamental in tropical and nearly frost-free areas. It is a useful ornamental as a dramatic strong-structured plant that can relieve the soft rounded leaves of many tropical plants. The sword-shaped variegated leaves work well combined with tropical plants of dramatic foliage and colors. This species also makes a fine specimen plant for a large container or courtyard corner. In areas where light frosts occur it should be planted in slightly protected areas next to buildings or beneath trees.

Hesperaloe campanulata Starr

COMMON NAME: Bell flower hesperaloe

SIZE: *Hesperaloe campanulata* is a stemless species usually about 3.25 ft. (1 m) tall and wide. It forms tight clumps of several rosettes.

LEAVES: The bright green leaves have a slight yellow tint

and are 23.5–39 in. (60–100 cm) long and 0.6 in. (1.5 cm) wide at their widest place, just above the base. They are rigid and narrow to a thin unarmed point. The leaf edges are turned slightly inward, giving them a somewhat concave shape in cross section. Strong, straight filaments separate from the edges of the leaves.

BLOOM: The tall flowering stalk can reach 9.75 ft. (2.9 m) tall and can have two to five branches. The flowers are bell-shaped, from which their common name is derived, and held upright on the stalk. The tepals are white on the inside and pink with a white margin on the outside.

DISTRIBUTION: *Hesperaloe campanulata* is found only in a limited range within the Mexican state of Nuevo León. It is new to horticulture and is just beginning to be planted in the southwestern United States, particularly in Arizona. Because of its cold tolerance, it could be planted in arid and semi-arid areas where winter temperatures are not too low.

PROPAGATION: Propagation is by seed or by removal of the offsets.

CULTURAL REQUIREMENTS: *Hesperaloe campanulata* performs best in full sun in well-drained even rocky soils. It is very drought tolerant and is moderately cold tolerant, being able to withstand temperatures down to at least 12–13°F (ca. (11°C). Like all hesperaloes, this one needs supplemental water in the driest times of the low desert summer. In cool coastal climates as much sun as possible should be provided.

SIMILAR OR RELATED SPECIES: Vegetatively, *Hesperaloe campanulata* is very similar to *H. funifera*. The leaves of both species are very similar in general appearance, but those of *H. campanulata* are shorter. *Hesperaloe campanulata* is somewhat similar to *H. parviflora* in length of the leaves and pink flower color; however, the leaves of *H. parviflora* are dark green with inrolled edges, making the leaves almost round in cross section. The flowers of *H. campanulata* are distinctly bell-shaped upon opening in the late afternoon and remain so during the night and into the next morning. In the heat of the day the flowers close down to a tubular shape and could be confused with those of *H. parviflora*.

Plate 53. *Beaucarnea guatemalensis*

Plate 54. *Beaucarnea recurvata*

Plate 55. *Beaucarnea stricta*

Plate 56. *Beschorneria yuccoides*

Plate 57. *Calibanus hookeri*

Plate 58. *Dasylirion acrotriche*

Plate 59. *Dasylirion quadrangulatum*

Plate 60. *Dasylirion wheeleri*

Plate 61. *Furcraea foetida* planted in pot

Plate 62. *Furcraea foetida* var. *medio-picta*

Plate 63. *Furcraea macdougalii*

Plate 64. *Furcraea roezlii*

Plate 65. *Furcraea selloa* var. *marginata*

Plate 66. *Hesperaloe funifera*

Plate 67. *Hesperaloe parviflora*

Plate 70. Flowers of *Manfreda guttata* showing highly exserted stamens and pistil

Plate 68. Fruit of *Hesperaloe parviflora*

Plate 69. *Manfreda maculosa*

Plate 71. *Nolina longifolia*

Plate 72. *Nolina matapensis*

Plate 73. *Nolina microcarpa*

Plate 74. *Nolina parryi*

Plate 75. *Nolina texana*

Plate 76. *Yucca aloifolia*

Plate 77. *Yucca baccata*

Plate 78. *Yucca baccata* var. *vespertina*

Plate 79. *Yucca brevifolia*

Plate 80. *Yucca elata*

Plate 81. *Yucca elephantipes*

Plate 82. *Yucca faxoniana*

Plate 83. Variegated *Yucca filamentosa*

Plate 84. Plant of the *Yucca filamentosa–Y. flaccida* complex

Plate 85. *Yucca filifera*

Plate 86. *Yucca glauca*. Photo by Edward Kutac

Plate 87. Flowers of *Yucca glauca*. Photo by Edward Kutac

Plate 88. *Yucca gloriosa*

Plate 89. *Yucca pallida*

Plate 90. *Yucca recurvifolia*

Plate 91. *Yucca rigida*

Plate 92. *Yucca rostrata*

Plate 93. *Yucca rostrata* planted in pot

Plate 94. *Yucca schidigera*

Plate 95. *Yucca schottii*

Plate 96. *Yucca torreyi*

Plate 97. *Yucca treculeana*

Plate 98. Fleshy fruit of *Yucca treculeana*

Plate 99. *Yucca whipplei*

Plate 100. Authors' garden in Scottsdale, Arizona

USES: *Hesperaloe campanulata* makes an excellent plant for sunny locations with poor rocky soils. The flowers are very attractive and, because the flowering stalk is not too large, they are visible easily. The relatively small size of the species makes it an excellent choice for use in mixed plantings of desert or drought-adapted small shrubs and succulents. It can also be used effectively as a potted plant, near pools, and in small corners of the garden where a dramatic shape but small size is needed.

Hesperaloe funifera (K. Koch) Trelease

PLATE 66; FIGURES 2-3, 3-1

SYNONYM: *Yucca funifera* K. Koch

COMMON NAMES: Giant hesperaloe, Samandoque

SIZE: *Hesperaloe funifera* is the largest of the hesperaloes and can form clumps of tightly grouped rosettes up to 6 ft. (1.8 m) tall and as wide. Each clump usually has fewer than 10 rosettes, but the large, heavy leaves make the clumps appear huge.

LEAVES: The leaves have a distinct yellow-green color and range from 3.75 to 6 ft. (1.1–1.8 m) long and from 1.25 to 2.5 in. (3.2–6 cm) wide at the widest part, which is approximately a third of the way up the leaf from the base. From the widest point the leaf slightly narrows towards the base and gradually narrows to an acute tip at the end. The leaves are straight, giving the plant a stiff and rigid appearance. The leaf edges are folded over completely into a rolled appearance towards the tip, slightly rolled to be crescent-shaped in cross section through most of their length, and flatten out towards the base. They are lined with light brown marginal stripes that separate into very thick, nearly straight marginal filaments.

BLOOM: The large flowering stalk is 12–15 ft. (3.7–4.6 m) tall and has a few (usually less than 10) lateral branches. The individual flowers are approximately 1 in. (2.5 cm) wide and greenish white with short stamens and styles that are exserted beyond the tepals. The flowers are arranged sparingly along the stalk.

DISTRIBUTION: *Hesperaloe funifera* is native to northeastern Mexico in the states of Coahuila, Nuevo León, and San Luis Potosí. Although it is not nearly as common in horticulture as *H. parviflora*, it is seen in small but increasing numbers in Arizona and Texas.

PROPAGATION: Propagation is by seed or by removal of the offsets.

CULTURAL REQUIREMENTS: *Hesperaloe funifera* requires well-drained soil in a sunny or partially shaded position. It is very drought tolerant and requires supplemental water only during the driest part of the summer. As an ornamental plant, it can be grown where winter temperatures are not too severe, although it tolerates temperatures down to 5–10°F (–15 to –12°C).

SIMILAR OR RELATED SPECIES: *Hesperaloe funifera* is rather distinct and rarely confused with other species. It can appear similar to small yuccas, particularly ones with bright green leaves such as *Yucca faxoniana*; however, the lack of terminal spine, the straight marginal filaments, and the clumping form of *H. funifera* help distinguish it from most young yuccas. It is distinguished readily from *H. parviflora* by its large, bright green leaves as opposed to the darker green leaves of *H. parviflora* that are rolled. Hybrids between *H. funifera* and *H. parviflora* occasionally are seen in horticulture. These plants vary in leaf size and shape, as well as flower color, size, and shape. Their flower stalks often are similar to those of *H. funifera* but with pink tubular flowers similar to the flowers of *H. parviflora*. *Hesperaloe funifera* also is very similar to *H. campanulata* but has longer leaves. The flowers of *H. funifera* are very similar to those of *H. nocturna*, but differ slightly in the size and position of the anthers. The leaves of *H. nocturna* are narrow and grasslike.

USES: The rigid, strong leaves of *Hesperaloe funifera* have a high fiber content and may have potential as a fiber crop. Recent studies of the fiber production show that this species may have productive capacities similar to those of commercial fiber-producing agaves such as sisal (*Agave sisalana*) and henequen (*A. fourcroydes*). The plant's drought and relative cold tolerance could allow fiber production in areas too cold or dry for production of traditional agave fiber crops. *Hesperaloe funifera* is an excellent tough ornamental plant for dry and rocky areas. Its rigid bright green leaves and relatively large size give it a unique appearance.

Hesperaloe nocturna Gentry

COMMON NAME: Night blooming hesperaloe

SIZE: *Hesperaloe nocturna* is a medium-sized clumping species with many narrow, stiff, grasslike leaves. The plants form dense clumps that can be 5–6 ft. (1.5–1.8 m) wide.

LEAVES: The dark olive green, stiff but arching leaves are up to 5 ft. (1.5 m) long but only 0.5–0.75 in. (1.3–2 cm) wide at the base. They narrow to a fine, but unarmed tip and are lined with numerous curling white filaments. The leaves are channeled on the upper side and rounded on the underside.

BLOOM: The thin curving inflorescence is 5–13 ft. (1.5–4 m) long and has several thin side branches. The flowers, which are night opening and held upright on the stalk, are 1–1.25 in. (2.5–3.2 cm) long and are greenish white in color with a lavender tint.

DISTRIBUTION: *Hesperaloe nocturna* has a limited natural distribution, being known only from north central and northeastern parts of the Mexican state of Sonora. It is seen sparingly as a cultivated plant in southwestern United States, particularly in Arizona.

PROPAGATION: Propagation is by seed or by removal of the offsets in cool weather.

CULTURAL REQUIREMENTS: *Hesperaloe nocturna* is a tough species that tolerates poor soils and hot full sun even in the warmest deserts. Supplemental irrigation in summer should be provided during extremely dry spells. This species is moderately cold hardy and has been reported to tolerate temperatures down to at least 10°F (−12°C).

SIMILAR OR RELATED SPECIES: Vegetatively, *Hesperaloe nocturna* is most similar to *H. parviflora*, but the leaves are longer and numerous, with a grassy appearance. Once the plants bloom they are easy to distinguish because of the differences in

flower color. The inflorescences also are different, with those of
H. nocturna being very thin and tall with highly arching
branches. When not in bloom *H. nocturna* might also be confused with *Nolina microcarpa* or *N. erumpens;* however, it
lacks the tiny but sharp marginal teeth of the nolinas, which in
turn lack the curling marginal filaments of *H. nocturna. Hesperaloe nocturna* has been reported to hybridize with *H. parviflora.* The resulting hybrids have flowers with the reddish color
of *H. parviflora,* a shape intermediate between the parent species, and the long and linear leaves of *H. nocturna.*

USES: *Hesperaloe nocturna* is well suited to hot and dry locations or locations where care is difficult or infrequent. Its
grasslike leaves can help soften the strong heavy forms of cactus, agaves, and other succulents. Because its highly arching
inflorescences are thin and long, the plant should be sited
where it is not too crowded so as to allow sufficient room for
the developing inflorescence.

Hesperaloe parviflora (Torrey) Coulter
PLATES 67, 68; FIGURES 1-2, 2-3, 4-3

SYNONYMS: *Hesperaloe yuccaefolia* Engelmann, *Aloe yuccifolia* Gray, *Yucca parviflora* Torrey, *Yucca parvifolia* Hemsley
COMMON NAMES: Red hesperaloe, Red yucca
SIZE: *Hesperaloe parviflora* is a stemless species, usually
about 3–4 ft. (1–1.2 m) tall. It spreads slowly by offsets to form
clumps 6 ft. (1.8 m) wide.
LEAVES: The dark olive green leaves are thin, hard, and linear. They measure 0.25–0.5 in. (0.6–1.2 cm) wide and up to 4 ft.
(1.2 m) long. They are numerous, clustering from the base of
the plants, commonly with white curling filaments that flow
freely from the smooth margin. The leaf edges almost join, giving the leaf a nearly round appearance. In cool weather the
leaves often have a reddish cast.
BLOOM: The inflorescence, which shows some definite variation in this species, is a raceme 5–9 ft. (1.5–2.7 m) tall or a
loose, open panicle rising high above the plant. In some plants
the pedicels are short, giving the appearance of a spike. The in-

Figure 4-3. Flowers, *Hesperaloe parviflora*

florescence can be erect or rise in a deep arch high over the plant, and it may have few or many flowers. The flowers are 1–2 inches (2.5–5 cm) long and tubular (some with wide flaring petals), opening irregularly along the stalk. They are diurnal and occur in a wide range of colors from deep carmine-red to coral and pink, often with a lighter interior than exterior. In some plants the stalk is pink, creating a graceful, eye-catching bloom. Some nurseries offer pale cream and bright yellow-flowered forms. Bloom is throughout the warm season, beginning as early as April and continuing through October.

DISTRIBUTION: *Hesperaloe parviflora* is distributed naturally in western Texas and in northeastern Mexico, but in Texas it is not abundant. Ornamentally, it is used throughout much of the southwestern United States. There also are reports of its use in the southeastern states in dry, well-drained locations.

PROPAGATION: Propagation is by seed or by removal of the offsets.

CULTURAL REQUIREMENTS: *Hesperaloe parviflora* requires full sun to grow and bloom best, even in the hottest regions of the southwestern United States. In hot climates it tolerates partial shade. Minimal supplemental irrigation in summer keeps plants fit. The species has no reported disease or pest problems beyond rabbits and deer that eat newly established plants. It has a reported cold tolerance to near 0°F (–18°C), but can probably tolerate temperatures to at least –5°F (–21°C).

SIMILAR OR RELATED SPECIES: Young yuccas could be mistaken for young container-grown plants of *Hesperaloe parviflora*, but leaves of the hesperaloe are harder and rolled, almost round. Older plants, particularly in bloom, are unmistakable. The reddish tubular flower of *H. parviflora* distinguishes it from all other hesperaloes, which tend to have bell-shaped flowers. Several other differences also exist between *H. parviflora* and other species. *Hesperaloe funifera* is a much larger plant, with very long, bright green, upright leaves, and a paniculate inflorescence that can rise to more than 15 ft. (4.6 m). *Hesperaloe campanulata* is similar in size to *H. parviflora*, but has leaves similar in shape and color to those of *H. funifera*. Hybrids, particularly between *H. parviflora* and *H. funifera*, are offered occasionally. These hybrids are attractive, combining the size and paniculate inflorescence of *H. funifera* with the red-pink flower color of *H. parviflora*. *Hesperaloe nocturna*, a species occasionally found in horticulture, is similar superficially to *H. parviflora*, but it has very narrow, almost grasslike leaves and whitish, nocturnal flowers that are borne on a very large branched stalk.

USES: *Hesperaloe parviflora* is a highly desirable ornamental species in the hot, arid low desert. It is extremely drought tolerant, requiring only minimal summer irrigation in the low desert, and cold hardy enough to be used regularly in higher desert locations. Because of its relatively small size, the species is suitable for use as a potted plant, near pools, patios, or walkways, or in any very hot location where summer color is desirable. It is particularly effective when planted in mass, a planting style seen with increasing frequency in public plantings in both Phoenix and Tucson. In cooler, coastal locations it must be sited in the hottest spot available for best performance.

Manfreda maculosa (W. Hooker) Rose

PLATE 69; FIGURES 3-3, 4-4

SYNONYMS: *Agave maculosa* W. Hooker, *Agave maculata* Engelmann

COMMON NAME: Spice lily

SIZE: *Manfreda maculosa* is a small species generally not more than 6 in. (15 cm) tall and spreading to 10–12 in. (25–30 cm) wide. It forms offsets.

LEAVES: The thin, fleshy, and brittle leaves are 0.5–1 in. (1.3–2.5 cm) wide and up to 14 in. (36 cm) long. They are spotted variously with irregular maroon spots and infrequently are solid green. They are guttered deeply, making them seem even thinner than they are. The teeth are very small, not sharp, and widely spaced.

BLOOM: The inflorescence is an open spike 16–52 in. (40–132 cm) tall. The flowers are fragrant, sessile, creamy white often streaked with pink, and age to a distinctive deep rose nearly brown color. They occur from late spring through the summer. An individual plant has flowers at all stages, therefore in many colors, on one stalk. Stamens in this species are barely exserted.

DISTRIBUTION: *Manfreda maculosa* occurs in sandy mesquite forests and scrubland of Texas from roughly Bracketville to San Antonio east to the coast and south into the Mexican state of Tamaulipas.

PROPAGATION: Propagation is by seed or by removal of offsets.

CULTURAL REQUIREMENTS: Whether in containers or in the ground, *Manfreda maculosa* is easy to cultivate. Plants can grow in strong sun in the low desert, but keep better leaf shape and color if there is some relief from the afternoon sun. In less rigorous summer climates plants should be grown in full sun. They require regular watering in the summer with good drainage. This manfreda has been reported to do well in gardens where low temperatures are near 10°F (–12°C).

SIMILAR OR RELATED SPECIES: *Manfreda maculosa* could be mistaken for *M. longiflora* (Rose) Verhoek-Williams (synonym *Runyonia longiflora* Rose), which usually is much smaller, has very thin leaves with tan striation rather than spots, and has a flower characterized by a very long tube with short included stamens that fade to pink rather than the dark rose-brown of *M. maculosa.* All other manfredas likely to be encountered in cultivation are much larger, with longer and wider leaves, and do not have flowers that fade to the deep pink-brown color so characteristic of this species.

USES: Like many manfredas, *Manfreda maculosa* was regarded by Native American cultures in its range and by early European settlers as an antidote to snakebite. Its roots are pounded and the resulting mash is used as a shampoo or a cleanser. Ornamentally, the species is a charming addition to any garden. The pattern on the leaf is interesting throughout the year, and the fragrant flowers add interest to a summer garden. The species is an excellent plant for a container or placed where the distinctive form and foliage can be enjoyed.

Figure 4-4. Flowers, *Manfreda maculosa*

Manfreda virginica (Linnaeus) Rose

SYNONYMS: *Agave virginica* Linnaeus, *Agave virginica* var. *tigrina* Rose

COMMON NAMES: False agave, Rattlesnake master, American aloe, Hauco, Amole

SIZE: *Manfreda virginica* is a small species rarely more than 18 in. (46 cm) tall. It has numerous soft, fleshy leaves and a true winter dormancy in temperate areas wherein the entire plant dies away to return in the warm weather. Plants can multiply rapidly from rhizomes or from buds at the leaf axils.

LEAVES: The leaves are 2.5–3 in. (6–8) wide and 5–16 in. (13–40 cm) long, soft, and semi-succulent. They are marked with varying amounts and sizes of brown-purple mottling; some individuals are entirely green and others so highly marked as to be nearly purple-leaved. Leaf size and shape can vary greatly over the life of the plant. Young or late-forming leaves are small, short, and broad, and held tightly on the plant, while older leaves or those formed earlier in the year spread from the center. The margin is finely toothed or smooth and straight.

BLOOM: The inflorescence is a spike up to 6 ft. (1.8 m) tall that forms in the early summer. The flowers, which are solitary or occasionally in pairs on the upper part of the stalk, are green to yellow-green in color and very fragrant, with long exserted cinnamon-brown stamens. The tepals are very erect and reflex upon maturity. This species does not necessarily flower every year, and it is common to skip years in its flowering cycle.

DISTRIBUTION: *Manfreda virginica* is found from West Virginia to Missouri and Florida. Within this range, it occupies several different habitats, including moist forest, prairie, and sandy lenses.

PROPAGATION: Propagation is by seed or offsets.

CULTURAL REQUIREMENTS: *Manfreda virginica* is the most cold tolerant manfreda, fully able to tolerate −20°F (−29°C). It can also withstand very warm summers if kept amply watered, but in the low desert requires afternoon shade in the summer. Gardeners in the southeastern United States can have problems with nematodes, but keeping the plants raised above grade and using rocks or limestone to improve and open the drainage is sufficient.

SIMILAR OR RELATED SPECIES: Manfredas often are difficult to separate and hybridize freely. *Manfreda virginica* can be distinguished from all other manfredas in horticulture by its style that is much shorter than the stamens. In addition, the green to yellow-green erect flowers with very long, brownish stamens, and finely toothed to smooth leaves help distinguish this species. Other larger-leaved manfredas are uncommon but deserve more attention in gardens. *Manfreda guttata* (Jacobi & Bouché) Rose (synonym *Agave guttata* Jacobi & Bouché) is an outstanding ornamental with large, nearly smooth gray-blue leaves (Plate 70). The leaf margin is rough, and the leaves can be spotted or not. This species creates numerous offsets, often making large clumps that are more than 4 ft. (1.2 m) in diameter. The blooming stalk is equally large, more than 10 ft. (3 m) tall. *Manfreda sileri* Verhoek is blue-leaved with purple marking on the leaves. It is the same general size as *M. virginica*. The flower stalks are very large, up to 5 ft. (1.5 m) tall, with upward-facing chartreuse flowers. *Manfreda undulata* (Jacobi) Rose (synonym *Agave undulata* Jacobi) has distinctive green to brown flowers with extremely elongated stamens, often extending more than 6 in. (15 cm) long, and silvery, undulating leaves. It is an extremely handsome plant. It has been observed to tolerate temperatures near 10°F (−12°C). Some authorities consider it the same as *M. guttata*. *Manfreda variegata* (Jacobi) Shinners (synonym *Agave variegata* Jacobi) is a name that is very common in the trade to describe a host of different-looking plants. In general, the plants have fleshy, semi-succulent leaves that are spotted but more narrow and succulent than those of *M. virginica*. The flowers are green-brown with long stamens. It is possible that these plants are hybrids, long known in gardens and passed along in varying clones for many generations. They have been observed to tolerate temperatures down to 15°F (−9°C).

USES: *Manfreda virginica* was used by Native Americans in many parts of the species's range. The roots were pounded with water to treat a host of illnesses ranging from colic to dyspepsia and dropsy. In the Carolinas, Native Americans reportedly pounded the roots with water and drank the mixture as an antidote to snakebite, but there is little evidence that it has any effect. This species is a valued addition to any garden with its unusual soft leaves, rosette form, and amazing flowers. It blends well with smaller-scale perennials and with other succulents and is excellent as a container plant.

Nolina bigelovii S. Watson

COMMON NAME: Desert nolina

SIZE: *Nolina bigelovii* is a large, rigid, shrublike plant with a trunk that is 3.25–9.75 ft. (1.1–2.9 m) high and topped with a rosette of stiff leaves. The trunk often is single-headed, but can have two or more rosettes.

LEAVES: The stiff, straight leaves are 0.5–1 in. (1.3–2.5 cm) wide and 2.5–4 ft. (0.8–1.2 m) long. They have well-defined striations along their length and are a dull blue-green to gray-green. The margin is smooth and lined with thin brown or tan stripes that separate into curling filaments particularly near the trunk.

BLOOM: The cream-colored flowers are small, about 0.1 in. (ca. 3 mm) long, and are borne on large inflorescences that are 3.5–6 ft. (1.1–1.8 m) long.

DISTRIBUTION: Native to rocky slopes of very arid deserts, *Nolina bigelovii* occurs naturally in the United States in southwestern Arizona, southeastern California, and southern Nevada and into the Mexican states of Sonora and Baja California. It is not common in horticulture but can be seen on occasion in the low desert within or near its natural range. It increased in the horticultural trade in the 1990s.

PROPAGATION: Propagation is by seed.

CULTURAL REQUIREMENTS: *Nolina bigelovii* is probably the most drought-tolerant nolina. It can tolerate full sun and poor rocky soils in the hottest deserts. Occasional summer watering in these areas helps speed growth, which normally is slow. Little is known specifically about the plant's cold tolerance, but because the species naturally occurs in warm deserts, it might be prudent not to plant it in areas where winter temperatures regularly fall below 20°F (–7°C).

SIMILAR OR RELATED SPECIES: *Nolina bigelovii* is very similar to *N. parryi*. Some botanical treatments even list *N. parryi* and *N. parryi* subsp. *wolfii* as varieties of *N. bigelovii*. These plants, however, are distinguished from *N. bigelovii* by their toothed leaf margin, and they lack the marginal leaf filaments of *N. bigelovii*. In the landscape and from a distance *N. bigelovii* could be mistaken for a small yucca with blue-green leaves such as *Yucca rostrata*, but it differs from *Y. rostrata* by having wider, striated leaves with marginal filaments.

USES: *Nolina bigelovii* is an excellent landscape plant for exposed areas and naturalistic planting in the hottest and driest desert climates. It combines well with cactus, yuccas, agaves, and other desert plants in native plantings, and its drought and sun hardiness make it a good choice for areas that are difficult to maintain and irrigate. The plant's rigid appearance makes it a good choice where a small but very sculptural plant is desired.

Nolina erumpens (Torrey) S. Watson

SYNONYM: *Dasylirion erumpens* Torrey
COMMON NAME: Bear grass
SIZE: *Nolina erumpens* is a stemless, clump-forming species that can grow to 8.25 ft. (2.5 m) wide.
LEAVES: The clumps can consist of more than a hundred coarse grasslike leaves that are erect but pliable, giving the plant the appearance of a coarse large brush. The dark green leaves are 0.25–0.75 in. (0.6–2 cm) wide at the base and 2–6.5 ft. (0.6–2 m) long. They have finely toothed, sharp edges with fibrous, somewhat frayed tips.
BLOOM: The inflorescence is a large-stalked panicle 2–8.25 ft. (0.6–2.5 m) tall. The flowers are tiny and dark cream in color with often a rosy pink to purple cast.
DISTRIBUTION: *Nolina erumpens* is a native of the rocky soils and brushlands of western Texas and the Mexican state of Chihuahua. It only occasionally is seen in cultivation.
PROPAGATION: Propagation is by seed or by removal of the offsets in cool weather.
CULTURAL REQUIREMENTS: *Nolina erumpens* requires a

well-drained soil that is allowed to dry out from time to time. It does well in full sun, but could probably tolerate partial shade. It tolerates heat and drought, requiring only supplemental irrigation in the hottest times of the year once it is established. It tolerates considerable cold, probably down to approximately 0°F (–18°C).

SIMILAR OR RELATED SPECIES: *Nolina erumpens* is somewhat similar to *N. texana* (Plate 75), which is a much smaller plant with fine leaves that are much shorter and narrower than those of *N. erumpens*. *Nolina microcarpa* is very similar to *N. erumpens* with only minor differences in their general appearance. The leaves of *N. microcarpa* are arched more than the somewhat erect leaves of *N. erumpens* and its leaf tips are frayed distinctly while those of *N. erumpens* tend to be less so.

USES: *Nolina erumpens* is an excellent plant for dry gardens. Its narrow leaves help lend a fine texture contrast to the often large bulky leaves associated with cacti, yuccas, agaves, and other sculptural plants. Its fine texture also allows it to soften walls and buildings near where it is planted. Because of its heat and cold tolerance, it can be planted in sunny and windy areas where other plants might struggle.

Nolina longifolia (Schultes) Hemsley   PLATE 71

SYNONYMS: *Dasylirion longifolium* Zuccarini, *Beaucarnea longifolia* Baker, *Yucca longifolia* Schultes, *Roulinia karwinskiana* Brongniart

COMMON NAME: Oaxacan tree nolina

SIZE: *Nolina longifolia* is a startling treelike species that consists of a trunk up to 10 ft. (3 m) tall from which several thick branches emerge toward the top. The ends of the branches bear large mops of long, hanging, strap-shaped leaves that droop down over the branches and the upper portion of the trunk. The trunk is covered by a thick corky bark and is expanded at its base.

LEAVES: The remarkable green to light green leaves are 0.5–1.25 in. (1.3–3.2 cm) wide at the base and gradually taper to a thread along their length, which can be more than 6.5 ft. (2 m).

They are very pliable and lax, hanging down from the growing tip with very little arch. The leaf margin is lined with very tiny teeth that create a razorlike edge.

BLOOM: The tiny white flowers are held on a panicle that can be up to 6.5 ft. (2 m) long.

DISTRIBUTION: *Nolina longifolia* occurs in the Mexican states of Oaxaca and Puebla at an elevation of approximately 3000 ft. (900 m).

PROPAGATION: Propagation is by seed.

CULTURAL REQUIREMENTS: The specific cultural requirements of *Nolina longifolia* are not well documented, but the species has had a long history of growing well in Mediterranean climates and prospers in full sun and partial shade in those areas. It should do well in warmer desert climates, but some shade as well as supplemental watering in the driest parts of the year would be advisable. As with other nolinas a well-drained soil should insure against root rot. The cold tolerance of the species is not well known. Because of its tropical origins, it may be sensitive to temperatures much below about 25°F (4°C), but some experimental plantings are beginning to indicate that it may potentially have much greater tolerance to 15°F (−9°C) or perhaps lower. More horticultural experience with this species is needed.

SIMILAR OR RELATED SPECIES: Few plants look anything like *Nolina longifolia*. The combination of an arborescent habit with very long, lax leaves distinguishes this species from all other nolinas. *Nolina longifolia* could be mistaken for *Beaucarnea recurvata*, except that its leaves are up to 6.5 ft. (2 m) long, flat, and very lax, while those of *B. recurvata* are only up to 5 ft. (1.5 m) long, recurved from the growing point, and twisted in the lower portions. While the base of the trunk of *N. longifolia* is somewhat expanded, it is not large and swollen as in the beaucarneas.

USES: *Nolina longifolia* makes a stunning specimen plant. Its large size and long hanging leaves give it a very unusual appearance. It also works well with other unusual xerophytic plants and with larger-leaved tropical plants in a planting where dramatic form is desired.

Nolina matapensis Wiggins

PLATE 72

COMMON NAMES: Sonoran tree bear grass, Tuya

SIZE: *Nolina matapensis* is a treelike species with a trunk 9.75–26 ft. (2.9–8 m) tall and one or sometimes three to four branches topped by a large head of grasslike leaves. The fissured and patterned trunk is very dark, almost black. It varies from 6 to 17.75 in. (15–45 cm) wide, and old plants can have a wide base.

LEAVES: The light green to yellow-green leaves are approximately 0.5 in. (1.3 cm) wide at the broad base and 2.25–4 ft. (0.7–1.2 m) long, gradually narrowing to a fine tip. They are slightly concave in cross section with a small but broad keel along the bottom side. The leaf margin is finely toothed. The leaves are neither rigid nor totally lax but are stiffly recurving, forming gentle yet distinct arches in the inner parts of the head. The outer leaves tend to hang down towards the trunk.

BLOOM: The inflorescence is an erect panicle approximately 6–14 ft. (1.8–4.3 m) tall. It resembles a large plume arising from the head of arching leaves The abundant, tiny cream-colored flowers are 0.08 in. (2 mm) long.

DISTRIBUTION: *Nolina matapensis* occurs naturally in a limited area in mountain woodlands in the Mexican states of Sonora and adjacent Chihuahua at an elevation from 3500 to 6000 ft. (1000–1800 m). It is cultivated to a limited extent in the warm deserts of Arizona, but is not widespread in cultivation. Since the 1990s it has been available occasionally in the horticultural trade.

PROPAGATION: Propagation is by seed.

CULTURAL REQUIREMENTS: *Nolina matapensis* grows well in Mediterranean climates and in drier climates of inland deserts where winters are not severe. It has, however, been reported to have some cold tolerance, even withstanding temperatures near 15°F (−9°C) for short periods. Like all nolinas, it should be planted in well-drained soils. In the low desert it benefits from some shade in the hottest part of the day as well as some additional water to maintain good growth.

SIMILAR OR RELATED SPECIES: The leaves of *Nolina mata-*

pensis are very similar to those of *N. microcarpa;* they are nearly identical in length and both have a yellow-green cast with a concave shape and a flattened keel on the bottom side. The leaves of *N. matapensis* are approximately 0.5 in. (1.3 cm) wide at the base, tend to be mostly narrowed into a single tip, and are slightly curved and arched, while those of *N. microcarpa* are generally narrower, somewhat shredded into brushy tips, and are more lax in the head. Once the plants mature, they are easily separated because *N. matapensis* develops a trunk and *N. microcarpa* does not. The arching leaves help distinguish *N. matapensis* from most other arborescent nolinas, such as *N. nelsoni*, which has straight, rigid leaves, and *N. longifolia*, which has very lax leaves that tend to hang down over the trunk.

USES: In Mexico the leaves of *Nolina matapensis* have been used for making baskets and the trunks for posts. In the 1990s the species began to appear in horticulture in limited numbers. It is spectacular when mature, making an excellent specimen plant for courtyards and large enclosed areas. It also is an excellent plant around pools, and when planted with other dramatic desert plants or large leaved tropical plants.

Nolina microcarpa S. Watson   PLATE 73; FIGURES 3-5, 4-5

COMMON NAME: Bear grass

SIZE: *Nolina microcarpa* is a stemless species forming large clumps of coarse grasslike leaves. The clumps reach approximately 4 ft. (1.2 m) tall and 7 ft. (2.1 m) wide.

LEAVES: The yellow-green to olive green leaves are 2–4 ft. (0.6–1.2 m) long and 0.25–0.5 in. (0.6–1.3 cm) wide. Gracefully arching, they have a flattened keel on the underside. The edges are sharp and finely toothed. The ends of the leaves split into a frayed brushlike tip that is 2–4.75 in. (5–12 cm) long.

BLOOM: The numerous tiny cream-colored flowers are borne on a highly branched panicle that is at least 3.25 ft. (1 m) long.

DISTRIBUTION: *Nolina microcarpa* is distributed naturally in southern Arizona, southern New Mexico, western Texas, and in the Mexican states of Sonora and Chihuahua. It is a spe-

225

Figure 4-5. Flowers, *Nolina microcarpa*

cies of the high grasslands and woodlands from 3500 to 5500 ft. (1000–1650 m). As an ornamental, it is often available from nurseries within or near its natural range that carry native and drought-adapted plants. It tolerates the harsh conditions of warm deserts at elevations lower than its natural range.

PROPAGATION: Propagation is by seed or by removal of the offsets.

CULTURAL REQUIREMENTS: *Nolina microcarpa* performs well in a sunny or partially shaded exposure in well-drained soils. Established plants are drought tolerant, but supplemental water helps maintain good vigor in hot desert climates. This species can tolerate cold down to at least –15°F (–26°C) and perhaps lower.

SIMILAR OR RELATED SPECIES: *Nolina microcarpa* is similar to other stemless clumping nolinas such as *N. erumpens* and *N. texana* (Plate 75). It differs from *N. texana*, a smaller and more delicate grasslike plant, by having much wider and longer leaves that are distinctly sharply toothed. It is very similar in size and shape to *N. erumpens* with the vegetative and form differences being very subtle. *Nolina microcarpa* has leaves that arch to a greater extent and tips that often are distinctly frayed into a brush, while *N. erumpens* has leaves that generally are erect with slight arching and frayed tips that often are present but less distinct.

USES: *Nolina microcarpa* is an excellent plant for softening the hard edges frequently associated with dry gardens composed of cacti, yuccas, agaves, and other stiff-leaved succulents. It works well when grouped with large shrubs or the small trees common to arid lands. The large plumelike inflorescence, while not spectacular, adds an interesting touch to gardens.

Nolina nelsoni Rose

FIGURE 2-4

COMMON NAME: Blue nolina

SIZE: *Nolina nelsoni* is small treelike species with a trunk that is 3–12 ft. (1–3.7 m) tall and topped by a head of stiff, rigid leaves.

LEAVES: The stiff blue-green leaves are 19.75–33 in. (50–84

cm) long and 0.75–1.5 in. (2–3.8 cm) wide. Although they are held in very rigid hemispherical heads, they are thin and pliable to the touch. The leaves have a slightly concave shape in cross section, and the leaf margin is lined with tiny teeth that are nearly invisible to the naked eye.

BLOOM: The tiny cream-colored flowers are borne on a large inflorescence 6.5–11 ft. (2–3.4 m) long.

DISTRIBUTION: *Nolina nelsoni* has a very limited natural distribution and is confined to small areas in the Mexican state of Tamaulipas. It is seen occasionally in cultivation, particularly in Texas.

PROPAGATION: Propagation is by seed.

CULTURAL REQUIREMENTS: *Nolina nelsoni* grows well in full sun or partial shade and in a well-drained soil. It is reportedly very cold tolerant, down to at least 10°F (–12°C). Although it is drought tolerant, the species requires deep waterings in the hottest desert areas or during long droughts in the summer to maintain best growth and condition of the plant.

SIMILAR OR RELATED SPECIES: *Nolina nelsoni* could be confused with *N. parryi,* but leaf tips of *N. parryi* are frayed slightly and leaves generally are less than 0.75 in. (2 cm) wide, while those of *N. nelsoni* are wider than 0.75 in. (2 cm). This difference makes the leaf heads of *N. parryi* more grassy-looking, while those of *N. nelsoni* look more like the heads of yuccas. *Nolina parryi* often lacks a trunk, although it can form a small trunk, while *N. nelsoni* always develops one. *Nolina parry* subsp. *wolfii* develops a large trunk, but it tends to have flattened leaves of a darker drab green color. *Nolina bigelovii* also is somewhat similar to *N. nelsoni,* but the brown filaments along the leaf margin help to distinguish it from *N. nelsoni. Nolina beldingii* Brandegee is another arborescent species with bluish but less rigid leaves; it rarely is seen in cultivation but is somewhat similar to *N. nelsoni.*

USES: *Nolina nelsoni* is a fine plant for use as a large ornamental specimen. Its rigid leaves give it a very structural appearance. It is attractive near buildings, walls, or pools. It can also be effectively combined with other dryland plants of bold leaf and trunk structure as a component in an exotic dry garden.

Nolina parryi S. Watson

PLATE 74

COMMON NAME: Parry's nolina

SIZE: *Nolina parryi* is a species of variable form and size. It has a short trunk 3.25–6.5 ft. (1–2 m) tall topped by a rosette of long leaves. *Nolina parryi* subsp. *wolfii* Munz is larger with a very thick trunk that can reach up to 15 ft. (4.6 m) tall. It has at times been placed as a variety of *N. bigelovii* and has been listed as a separate species. Botanical sources vary considerably over the treatment of this taxon.

LEAVES: The gray-green to olive green leaves are 0.25–0.75 in. (0.6–2 cm) wide and 1.5–3 ft. (0.5–1 m) long. They are concave on the top, and the margin is lined with tiny teeth that give the leaf a sharp edge. The leaves are rigid but can have a slight arch. *Nolina parryi* subsp. *wolfii* has larger leaves, approximately 1.5 in. (3.8 cm) wide and up to 5 ft. (1.5 m) long, and they are flat rather than concave, and are olive green in color. The leaves of the subspecies, like those of the species, are lined with small teeth that give them a sharp edge.

BLOOM: The inflorescence bears large numbers of tiny cream-colored flowers and is approximately 6 ft. (1.8 m) tall. Subspecies *wolfii* has a larger inflorescence, up to 12 ft. (3.7 m) tall.

DISTRIBUTION: *Nolina parryi* is found on the dry hillsides of southern California's coastal hills and mountains below 3000 ft. (900 m) in elevation. It also ranges southward into Baja California. Subspecies *wolfii* occurs in the inland desert mountains of southern California where it grows in mixed open woodlands of pinyon pine (*Pinus cembroides*), juniper (*Juniperus* spp.), and Joshua tree (*Yucca brevifolia*), at elevations to 5500 ft. (1650 m). A few collections of plants whose descriptions seem to fit subsp. *wolfii* have been cited for isolated locations in northern Arizona. *Nolina parryi* occasionally is available from nurseries that specialize in California native plants. It can be seen in native gardens and landscapes in California, but is not as common as one would expect considering its beauty and hardiness.

PROPAGATION: Propagation is by seed. The plants take approximately seven to eight years to reach full flowering stage.

CULTURAL REQUIREMENTS: *Nolina parryi* performs best in a

well-drained soil with full sun. It is very drought tolerant, so that in coastal or Mediterranean climates only occasional summer watering is needed. In the hottest desert climates, intermittent summer watering is needed to insure the plant's best performance. The species's cold tolerance is not reported often, but because the species occurs in mountainous areas it could be expected to have some cold hardiness. The populations referred to the type species might tolerate temperatures down to 10°F (−12°C). Subspecies *wolfii* is likely even more cold tolerant. Both taxa are expected to tolerate these temperatures on an intermittent, not sustained basis.

SIMILAR OR RELATED SPECIES: *Nolina parryi* is somewhat similar to *N. bigelovii*, although it lacks the marginal leaf filaments that are a distinct feature of the latter. *Nolina parryi* is similar to *N. nelsoni*, except that its leaves are less than 0.75 in. (2 cm) wide, while those of *N. nelsoni* are more than 0.75 in. (2 cm) wide and are very rigid.

USES: As with many of the other nolinas, *Nolina parryi* blends well with other native plants to create a naturalistic garden. It also works well with cacti, yuccas, and agaves in plantings of strong form. Its tolerance of dry conditions allows it to be used in areas where irrigation is infrequent or difficult to achieve.

Nolina texana S. Watson   PLATE 75

COMMON NAMES: Sacahuista, Bear grass

SIZE: *Nolina texana* is a stemless, clumping plant consisting of hundreds of wiry, very narrow leaves. It resembles a medium-sized clumping grass approximately 4–5 ft. (1.2–1.5 m) in diameter.

LEAVES: The narrow dark green to yellow-green leaves are only 0.08–0.16 in. (2–4 mm) wide and 1.5–2.5 ft. (0.5–0.8 m) long. They are fairly straight near the center of the clump, but near the edges of the clump the leaves arch gently towards the ground. The margins are smooth, but some plants have a few scattered teeth, giving the margins a slightly rough feel. The leaf tips are pointed but soft.

BLOOM: The inflorescence is 1–2 ft. (0.3–0.6 m) tall and mostly contained within the leaves, not extending much if at all beyond their length. The tiny flowers are white to creamy white in color.

DISTRIBUTION: *Nolina texana* has a wide geographic range that extends from the eastern edge of the Edwards Plateau in central Texas westward into southern New Mexico and Arizona and southward into the Mexican states of Sonora and Chihuahua. The species has been known to grow up to 5500 ft. (1650 m) in elevation in the western parts of its range. It is grown as an ornamental plant primarily in Texas and New Mexico.

PROPAGATION: Propagation is by seed, which should be planted in cool weather. Moist pre-chilling of approximately three months has been reported to assist in germination. The plant also can be propagated by removal of the offsets.

CULTURAL REQUIREMENTS: *Nolina texana* is a tough undemanding species that can tolerate full sun to nearly full shade if the roots are kept on the dry side. It is drought tolerant, only needing supplemental summer water in the driest climates. It also is very cold tolerant, reportedly withstanding temperatures down to −15°F (−26°C).

SIMILAR OR RELATED SPECIES: *Nolina texana* is somewhat similar to *N. microcarpa* and *N. erumpens*, both of which are stemless clumping plants with narrow leaves. Their leaves and inflorescences, however, are much larger than those of *N. texana*. A similar species that might occasionally be seen in cultivation is *N. lindheimeriana* (Scheele) S. Watson (synonym *Dasylirion lindheimeriana* Scheele), often known as devil's shoestring. *Nolina lindheimeriana* differs from *N. texana* by having flattened rather than wiry leaves: its leaves are distinctly sharp with many fine teeth while those of *N. texana* are smooth or only slightly roughened from having a few small teeth.

USES: The wide environmental tolerance of *Nolina texana* allows it to be used in a variety of situations. It is an excellent plant for smoothing the rough textures of cactus, agaves, yuccas, and other heavy-leaved plants in desert or dryland gardens.

It also is small enough to be used as an accent plant in dry rock gardens and to add a fine texture to plantings of smaller drought-tolerant perennial plants.

Polianthes tuberosa Linnaeus

COMMON NAME: Tuberose

SIZE: An herbaceous species, *Polianthes tuberosa* consists of soft grasslike leaves arising from underground tuberous structures. It produces offsets that result in small clumps of leaves. Plants are from 12–18 in. (30–46 cm) tall.

LEAVES: The dull green leaves are approximately 1–1.5 ft. (0.3–0.5 m) long, often with a slight reddish cast, and approximately 0.5 in. (1.3 cm) wide at the base. They are thin, linear, slightly succulent, and are borne in sets of six to nine arising from the tuber. As the tuber produces more offsets, more leaves develop, increasing the size of the grasslike clump. Some leaf variation has been developed through horticultural selection. The selection known as *Polianthes tuberosa* 'The Pearl' has broader and darker leaves than the species. Variegated leaf forms with narrow gold or silver stripes also have been selected.

BLOOM: The inflorescence is a spike 3 ft. (1 m) tall. The pure white flowers, which are borne on the upper part of the stalk, emit a strong sweet fragrance. They are waxy and consist of a funnel-shaped tube 1.5–2.5 in. (3.8–6 cm) long. The tube is narrow at its base and separates into six segments approximately two-thirds of the way from the base to the end of the flower. The segments flare open and show six stamens inserted within the floral tube and a three-parted stigma. Often several spikes will emerge from the tubers at flowering time. The double-flowered horticultural variety called 'The Pearl' is borne on shorter spikes only 1.5–2 ft. (0.5–0.6 m) tall. Orange-flowered forms of the species also have been reported.

DISTRIBUTION: *Polianthes tuberosa* is not known in the wild and is thought to have been domesticated by the Aztecs in central Mexico. It currently is grown over much of the tropical and temperate world and is valued highly for its very fragrant flowers. Because it requires a moist but warm soil, it generally is grown as a greenhouse plant in northern Europe and in the cold parts of the United States. Where soils do not stay cold and damp too long, such as in the warmer parts of the southeastern United States, it can be grown outdoors.

PROPAGATION: Propagation is by removal of the tuberlike bulbs, which are planted in the spring once the weather has warmed.

CULTURAL REQUIREMENTS: The plants should generally be given full sun, but partial shade would be best in very hot and sunny climates. In more northerly areas with warm summers, such as much of the eastern United States, *Polianthes tuberosa* can be grown as a summer annual, renewed each year by planting more tubers. In the Gulf Coast and South Atlantic states the tuber can overwinter if covered with mulch to protect it from freezes, particularly when temperatures are expected to go below 10°F (−12°C). If, however, the winter is cold or too damp, the plants may not reliably bloom the next summer. During the summer growing season the plants should not be allowed to become excessively dry.

SIMILAR OR RELATED SPECIES: Several white-flowered species are similar to *Polianthes tuberosa* but rare in cultivation: *P. nelsoni* Rose, *P. palustris* Rose, and *P. pringlei* Rose. Two other species also not common in cultivation but having interesting flowers are *P. geminiflora* (Llave) Rose (synonym *Bravoa geminiflora* Llave), with paired red flowers, and *P. howardii* Verhoek, which has red and green flowers with dark, almost black interiors. It is expected that many of these species have similar cultural requirements to *P. tuberosa*; however, *P. geminiflora* has been reported to successfully overwinter against warm fences in south England, so it may have greater tolerance to cold and moist conditions than *P. tuberosa*. An orange-colored hybrid, reportedly of *P. geminiflora* and *P. tuberosa*, has often been referred to in horticultural literature as *P. blissi* Hort.

USES: *Polianthes tuberosa* is best known as a cut-flower species grown for its sweet heady fragrance. This use extends to before the Spanish conquest of Mexico. The species was a popular conservatory plant for many years in Europe and North America, reaching the height of its popularity in the late nineteenth century. It unfortunately became associated with funeral use and eventually declined in popularity. The species has been grown commercially in various parts of the world including Italy, South Africa, and North Carolina in the United States. Near the city of Grasse in southern France the species is grown to extract oils from its flowers as an additive to perfume. It is used as a garden annual or tender perennial, valued for its fragrant late-summer flowers, or as a conservatory plant.

Yucca aloifolia Linnaeus   PLATE 76

COMMON NAMES: Aloe yucca, Spanish dagger

SIZE: *Yucca aloifolia* is a single-stemmed or simply branched plant to 10 ft. (3 m) tall. Several stems sometimes emerge from the base of the plant. Branches, if they appear, are located near the tops of stems.

LEAVES: The flat or slightly concave, linear leaves are arranged in a spiral and crowded tightly around the stem. Many live leaves form elongated heads along the stem. Each leaf is 12–20 in. (30–51 cm) long and 1–1.5 in. (2.5–3.8 cm) wide with small sharp teeth along the edge and a very sharp dark-colored terminal spine. *Yucca aloifolia* is among the oldest yuccas in cultivation, and many of its forms have been cultivated since 1605. William Trelease in his famous 1902 survey of the genus *Yucca* identified many varieties and horticultural forms, which are listed here. *Yucca aloifolia* var. *arcuata* (Haworth) Trelease (synonym *Y. arcuata* Haworth) has short stems from a prostrate caudex. The smooth-margined leaves are 1–1.5 ft. (0.3–0.5 m) long. This variety is from shaded areas near the Carolina coast. *Yucca aloifolia* f. *conspicua* (Haworth) Engelmann (synonym *Y. conspicua* Haworth) has broad, lax, and recurved leaves and clustered trunks. *Yucca aloifolia* var. *draconis* (Linnaeus) Engelmann (synonym *Y. draconis* Linnaeus) has leaves wider than the type at 2–3 in. (5–8 cm) wide. Furthermore, the leaves are flexible and recurved, and the trunks generally are branched towards the top of the stems. *Yucca aloifolia* f. *marginata* Bommer is fairly common in horticulture. The leaves of this variegated form have a yellow or white margin and often have a red tinge, particularly when young. *Yucca aloifolia* f. *menandi* Trelease is similar to f. *tricolor* but has rigidly curved leaves that are somewhat rough on the margin and on the dorsal ridges. *Yucca aloifolia* f. *purpurea* Baker has purple-green leaves that are similar in form to those of var. *arcuata*. *Yucca aloifolia* f. *tenuifolia* (Haworth) Trelease (synonym *Y. tenuifolia* Haworth) has a habit similar to that of var. *arcuata*, but with roughened dorsal ridges and sharp fine teeth along the edges of the often purplish leaves. *Yucca aloifolia* f. *tricolor* Bommer is a garden sport with yellow and white center stripes, often tinged with red. *Yucca aloifolia* 'Vittorio Emmanuel II' has heavy purple staining on the stems and on the outside of the petals. It is thought to be a hybrid of *Y. aloifolia* originating in Europe. *Yucca aloifolia* var. *yucatana* (Engelmann) Trelease (synonym *Y. yucatana* Engelmann) is an unusually tall variety, up to 23 ft. (7 m). It comes from Mexico and has a tomentose panicle and rather flexible leaves.

BLOOM: The inflorescence is a stout panicle 1–1.5 ft. (0.3–0.5 m) long and 6–10 in. (15–25 cm) wide. One-fourth to one-half the length of the panicle is set into the head of leaves. The waxy white flowers, often tinged with purple or green, are 1–1.25 in. (2.5–3.2 cm) long and 0.3–0.5 in. (0.8–1.3 cm) wide. The fruit is 1.5–2 in. (3.8–5 cm) long, and dark green on the outside and purplish to black on the inside.

DISTRIBUTION: *Yucca aloifolia* is widely distributed along the southern coast of the United States from Louisiana to Florida and as far north as Virginia. In the Caribbean basin area it is found from the Virgin Islands to Jamaica and west to Mexico. It grows most commonly on sand dunes or shell mounds near the coast. The species is among the oldest and most common yuccas in horticulture and has a very widespread distribution as an ornamental plant. It is very common throughout the southeastern and southwestern United States where winter temperatures stay generally above 0°F (–18°C).

PROPAGATION: Propagation is by seed, by removal of the offsets, and by root or stem cuttings.

CULTURAL REQUIREMENTS: *Yucca aloifolia* tolerates a wide variety of garden conditions. It grows well in full sun or partial shade. It tolerates dry sandy soils or even soils that are moist for some parts of the year. It survives on natural rainfall in the southeastern United States and in Europe, but should be given supplemental summer water when planted in the driest parts of deserts in the Southwest. As winter temperatures approach 0°F (–18°C), this species should be planted in protected locations only.

SIMILAR OR RELATED SPECIES: *Yucca aloifolia* is most similar to *Y. gloriosa* to which it certainly is related closely. The sharp-pointed terminal leaf spine of *Y. aloifolia* serves to differentiate the two species. *Yucca aloifolia* also generally has narrower, rigid sharp-toothed leaves, whereas the leaves of *Y. gloriosa* generally are wider and often somewhat lax and smooth or with only very minute marginal teeth. Both species have many horticultural forms with many overlapping characteristics. No doubt hybrid forms between the two species exist.

USES: The leaves of *Yucca aloifolia* were used traditionally by settlers in the southeastern United States to make string and twine that often was used to hang cured meats. As an ornamental plant *Y. aloifolia* has been valued for its relative hardiness and semi-arborescent habit for centuries particularly in southern Europe and along the East Coast of the United States. Its tolerance of humid climates coupled with its dramatic hard structural appearance make it a unique landscape plant for much of the eastern United States south of Virginia and for most of southern and maritime Europe. It can be planted anywhere a dramatic form is needed. Because it has sharp terminal spines, it should be sited where it cannot cause injury.

Yucca baccata Torrey — PLATES 77, 78; FIGURES 2-2, 2-3

COMMON NAMES: Banana yucca, Blue yucca, Datil yucca

SIZE: *Yucca baccata* usually is a small-trunked species with one or up to 10 trunks. Plants can form clusters up to 16.5 ft. (5 m) wide. The individual trunks often curve and branch. Large clusters of stems can have up to 70 rosettes of leaves, although 5–20 rosettes are much more common. The trunk can be up to 8 ft. (2.4 m) tall with typically two to five branches. The number of trunks and the number of branches vary considerably for plants in nature and under cultivation. The trunked populations usually are referred to as *Y. baccata* var. *baccata*. Trunkless individuals or those with very short trunks and dense clusters of leaves often are referred to as *Y. baccata* var. *vespertina* McKelvey.

LEAVES: The deeply concave leaves vary greatly in color and size. They may be blue-green, gray-green, or, in some populations, a light blue-gray color. In size they are 1.25–2.5 ft. (0.4–0.8 m) long and 1.25–2.25 in. (3.2–5.7 cm) wide. Thick and scabrous, the leaves bear numerous coarse or fine curled filaments along the margin. The leaves are often straight and rigid, but in some populations are twisted.

BLOOM: The inflorescence is an elongated panicle 1.75–2.5 ft. (0.5–0.8 m) long. Generally more than half the length of the panicle is within the head of leaves. The flowers are elongated, being 1.5–4 in. (3.8–10 cm) long and 0.5–1 in. (1.3–2.5 cm) wide, and are pendant. They expand very little so that they appear as elongated bells upon the panicle branches. The flowers are white or cream in color often with purple or reddish brown tinges. Some populations of *Y. baccata* var. *vespertina* are known to have flower stalks and buds that are solid maroon in color. The maroon of these individuals contrasts with the bright blue-green leaves, making them striking ornamental plants.

DISTRIBUTION: *Yucca baccata* has a very large range over much of southwestern United States and northern Mexico. It occurs in western Texas, southwestern Colorado, southern Utah, southern Nevada, most of New Mexico except the eastern plains section, most of Arizona except the lowest desert regions, and into the edges of the Mohave Desert of California. It also occurs in most of the northern states of Mexico south to the state of Querétaro. It has an equally large elevational range, occurring from 2000 to 8000 ft. (600–2400 m). This species is planted as an ornamental throughout its natural range and into desert areas below its natural elevational range.

PROPAGATION: Propagation is by seed or by removal of young offsets.

CULTURAL REQUIREMENTS: *Yucca baccata* requires full sun or partial shade and a well-drained soil. It can occur mixed with small trees or shrubs in its natural range and thus generally tolerates partial shade. It is very hardy, tolerating extremes of temperature. It performs well in the hottest desert regions if given supplemental summer water. It also is very cold tolerant, perhaps more so than any other trunked yucca, tolerating temperatures down to at least −20°F (−29°C) with certain populations probably tolerating even colder temperatures.

SIMILAR OR RELATED SPECIES: The leaves of *Yucca baccata* are similar to those of *Y. schidigera* and *Y. torreyi*, two species with which it has been known to hybridize. The leaves of *Y. torreyi* generally are longer than those of *Y. baccata*, and those of *Y. schidigera* are broadened somewhat in the middle as opposed to the leaves of *Y. baccata* that gradually narrow towards the tip. The clustering stem habit with short, usually curving trunks, as well as the elongated flowers help to distinguish *Y. baccata* from similar species with filament-lined rigid leaves. *Yucca baccata* also is similar to *Y. arizonica* McKelvey, a very attractive plant that has heads of dense, very straight, and upright leaves borne on stems that can reach up to 8.2 ft. (2.5 m) tall. A shorter plant with similar leaves, reportedly a hybrid between *Y. baccata* and *Y. arizonica*, often is referred to as *Y. thornberi* McKelvey. *Yucca baccata* also is known to hybridize with *Y. elata* to produce a very attractive plant.

USES: The large fleshy fruits of *Yucca baccata* were an important food for the native peoples living within its natural range. The fruits were eaten raw or roasted and were often ground and made into small cakes used for winter food stock. The leaves and extracted fibers were used to make baskets, sandals, and mats. Soap was extracted from the plant's roots. Because of its wide range of growing conditions and extreme hardiness, *Y. baccata* is among the most widely used yuccas for ornamental plantings in the southwestern United States. It is planted in warm and relatively cold desert regions. Its leaning and branching trunks and clustering habit make it particularly useful in gardens of native plants or in transitional areas where more formal plantings mix with native vegetation. This species may be very sensitive to cold damp soils because, despite the plant's cold hardiness, some experiments with growing it in very humid climates such as the eastern United States have not met with success.

Yucca brevifolia Engelmann   PLATE 79

COMMON NAME: Joshua tree

SIZE: The largest of all native yuccas in the United States, *Yucca brevifolia* is a treelike species that reaches 30 ft. (9 m) tall, with extremely large individuals known to be 50 ft. (15 m) tall. An exceptionally large plant near Lancaster, California, was estimated to be nearly 80 ft. (24 m) tall. Older plants have a heavy trunk that can reach 5 ft. (1.5 m) wide; they have many branches so that the spread can be 30 ft. (9 m) wide. The branches often bend at right angles or downward in a complex pattern, giving the tree a very distinctive silhouette. *Yucca brevifolia* var. *jaegeriana* McKelvey generally has shorter trunks, 10–20 ft. (3–6 m) tall, and a dense branch pattern. *Yucca brevifolia* var *herbertii* Munz has strong underground rhizomes that produce aerial stems and eventually lead to dense clusters of single or slightly branched stems. The leaves of Y. *brevifolia* cling to the branches after they die, but very old trunks often are clean, exposing the wood that weathers into a dark brown color and often separating into a pattern of small plates.

LEAVES: The rigid leaves are 6–14 in. (15–36 cm) long and 0.5 in. (1.3 cm) wide. They are arranged tightly at the ends of the branches and range in color from gray-green to a light blue-green. They are sharp pointed and have minute teeth along the edge. Variety *jaegeriana* has shorter leaves, only 4 in. (10 cm) long.

BLOOM: The inflorescence is a nodding panicle 11.75–19.75 in. (29.5–50 cm) long with flowers arranged on it densely. The flowers are cream to greenish white in color, 1.5–2.75 in. (3.8–7 cm) long, tough, and leathery. They remain closed except for a small opening where the ends of the tepals come together. The flowers produce a distinct and slightly unpleasant odor.

DISTRIBUTION: *Yucca brevifolia* is the classic indicator species of the Mohave Desert. It occurs most abundantly in southeastern California but also is found in parts of southern Nevada, northwestern Arizona, and extreme southwestern Utah. It occurs on desert flats and slopes from 1500 to 6500 ft. (460–1950 m) in elevation. Ornamentally, it is used throughout its natural range as well as in the Sonoran and Chihuahuan desert areas. Because of its cold tolerance, this species can be used ornamentally at moderate elevations in southwestern United States, such as the Albuquerque, New Mexico, area.

PROPAGATION: Propagation is by seed or by stem tip cuttings; however, success rates for the latter method are often low.

CULTURAL REQUIREMENTS: *Yucca brevifolia* performs best in full sun in sandy or well-drained soils. Long cool, damp periods can be fatal to the plant, particularly if the soil is not well drained. This species is slow growing, but occasional deep waterings can help maintain best growth. It is fairly cold tolerant, being known to tolerate temperatures as low as 0°F (–18°C). Plantings in Denver suggest it may be even more cold tolerant, down to –10°F (–23°C).

SIMILAR OR RELATED SPECIES: A distinctive species, *Yucca brevifolia* is not easily confused with other yuccas. Its large size combined with the short light-colored leaves tends to separate it from all other tree yuccas. It is most similar in general appearance to the Mexican tree yuccas, such as *Y. decipiens* Trelease, *Y. filifera*, *Y. periculosa* Baker, and *Y. valida* T. Brandegee, but all these plants have dark green leaves. The only other large arborescent yucca with light-colored leaves is the rare *Y. jaliscensis* (Trelease) Trelease (synonym *Y. schottii* var. *jaliscensis* Trelease), which has longer leaves with smooth edges similar in nature to those of *Y. schottii*.

USES: *Yucca brevifolia* has had various uses. The wood was utilized to make high-quality paper in the early twentieth century; the paper was shipped as far away as England. In 1893 Messrs. Densmore, Means, and Fleming opened a factory in Los Angeles to cut *Y. brevifolia* wood into various products, such as book covers and veneer sheets for novelties. The wood's greatest use was for surgical splints during World War I. It had ideal properties for this purpose: it was lightweight but strong, and thin sheets could be cut with scissors. Because of its porous nature, it allowed excellent air circulation but held its strength even when wet. The plant's greatest use today is as an ornamental for desert gardens that seek a natural appearance. Its large dramatic form makes it an excellent low-care specimen plant. It also is very attractive in informal gardens composed of various native shrubs, cacti, and other succulents.

Yucca elata (Engelmann) Engelmann

PLATE 80; FIGURES 2-2, 2-3

SYNONYMS: *Yucca angustifolia* var. *radiosa* Engelmann, *Yucca angustifolia* var. *elata* Engelmann

COMMON NAME: Soaptree yucca

SIZE: *Yucca elata* is a variable, but often large species that can reach 30 ft. (9 m) tall under ideal conditions, but usually is 6–15 ft. (1.8–4.6 m) tall. Plants have one to ten trunks, which generally are 6–12 in. (15–30 cm) wide and which frequently branch once or twice near the top. Some populations are stemless.

LEAVES: The numerous leaves are arranged in a dense radial head. They are thin and flexible, up to 3 ft. (1 m) long and less than 0.25 inch (6 mm) wide, and a dull green in color. The smooth white margin is composed of compressed fibers, which are most noticeable as a dense filament mass at the base of the leaves. As a result, from a distance the head of leaves appears more gray than green. As the leaves die they remain attached, forming a thick mat along the trunk.

BLOOM: The inflorescence is a large open panicle 3–7 ft. (1–2.1 m) tall. It is held high above the head of leaves on a long stalk with up to 20 stalks on some plants, creating a spectacular sight in bloom. The fragrant, bell-shaped flowers are white to green-white. *Yucca elata* is the official state flower of New Mexico.

PROPAGATION: Propagation is by seed. Although multiple stems can arise from the base of the plant, these stems are difficult to remove and root. Transplanting of older plants is likewise difficult because this species has a large fleshy underground stem, often many feet deep in old plants, from which the roots arise. Injury to this stem, or removal of parts of it, usually results in the death of the transplanted yucca.

DISTRIBUTION: *Yucca elata* is found in the high deserts and desert grasslands of southwestern United States and northern Mexico. It occurs from southwestern Texas through the southern portions of New Mexico and Arizona at an elevation of 2000–5500 ft. (600–1650 m). This species is a common ornamental in the same area but is used in the deserts below its natural range as well.

CULTURAL REQUIREMENTS: *Yucca elata* requires a well-drained soil and full sun. It tolerates extreme heat, but should be given deep irrigation once every three weeks for established plants in the low desert. The species tolerates cold temperatures down to approximately –10°F (–23°C).

SIMILAR OR RELATED SPECIES: Especially when young, *Yucca elata* is difficult to distinguish from *Y. angustissima* Engelmann ex Trelease, *Y. glauca,* and other yuccas with grasslike heads of leaves. *Yucca elata,* however, is the only arborescent yucca with the combination of thin green leaves, numerous white filaments along the leaf margin, and a blooming stalk that rises far above the plant. This combination of characters distinguishes it from *Y. rostrata,* which lacks the white leaf margin filaments and has grayish blue leaves. *Yucca elata* hybridizes with *Y. baccata* in nature to produce an attractive plant.

USES: The roots and stems of *Yucca elata* are high in saponin and were used frequently by native peoples and European pioneers to make a frothy soap, hence the plant's common name. The species is important for its fiber that is used for baskets by native peoples, and for its leaves and stems that have been chopped for cattle feed in times of drought. Because of its great size, *Y. elata* often is used as a specimen or focal plant in gardens. In general, it looks best as part of a mixed planting with other desert native plants to create a natural desert look. It is an important ornamental in colder desert climates because it is among the most cold-tolerant arborescent yuccas.

Yucca elephantipes Regel   PLATE 81

SYNONYM: *Yucca guatemalensis* Baker

COMMON NAME: Giant yucca

SIZE: *Yucca elephantipes* is a large arborescent species with multiple stems that can reach up to 30 ft. (9 m) tall at maturity. As the plant ages, the base becomes very large and swollen. As many as 50 stems can develop.

LEAVES: The relatively large leaves are 2–3 in. (5–8) wide and up to 4 ft. (1.2 m) long. They are a dark rich green in color and have a slightly shiny or glossy surface. The leaf margin is smooth, and there is no terminal spine. The leaves are pliable and flat, with usually faint irregular ridges that run through the long direction of the leaf. The arrangement of the leaves in the head appears to vary in this species. In some individuals the head of leaves is relatively spherical, and in most individuals the youngest leaves are straight and radiate from the top of the stem while the oldest leaves are lax and hang down. In other individuals this characteristic is exaggerated and the leaves hang down along the stem, giving the plant a weeping appearance.

BLOOM: The inflorescence is a panicle with a short stalk, often primarily within the head of leaves. The small, bell-shaped creamy white flowers are numerous and are arranged densely on the panicles.

DISTRIBUTION: A tropical species that grows from the Veracruz coast of Mexico southward into Guatemala, *Yucca elephantipes* is distributed horticulturally in warm winter and tropical areas throughout the world. It has been planted as an ornamental along the Mediterranean coast since the late nineteenth century. In the United States it is most common in the relatively frost-free portions of central and southern Florida and southern California.

PROPAGATION: Propagation is by stem cuttings of any size.

CULTURAL REQUIREMENTS: Because of its tropical origins, *Yucca elephantipes* is cold tender. It is grown primarily in frost-free areas and tolerates temperatures only down to about 27°F (–3°C). Where frost is very light, it can be grown in protected areas, near a building or under large evergreen trees. This species should be planted in well-drained soil and given moderate watering and fertilizer. It can be grown in full sun, partial shade, or nearly full shade. Where the sun is intense, the leaves should receive some shade, particularly in the afternoon, to prevent sunburning.

SIMILAR OR RELATED SPECIES: *Yucca elephantipes* is most easily confused with *Y. gloriosa.* Its leaves are larger than those of *Y. gloriosa,* generally are darker green, and have a shiny or glossy surface, whereas those of *Y. gloriosa* tend to be lighter in color and not shiny or glossy. The flowers of *Y. elephantipes* are smaller and more numerous than those of *Y. gloriosa.*

USES: The flowers of *Yucca elephantipes* have been used as a food source by the native peoples of Guatemala. They have been sold in the market places and often are fried with eggs. This species has been used as an ornamental in Central America and Mexico as well as the Mediterranean coast, Florida and California in the United States, and in other nearly frost-free and tropical areas worldwide. It is an excellent focal plant to create dramatic sculptural displays in a courtyard, against a building, or near a pool. The plant also is excellent in mixed plantings with other large-leaved tropical plants, such as palms, cordylines, elephant ears, or bananas and their relatives. *Yucca elephantipes* lends a very exotic look to any planting into which it is incorporated. It is the yucca most commonly used as an indoor container plant because of its ability to tolerate low light conditions.

Yucca faxoniana Sargent   PLATE 82

SYNONYMS: *Yucca carnerosana* (Trelease) McKelvey, *Samuela faxoniana* Trelease

COMMON NAMES: Faxon yucca, Spanish dagger, Palma samandoca

SIZE: A large imposing plant, *Yucca faxoniana* usually is 6.5–19.5 ft. (2–6 m) tall, but exceptionally large plants can be 29.5 ft. (8.7 m) tall. Plants usually have a single trunk, but can have up to six trunks that are often of different heights. The trunks are wide, 1–1.5 ft. (0.3–0.5 m), and unbranched, or with a few branches near the top.

LEAVES: The dark yellow-green leaves are 2–4 ft. (0.6–1.2 m) long and 2–3 in. (5–8) wide. They are narrowed slightly at the base, being widest approximately three-fourths of the way up the leaf from the base. From this widest point the leaf narrows to a sharp, dark brown terminal spine. The leaf margin has a dark brown stripe from which thick, curling white filaments are produced. The rigid leaves are arranged in a very symmetrical head and, after dying, they remain attached and form a skirt along the length of the trunk.

BLOOM: The inflorescence is a panicle 3–4 ft. (1–1.2 m) tall with 25–40 branches. It usually is held completely above the leaves; otherwise only the lower one-fourth of the panicle is within the leaves with the remainder emerging above the leaves. The flowers are numerous, 2–3.5 in. (5–9 cm) long, and white to greenish white in color. They are unique in the genus. The outer three tepals are fused approximately one-fourth to one-half through their length into a tube. Plants with a tube at least 1 in. (2.5 cm) long have been referred by some authorities to *Yucca carnerosana*.

DISTRIBUTION: The natural distribution of *Yucca faxoniana* is northeastern Mexico from the states of Zacatecas and San Luis Potosí north to the U.S. border. This species also is found in western Texas west of the Pecos River. In horticulture it commonly is planted as an ornamental in western Texas as far north as Amarillo and in New Mexico as far north as Albuquerque. It is planted to a much lesser extent elsewhere in the southwestern United States.

PROPAGATION: Propagation is by seed.

CULTURAL REQUIREMENTS: *Yucca faxoniana* grows best in full sun, although it tolerates partial shade. Good drainage should be supplied. This species is very drought tolerant, but should be given supplemental summer watering approximately every three weeks in the driest and hottest deserts; otherwise it requires little supplemental irrigation. It tolerates extreme cold, down to approximately 0°F (–18°C).

SIMILAR OR RELATED SPECIES: *Yucca faxoniana* is similar in

appearance to several fleshy-fruited arborescent yuccas. It can be confused with *Y. torreyi*, but it has a more symmetrical head of leaves whereas the leaves of *Y. torreyi* are arranged haphazardly resulting in an unkempt appearance. *Yucca faxoniana* may also be confused with *Y. treculeana*, but the latter has very few or no leaf filaments. *Yucca faxoniana* has straight, rather thick trunks and branches, whereas *Y. torreyi* and *Y. treculeana* tend to have thinner, often leaning or curving trunks or branches.

USES: *Yucca faxoniana* has several traditional economic uses within its range in Mexico. The trunks have been used for palisade construction, and the leaves have been used as thatching for structures. Cattle have been fed the split-open trunks as well as the large flower stalks. Humans have consumed the flowers, often in scrambled eggs. Extracted fibers from the leaves are made into a wide variety of products, such as rope, twine, saddle blankets, mats, and rugs. As an ornamental plant *Y. faxoniana* is outstanding. Its large size, heavy thick trunk, and symmetrical head of long rigid leaves create an imposing appearance in the landscape. As a specimen plant it creates a dramatic statement, but it should be used with some caution so that it does not overwhelm other plantings. It is particularly useful in areas that receive regular frost during the winter because fewer arborescent yuccas are available for such climates.

Yucca filamentosa Linnaeus   PLATES 83, 84

SYNONYMS: *Yucca concava* Haworth, *Yucca smalliana* Fernald

COMMON NAMES: Adam's needle, Adam's thread

SIZE: *Yucca filamentosa* is a stemless species that can produce abundant offsets. The rosette is up to 4.25 ft. (1.3 m) wide, and a clump can spread to twice that size.

LEAVES: The green leaves often have a slight bluish tint, are approximately 1.5 ft. (0.5 m) long and 1 in. (2.5 cm) wide, and have a slightly spatulate shape. They are thin, flexible, and generally straight rather than recurving, particularly the newer leaves in the center of the head. The abundant curling marginal filaments give the plant its specific epithet. Many varieties and horticultural forms have been identified during the plant's long botanical and horticultural history. William Trelease in his 1902 work on yuccas identified several of these, some of which are listed below with other more modern horticultural selections. *Yucca filamentosa* 'Blue Sword' has blue-green leaves. *Yucca filamentosa* var. *bracteata* Engelmann is found along the coasts of South Carolina and Georgia. It has very long leaves in which the outer sets are recurved. *Yucca filamentosa* 'Bright Edge' has leaves with marginal stripes of a creamy yellow color. *Yucca filamentosa* 'Bright Eye' has leaves with a yellow central stripe. *Yucca filamentosa* 'Color Guard' has cream-colored leaves edged with green. *Yucca filamentosa* var. *concava* (Haworth) Baker, known as the spoon leaf yucca, has broad and stiff, very spatulate shaped leaves with a silvery sheen. The leaves often are tinged with red in winter. *Yucca filamentosa* 'Garland's Gold' has leaves with a vivid yellow central stripe. *Yucca filamentosa* var. *media* Carrière has erect and lanceolate leaves in which the outer sets are recurved distinctly. *Yucca filamentosa* var. *patens* Carrière has narrow very rigid leaves that give the plant a distinct spreading appearance. *Yucca filamentosa* f. *variegata* Carrière is the general name for forms with white or yellow leaf variegation.

BLOOM: The inflorescence is an elongated open panicle held well above the rosette of leaves. The flowering stalk and panicle can vary from 4 ft. (1.2 m) to as much as 15 ft. (4.6 m) long. The flowers are approximately 2 in. (5 cm) long, expanding to 2–3 in. (5–8 cm) wide. They are white to cream in color, sometimes tinged with pink or brown. The flowers of a named selection, 'Rosenglocke', have distinct pinkish tints.

DISTRIBUTION: *Yucca filamentosa* is found in the South Atlantic and Gulf coastal plain from Florida west to Mississippi and north to New Jersey. Horticulturally, this species has a much larger range, being grown over most of the United States including areas in the Northeast as far north as Maine and Vermont and over much of the southern half of the midwestern states. It also is commonly planted in Britain and Europe.

PROPAGATION: Propagation is by seed or by removal of the offsets.

CULTURAL REQUIREMENTS: *Yucca filamentosa* performs best with a moderately rich but well-drained or sandy soil. It can tolerate full sun or partial shade. It is among the most cold hardy yuccas, tolerating temperatures down to at least –20°F (–29°C).

SIMILAR OR RELATED SPECIES: The taxonomic status of *Yucca filamentosa* has been complicated and controversial for many years. Some authorities consider it and *Y. flaccida* one species. Some authorities recognize *Y. smalliana* as a separate species and as a part of this complex of closely related taxa. Naturally occurring hybridization, the large number of naturally occurring varieties, and the large number of horticultural selections have created confusion in the identification of these plants. Although the plants are very easy to confuse, some characteristics seem to be associated with each name. The leaves of *Y. filamentosa*, particularly those at the center of the head, are straight and rigid while those of *Y. flaccida* are flaccid and recurving. Furthermore, the marginal leaf filaments of *Y. filamentosa* tend to be thick and curled while those of *Y. flaccida* are fine and straight. The panicle of *Y. filamentosa* is held high above the head of leaves and is narrower than that of *Y. flaccida*, which is wider and is held only slightly above the head of leaves. *Yucca smalliana* occurs in the southeastern United States from South Carolina to Florida and Mississippi and has sometimes been called *Y. filamentosa* var. *smalliana* (Fernald) Ahles (synonym *Y. smalliana* Fernald). It is very similar to *Y. flaccida* (see below).

USES: *Yucca filamentosa* is among the oldest and most widespread yuccas in horticulture. Its use as an ornamental began in the sixteenth century in Europe where it appeared in some of the early collections of North American plants in British gardens. It was used in gardens of the colonial period in eastern North America as well. Its outstanding value in providing strong structural relief to perennial gardens and evergreen color to winter gardens has made it a very popular ornamental plant. Its many variegated selections add a bright touch to dark garden locations and provide additional contrast to the dark and rounded forms of many perennial plantings. *Yucca filamentosa* is a good container plant for sunny or partially shaded conditions.

Yucca filifera Chabaud   PLATE 85

COMMON NAMES: Palma china, Izote

SIZE: *Yucca filifera* is among the largest yuccas and is perhaps the best-known and most common Mexican tree yucca in cultivation. This highly branched tree can reach 30 ft. (9 m) tall with a trunk up to 5 ft. (1.5 m) wide. It is a spectacular sight when full grown. Several very large and old plants can be seen at the Huntington Botanical Garden in San Marino, California.

LEAVES: The sharp-pointed, rigid leaves are approximately 19.75 in. (50 cm) long and approximately 1.5 in. (3.8 cm) wide. They form spherical heads on the ends of the many branches. The leaves are an olive green color and bear numerous curled marginal filaments, although the amount of filaments is variable, with some individuals seeming to be relatively free of filaments while others are quite filiferous. The leaves end in a sharp terminal spine.

BLOOM: *Yucca filifera* has a very unusual blooming style that gives the plant a distinct look when it is in flower. The inflorescence, a dense panicle up to 5 ft. (1.5 m) long, is strongly pendulous, hanging nearly or completely straight down from the head of leaves. The flowers are creamy white and are 1.5–2.25 in. (3.8–5.7 cm) long.

DISTRIBUTION: A species of the Chihuahuan desert and semi-arid lands of northeastern Mexico, *Yucca filifera* is found in the states of Coahuila and Nuevo León south to the states of Hidalgo and Mexico.

PROPAGATION: Propagation is by removal of the offsets.

CULTURAL REQUIREMENTS: Like most yuccas from warm desert climates, *Yucca filifera* does well in a sunny location with well-drained soils. It prospers in cool dry Mediterranean climates. Large specimens have been grown not only in southern California but also along the French Riviera, where a large plant flowered in Antibes in the 1880s. This species also does well in the warm deserts of Arizona. Its cold tolerance is not well documented; however, it is known that temperatures as low as 25°F (–4°C) cause no problems and it is probable that this species can tolerate temperatures down to at least 20°F (–7°C). It has been known to die at 4°F (–16°C).

SIMILAR OR RELATED SPECIES: *Yucca filifera* can be confused with other arborescent yuccas, of which the most common in cultivation is the Joshua tree, *Y. brevifolia*. The Joshua tree, however, has gray to blue-gray leaves without marginal filaments and fine teeth as opposed the smooth but filament-edged olive green leaves of *Y. filifera*. Several Mexican tree yuccas are similar to *Y. filifera*, such as *Y. decipiens*, *Y. periculosa*, and *Y. valida*, but their inflorescences are erect within the head of leaves rather than pendant. *Yucca periculosa* has shorter leaves, only to 11.75 in. (29.5 cm), but is otherwise vegetatively very similar to *Y. filifera*. *Yucca valida* also has short leaves that are arranged as elongated heads of leaves rather than the spherical heads of *Y. filifera*. *Yucca valida* is relatively unbranched except near the top of the plant where stems have a few branches. *Yucca decipiens* probably is most like *Y. filifera*, but it is an even larger tree, up to 49 ft. (15 m) tall.

USES: Ornamentally, *Yucca filifera* is a spectacular specimen plant. Its large size, however, dominates the landscape, so it is best to use the plant in large landscapes where it has plenty of room to spread its tremendous branches. In warm winter climates where plenty of room is available, few plants are more exotic and dramatic than *Y. filifera*.

Yucca flaccida Haworth

SIZE: *Yucca flaccida* is a small stemless species that produces numerous offsets to form small clumps. Rosettes are 5 ft. (1.5 m) in diameter and 3 ft. (1 m) tall.

LEAVES: The thin, flexible leaves are lanceolate, approximately 2.5 ft. (0.8 m) long and 0.5–1.5 in. (1.3–3.8 cm) wide, and narrow towards the base and the tip. The outer leaves are always recurved, giving the plant a flaccid look. The leaf margin bears straight, fine, long filaments. William Trelease identified one variety and several horticultural forms with varying leaf characteristics in his 1902 work on yuccas. These are listed below with one modern horticultural selection. *Yucca flaccida* f. *exigua* (Baker) Trelease (synonym *Y. exigua* Baker) is similar to var. *glaucescens* but without marginal filaments. *Yucca flaccida* var. *glaucescens* (Haworth) Trelease (synonym *Y. glaucescens* Haworth) has leaves that are more glaucous than the type, broader, and more erect. *Yucca flaccida* 'Ivory' has soft flexible grayish green leaves with cream-colored variegation. *Yucca flaccida* f. *lineata* Trelease is a horticultural form in which the young leaves have slight yellow or white stripes that fade as the plant matures. *Yucca flaccida* f. *orchiodes* (Carrière) Trelease (synonym *Y. orchiodes* Carrière) has stiff, erect leaves without marginal filaments.

BLOOM: The inflorescence is 4–7 ft. (1.2–2.1 m) tall and held slightly above the leaves. The flowers are borne in open clusters and are creamy white and lightly fragrant, particularly in the evening.

DISTRIBUTION: *Yucca flaccida* is naturally distributed in the southern Appalachian Mountains from western North Carolina to northern Alabama. In the United States it can be planted in the lower midwestern states from Ohio to Iowa and in the northeastern states as far north as coastal Maine. It also is used in Britain and Europe as an ornamental plant.

PROPAGATION: Propagation is by seed or by removal of the offsets.

CULTURAL REQUIREMENTS: *Yucca flaccida* performs well in either full sun or partial shade. A moderately rich soil with good drainage is best, but this species can tolerate short periods of saturated soils. It also is known for its cold tolerance, being able to tolerate winter temperatures down to at least –20°F (–29°C).

SIMILAR OR RELATED SPECIES: The taxonomic status of *Yucca flaccida* has been complicated and controversial for many years. Some authorities consider it and *Y. filamentosa* one species. A third species, *Y. smalliana* Fernald, also is often considered part of this complex of closely related taxa. Naturally occurring hybridization, the large number of naturally occurring varieties, and the large number of horticultural selections have created confusion in the identification of these plants. Although the plants are very easy to confuse, some characteristics seem to be associated with each name. The leaves of *Y. flaccida* are flaccid and recurving throughout the entire head, while those of *Y. filamentosa* are flexible but stiff and straight, particularly the newer leaves at the center of the head. Leaf shape differs with the leaves of *Y. flaccida* being sharply narrowed at the base and tip, while those of *Y. filamentosa* are somewhat spatulate. The marginal leaf filaments of *Y. flaccida* are straight while those of *Y. filamentosa* are curled. The panicle of *Y. flaccida* tends to be broad and open and is held slightly above the leaves, while that of *Y. filamentosa* is narrower and held high above the head of leaves. *Yucca smalliana*, now a synonym of *Y. filamentosa*, is very similar to *Y. flaccida* except that its short 2 ft. (0.6 m) long leaves are more erect than those of *Y. flaccida*.

Uses: Unlike most other yuccas, *Yucca flaccida* is tolerant of cold and damp climates. Along with *Y. filamentosa* it is among the few plants in horticulture with a strong rosette form that can be used effectively in cold and damp conditions of much of the northern United States and northern Europe. It can be used to provide strong contrast to perennial border plantings or in other locations where a bold form may be wanted, such as against rock walls or in containers. The large attractive flowering stalks add to the plant's utility.

Yucca glauca Nuttall

PLATES 86, 87

Synonym: *Yucca angustifolia* Pursh
Common names: Soapweed yucca, Plains soapweed
Size: *Yucca glauca* is a mostly stemless species that can have short prostrate branching trunks, which produce heads of narrow stiff leaves. *Yucca glauca* var. *stricta* is more robust and can have a stem to 1 ft. (0.3 m) tall. Its inflorescence is larger than that of the type species and branched.
Leaves: The very narrow leaves, 0.25–0.5 in. (0.6–1.3 cm) wide, vary considerably in length from 8 to 36 in. (20–91 cm), even within the same rosette. They are arranged in a radial pattern, are gray-green in color, and are bordered by thin white

marginal stripes from which filaments are borne. The filaments are most abundant near the leaf base.

BLOOM: The flowers are interesting on the inflorescence and as individuals. The inflorescence is an elongated tight spike 3–6 ft. (1–1.8 m) tall. It is held slightly above the head of leaves. The often fragrant, pendulous, bell-shaped flowers are 1.5–2.5 in. (3.8–6 cm) long and generally greenish white. The flowers of Y. glauca var. rosea D. M. Andrews have dark pink or reddish buds with the outer tepals of the expanded flower maintaining a strong pink coloration.

DISTRIBUTION: Yucca glauca ranges from northwestern Texas, Oklahoma, and New Mexico north to Alberta and Saskatchewan in Canada. It probably has the largest geographical range and is the most cold hardy of any yucca. Because it tolerates extreme heat and cold, it can be grown in an extremely wide range of habitats. In fact, it can be grown virtually throughout North America where good drainage and a sunny exposure can be supplied. This species also has been cultivated in northern Europe—in England and the Netherlands.

PROPAGATION: Propagation is by seed or by removal of the offsets.

CULTURAL REQUIREMENTS: Yucca glauca requires full sun and a well-drained soil. Its tolerance of extreme heat and cold down to at least −35°F (−37°C) allow it to be planted in nearly any climate. If planted in extremely dry climates, additional summer water should be applied to keep the plant in good condition. Good drainage and full sun are necessary if the climate is humid.

SIMILAR OR RELATED SPECIES: Yucca glauca is similar in form and flower to several acaulescent, narrow-leaved species from Texas, New Mexico, Arizona, or Utah. The following species, some of which are often subsumed with each other, are similar in general appearance to Y. glauca: Y. angustissima, Y. baileyi Wooten & Standley, Y. constricta Buckley, Y. intermedia McKelvey, Y. kanabensis McKelvey, Y. navajoa J. M. Webber, and Y. standleyi McKelvey. None of these species is common in horticulture at this time, and it is probable that future taxonomic work will redefine their relationships. Yucca filamen-

tosa and *Y. flaccida*, two other acaulescent yuccas with leaves bearing leaf filaments, have leaves that are considerably wider than those of *Y. glauca* and lack the white marginal striping. *Yucca ×karlsruhensis* Graebner, a hybrid created in 1899 between *Y. glauca* and *Y. filamentosa*, has leaves approximately 0.75 in. (2 cm) wide and an inflorescence branched below the middle.

USES: Native Americans had a variety of uses for *Yucca glauca*. Fibers processed from the leaves were used for many purposes, such as making baskets, mats, sandals, belts, rope, and fishnets. The saponin-rich roots were used to make a cleansing lather. Recently *Y. glauca* has been used to create extracts for making skin care cosmetics. Because of its tolerance of extreme cold, this species is a useful ornamental in northerly climates where a strong rigid accent is needed and no other yuccas are hardy. The plant adds a very distinctive accent to native prairie gardens.

Yucca gloriosa Linnaeus   PLATE 88

COMMON NAMES: Moundlily yucca, Soft-tipped yucca

SIZE: *Yucca gloriosa* is a sometimes simple but usually few-branched arborescent species ranging from 6 to 15 ft. (1.8–4.6 m) tall. It usually has multiple stems arising from a base that is often swollen in old age. The stems may branch once or twice near the tops. The thin stems frequently are clear of dead leaves, giving old plants a very refined and exotic look.

LEAVES: The leaves generally are straight but can be reflexed in the middle or towards the ends in some forms of the plant. They also are thin and pliable, approximately 13–20 in. (33–51 cm) long and 1.5–2 in. (3.8–5 cm) wide. They are a light glaucous blue-green when they emerge, turning smoother, light green as they age. The leaf margin appears at first to be smooth, but very minute serrations can be detected by running a hand along the edges. The leaves terminate in an acute but spineless tip, hence the origin of one of the plant's common names. Variability in the leaves distinguishes several varieties and horticultural forms. William Trelease identified the following variations in his 1902 work entitled *The Yuccae*. One group, with leaves spreading and rigid, includes *Yucca gloriosa* f. *mediopicta* Carrière (synonym *Y. gloriosa* f. *medio-striata* Planchon), with white median variegation; *Y. gloriosa* f. *minor* Carrière, a dwarf garden form with smaller leaves; and *Y. gloriosa* f. *obliqua* Haworth, with leaves twisted to one side and more glaucous than those of the type. A second group, with leaves conspicuously folded towards the end, very concave but not recurved, includes *Y. gloriosa* f. *maculata* Carrière, with long dark green leaves, persistent small marginal teeth, and red-tinged flowers for which it was named (the red tinge has a mottled appearance); *Y. gloriosa* var. *plicata* Carrière, with leaves persistently glaucous, short, and broad; *Y. gloriosa* f. *superba* (Haworth) Baker (synonym *Y. superba* Haworth), a tall form up to 9.75 ft. (2.9 m) with leaves greener than those of the type; *Y.* ×*carrierei* Hort., with olive green leaves and a slightly pointed leaf tip; *Y.* ×*deleuii* Hort., a hybrid with purplish leaves; and *Y.* ×*sulcata* Hort., with leaves that are greener than those of the type and very broad. A third group, with outer leaves recurved, includes *Y. gloriosa* f. *longifolia* Carrière, which is similar to f. *nobilis* but with narrower leaves; *Y. gloriosa* f. *nobilis* Carrière, with persistently glaucous leaves (probably a hybrid with *Y. recurvifolia*); and *Y. gloriosa* var. *robusta* Carrière, which is similar to *Y. recurvifolia* and which has leaves that are transiently glaucous and stiffly recurved.

BLOOM: The inflorescence is a narrow but showy panicle on a short stalk 2–4 ft. (0.6–1.2 m) long. The panicle is set partially within the head of leaves. The white flowers are 1.5–2 in. (3.8–5 cm) long and occasionally are tinged with purple or red. Unlike most yuccas, *Yucca gloriosa* is not a spring bloomer, but blooms in the mid to late summer and sometimes into the fall.

DISTRIBUTION: *Yucca gloriosa* has a limited natural distribution on dunes of sea islands and along the coast from Louisiana to Florida and north to South Carolina. Within its natural habitat, it has to tolerate warm and dry conditions at times, as well as humid and moist. This adaptability and outstanding ornamental characteristics have made this species one of the most popular and widespread yuccas in cultivation worldwide.

It seems to be grown nearly everywhere that winter temperatures are mild. In the United States it is common in humid subtropical parts of Florida and protected areas along the northern
coast of the Gulf of Mexico as well as the deserts of Arizona. In
California it is extremely widespread, being planted by the
thousands throughout much of the state. It also is common in
other Mediterranean climates and warm winter climates
throughout the world.

PROPAGATION: Propagation is by seed, by removal of the offsets, or by stem cuttings.

CULTURAL REQUIREMENTS: Throughout most of its ornamental range *Yucca gloriosa* performs best in full sun with good
soil drainage. It, however, can tolerate partial shade and occasionally saturated soils. In extremely hot and dry climates such
as the desert regions of Arizona, it is best if it receives some
shade during the afternoon. Extreme sun exposure in these
climates can lead to yellowing and sunburning of leaves. Supplemental water during the summer months is important to
maintain the best condition in these climates. In much of
Florida and California this species is nearly carefree. *Yucca
gloriosa*, however, is relatively tender to cold. Temperatures
below approximately 22°F (–6°C) can cause leaf damage, those
below approximately 20°F (–7°C) can cause stem damage, and
as temperatures decline towards 15°F (–9°C) this species will be
killed.

SIMILAR OR RELATED SPECIES: *Yucca gloriosa* can often be
confused with two other species, *Y. aloifolia* and *Y. elephantipes*. The sharp-pointed terminal spine of *Y. aloifolia* is the
most reliable characteristic distinguishing that species from *Y.
gloriosa. Yucca aloifolia* also generally has narrower, rigid
sharp-toothed leaves, whereas the leaves of *Y. gloriosa* generally are wider, and often lax and pliable. Both species have several horticultural forms with similar or even overlapping characteristics, and no doubt hybrids exist between the two species.
Yucca elephantipes differs from *Y. gloriosa* by having larger
leaves, up to 4 ft. (1.2 m) long, which are dark green, glossy or
shinny. Often the head of leaves on *Y. elephantipes* tends to be
lax, sometimes with most leaves hanging from the top of the

stem and with only a few erect leaves. *Yucca elephantipes* also is a larger plant at maturity, to 30 ft. (9 m) tall, and has a larger head of flowers than *Y. gloriosa.*

USES: An outstanding ornamental, *Yucca gloriosa* excels where an exotic, tropical look is desired. As a focal point planted in a courtyard or against walls and buildings the plant lends a dramatic touch to the garden. Planting in such intimate places is aided by the spineless nature of this species. As a multistemmed plant it often is seen with the stems cleaned of any dead leaves. This treatment turns *Y. gloriosa* into a very sculptural form. It often is planted with other large-leaved or strong-formed tropical plants.

Yucca grandiflora Gentry

COMMON NAME: Sahuiliqui

SIZE: *Yucca grandiflora* is an arborescent species 13–20 ft. (4–6 m) tall. It has a few branches sometimes at the base and often near the top.

LEAVES: The thick, dark green leaves are 2.25–3.25 ft. (0.7–1 m) long with some individuals having leaves up to 4.5 ft. (1.4 m) long. The leaves are widest near the middle of the blade, being approximately 1.5 in. (3.8 cm) wide, and slightly narrowed at the base. They terminate in a stout, dark brown spine. The margin is lined with a thin brown inner stripe and a wider cream-colored outer stripe from which a few thin filaments originate as the plant ages. The leaves are smooth particularly on the upper surface and have a regular and refined appearance.

BLOOM: The inflorescence is a panicle 2.25–3.25 ft. (0.7–1 m) long and is held just above the leaves. It is irregular and emerges either directly atop the head of leaves or leaning as much as 90 degrees toward one side. The large creamy white flowers are 2.5–3.5 in. (6–9 cm) long.

DISTRIBUTION: *Yucca grandiflora* is found in the mountains and foothills of the Mexican state of Sonora with perhaps small populations in the state of Chihuahua. It has rather limited natural distribution and is not widespread or common in its native habitat. It rarely is seen in cultivation.

PROPAGATION: Propagation is by seed or by removal of the occasional basal offsets.

CULTURAL REQUIREMENTS: *Yucca grandiflora* is relatively new to horticulture, and its cultural requirements are not well known. It seems to perform well in full sun and well-drained soil in a variety of climates including the cool Mediterranean climate of southern California and the hot inland deserts near Phoenix, Arizona. Its cold tolerance is not well known, but it probably is safe to assume that this species can tolerate at least light freezes down to 25°F (−4°C) and perhaps as low as 20°F (−7°C).

SIMILAR OR RELATED SPECIES: *Yucca grandiflora* is most similar in appearance to *Y. torreyi* and *Y. treculeana*. *Yucca torreyi* has a rather disheveled arrangement of leaves and abundant thick curly marginal filaments, while the leaves of *Y. grandiflora* are arranged in regular heads and tend to have no or few marginal filaments, which are thin and straight. When not in flower *Y. grandiflora* may be difficult to distinguish from *Y. treculeana*; however, the latter tends to be single-trunked while the former often puts out a few basal suckers. The leaf surface of *Y. grandiflora* is smoother than that of *Y. treculeana*, which is rough to the touch. *Yucca treculeana* is free of marginal leaf filaments while *Y. grandiflora* can have some thin, straight filaments, particularly on the older leaves. When in bloom the plants are very different: *Y. grandiflora* has large flowers and irregular panicles while *Y. treculeana* has a regular, elongated panicle consisting of many small flowers.

USES: *Yucca grandiflora* has large fruits that can be up to 8 in. (20 cm) long by 2 in. (5 cm) wide and weigh up to 2 lbs. (ca. 1 kg). When ripe the sweet fruits have been consumed by Mexicans living in the area where this species is distributed naturally. It is reported that roasting the fruit enhances its flavor. As an ornamental plant *Y. grandiflora* makes an arresting specimen with its large size and refined appearance. Since it is relatively new in horticulture, the distribution of this species as an ornamental is not well documented. It should do well in all arid and semi-arid climates where winters are relatively mild. Supplemental summer water should help its appearance in the hottest and driest climates.

Yucca harrimaniae Trelease

COMMON NAME: Harriman's yucca

SIZE: *Yucca harrimaniae* is a short species, as small as 5 in. (13 cm) tall, but can be up to 22 in. (57 cm). Rosettes are stemless, but occasionally with short stems, and are 8–36 in. (20–91 cm) in diameter. The species occurs as a single plant or in clumps of rosettes.

LEAVES: The leaves are highly variable, ranging from 4 to 18 in. (10–46 cm) long and from 0.5 to 1.5 in. (1.3–3.8 cm) wide. They range in color from yellow to blue-green, and are rigid and thin but somewhat flexible. They have a brown marginal stripe from which appear white filaments.

BLOOM: The inflorescence is a raceme 1–3 ft. (0.3–1 m) long. The flowers are greenish white with a green style and 2–2.5 in. (5–6 cm) wide.

DISTRIBUTION: A species of the high plateaus and mountains of the southwestern United States, *Yucca harrimaniae* is found in northern Arizona and New Mexico and southern Utah and Colorado, generally at an elevation of 7500–8500 ft. (2250–2550 m). It is a useful ornamental in Colorado and other Rocky Mountain states where few other yuccas can survive the cold winters.

PROPAGATION: Propagation is by seed or by removal of the offsets.

CULTURAL REQUIREMENTS: *Yucca harrimaniae* requires full sun and a well-drained soil for best performance. It is among the most cold hardy yuccas, being able to tolerate temperatures down to at least –20°F (–29°C). Because it tolerates cold, sun, and drought, it can be used in plantings where little care can be provided.

SIMILAR OR RELATED SPECIES: *Yucca harrimaniae* is somewhat similar in appearance to several stemless yuccas of the high plains and mountain foothills in the southwestern United States. Few of these species, however, are in horticulture, and it would be unusual to encounter most of them except in their native habitat. One similar species found in horticulture is *Y. glauca*. The leaves of *Y. harrimaniae* are 0.5 in. (1.3 cm) wide and lined with a tan or brown stripe, while leaves of Y. *glauca* are less than 0.5 in. (1.3 cm) wide and are lined with white stripes.

UsES: *Yucca harrimaniae* is an excellent small yucca for landscapes where winter temperatures stay below freezing for long periods of time. Its strong rosette form combines well with small shrubs and perennial plants, particularly in rock gardens or in dry gardens. The rosette form gives a distinctive look to gardens of introduced and native species in climates where the rosette shape is not commonly seen.

Yucca pallida McKelvey   PLATE 89

Size: *Yucca pallida* is an acaulescent species that forms 7.5–20 in. (19–51 cm) tall rosettes that are 12–32 in. (30–81 cm) in diameter. The plant forms open clumps of widely separated heads, which have been known to contain up to 30 rosettes, although usually they have fewer.

LEAVES: The pale blue-gray to sage green leaves are 6–16 in. (15–40 cm) long and 0.75–1.25 in. (2–3.2 cm) wide, with the widest part near the midpoint. The leaves are lined with minute teeth and a thin yellow to brown marginal stripe. They terminate in a blunt yellow to brown spine. The leaves generally are flattened but can have the edges rolled slightly inward.

BLOOM: The inflorescence is a panicle 3–7.5 ft. (1–2.3 m) long with up to 100 bell-shaped pendant flowers. The flowers are 2–2.7 in. (5–7 cm) long and pale green to cream colored with a lighter colored margin.

DISTRIBUTION: *Yucca pallida* occurs in a rather limited distribution on the blackland prairies of northern and central Texas from the Dallas–Ft. Worth area south to the Waco and Killeen area. It is not very common in horticulture, but its use appears to be increasing in its natural range and in areas in the Southwest suitable for its growing.

PROPAGATION: Propagation is by seed or by removal of the offsets.

CULTURAL REQUIREMENTS: *Yucca pallida* tolerates full sun or partial shade and well-drained or heavy clayey soils. It has moderate cold tolerance, down to at least 0°F (–18°C).

SIMILAR OR RELATED SPECIES: *Yucca pallida* is similar to *Y. rupicola* with which it no doubt hybridizes. Intermediate forms between the two species appear in nature and in horticulture. *Yucca pallida*, however, has flattened leaves or leaves with up-turned edges but lacks the twisted and curved nature of the leaves of *Y. rupicola*. *Yucca pallida* also has much lighter colored leaves than the bright olive green leaves of *Y. rupicola*. *Yucca pallida* might be confused with several other acaulescent yuccas, such as *Y. filamentosa* or *Y. flaccida*, but the two latter have dark green leaves with marginal filaments.

USES: *Yucca pallida* is a very attractive small-leaved yucca that is excellent for small or confined spaces in either full sun or partial shade. It is small enough to fit comfortably into a perennial or rock garden planting, and its light-colored leaves offer excellent contrast with darker colored perennial plantings. Its moderate cold tolerance and its tolerance of heavier soils should allow it to be grown in the southeastern United States in well-drained areas. Because of the plant's outstanding ornamental characteristics, it should continue to gain in popularity over time.

Yucca recurvifolia Salisbury   PLATE 90; FIGURES 2-2, 4-6

SYNONYMS: *Yucca gloriosa* var. *recurvifolia* Engelmann, *Yucca gloriosa* var. *mollis* Carrière, *Yucca recurva* Haworth, *Yucca pendula* Groenland

SIZE: *Yucca recurvifolia* is a shrubby plant that can eventually become 6–10 ft. (1.8–3 m) tall and can spread by developing multiple trunks from basal offsets. The trunks are often curved or bent at strong angles, giving the plant a haphazard look, and are unbranched or with one or two branches.

LEAVES: The dark blue-green leaves are 2–3 ft. (0.6–1 m) long and 2 in. (5 cm) wide with a lax and recurved habit that gives this species its scientific name. This habit is sometimes strong enough that it results in the sharp-tipped leaves pointing downward, particularly the outer leaves. The leaves are flat, have no marginal filaments, and have slight but distinctive raised ridges running lengthwise. The leaf margin has narrow yellow or

261

brown stripes. This species has a long horticultural history, and several forms with varying leaf characteristics have been selected. William Trelease reported the following forms in his 1902 work entitled *The Yuccae: Yucca recurvifolia* f. *elegans* Trelease, with a median reddish stripe; *Y. recurvifolia* f. *marginata* (Carrière) Trelease (synonym *Y. gloriosa* f. *marginata* Carrière), with yellow marginal stripes; *Y. recurvifolia* f. *rufocincta* Baker, a low-growing form with a more pronounced brown leaf margin; *Y. recurvifolia* f. *variegata* (Carrière) Trelease (synonym *Y. pendula* f. *variegata* Carrière), with soft yellow median variegation; *Y.* ×*andreana* Hort., with dark green broad leaves up to 3 in. (8 cm) wide; and *Y.* ×*dracaenoides* Hort., with short broad leaves and pale or purplish stripes.

BLOOM: The inflorescence is a large, loose, open panicle 3–5 ft. (1–1.5 m) tall. The flowers are cream colored. When clumps are large, the collections of large blooming stalks make a spectacular sight. A horticultural form, f. *tristis*, has purplish brown to black bracts on the flower stalks.

DISTRIBUTION: A species of dunes and sandy soils of the South Atlantic and Gulf coastal plain, *Yucca recurvifolia* occurs in Georgia, Mississippi, and Louisiana. Ornamentally, it is among the most popular and widespread yuccas. Its tolerance of heat and cold as well as dry and temporarily wet conditions allows it to grow in desert gardens in the American Southwest and in sunny and well-drained lawns in the Southeast. This species also is grown in Europe and other areas where winter temperatures stay generally above 10–15°F (–12 to –9°C).

PROPAGATION: Propagation is by seed or by removal of the offsets.

CULTURAL REQUIREMENTS: *Yucca recurvifolia* is an easy plant to grow and undoubtedly is the most common yucca in horticulture in North America. It is very hardy to heat and cold and can be grown over a large geographic area. It tolerates full sun and partial shade as well as dry and occasionally moist soils. If planted near or in lawns, care should be taken so that water does not pond and stand near the base of the plant.

SIMILAR OR RELATED SPECIES: *Yucca recurvifolia* is a fairly distinct species. Its shrubby habit and broad drooping leaves

Figure 4-6. Flowers, *Yucca recurvifolia*

make it difficult to confuse with other species. It can sometimes be confused with *Y. gloriosa,* but the sharp-pointed leaf tip and ridged leaves of *Y. recurvifolia* are lacking in *Y. gloriosa.*

USES: *Yucca recurvifolia* is among the most ornamentally versatile yuccas. Its tolerance of heat, cold, moist soils, drought, sun, and partial shade allows it to grow in various climates and situations. Its moderate size also allows it to be used in various planting locations in which smaller or larger yuccas would be difficult. Mixed shrub borders or borders of tall herbaceous perennials can often be enhanced by the strong contrast offered by *Y. recurvifolia.* The plant also works well as an accent in small courtyards, against stone fences, near wide entryways, and in large pots. Its broad and recurving leaves can lend an exotic almost tropical touch to gardens with regular, but not extremely cold, freezing weather.

Yucca rigida (Engelmann) Trelease   PLATE 91

SYNONYM: *Yucca rupicola* var. *rigida* Engelmann
COMMON NAME: Blue yucca
SIZE: *Yucca rigida* is a medium-sized species ultimately reaching 12–15 ft. (3.7–4.6 m) tall. It generally is single-trunked but occasionally has multiple stems. The tops of the stems usually have several branches.

LEAVES: The beautiful light blue-gray leaves give this species its common name and make it one of the most attractive yuccas. Leaf color varies, with some individuals having leaves that are almost a pale blue in color. The rigid leaves are 2–3 ft. (0.6–1 m) long and 1 in. (2.5 cm) wide and end in a stiff dark brown spine. They are lined with an attractive yellow margin and very tiny teeth, and appear in a regular arrangement forming a half sphere on top of the stems. Numerous dead leaves usually remain attached to the stem.

BLOOM: The inflorescence is a panicle 2 ft. (0.6 m) tall and is at least partially hidden by the leaves. The flowers are creamy white and 1.5–2.5 in. (3.8–6 cm) long.

DISTRIBUTION: *Yucca rigida* is found only in northern Mexico where it grows on rocky hillsides in the states of Chihuahua, Coahuila, Durango, and Zacatecas. Because of its very attractive appearance, it is planted as an ornamental over much of the southwestern United States where temperatures do not stay below freezing for long periods.

PROPAGATION: Propagation is by seed.

CULTURAL REQUIREMENTS: *Yucca rigida* is best grown in full sun, but like most yuccas can also be grown in partial shade. It should be planted in a well-drained soil to prevent root rot in winter. It is very drought tolerant once established, requiring only occasional supplemental water in the most hot and arid climates. It also is relatively cold tolerant and can survive temperatures of approximately 5–10°F (–15 to –12°C).

SIMILAR OR RELATED SPECIES: *Yucca rigida* is most easily confused with *Y. rostrata*, which also has leaves with a bluish cast. The leaves of *Y. rostrata*, however, are narrower, more abundant, and often have a slight twist or are reflexed slightly towards the end; they are arranged in nearly complete spherical heads, whereas the leaf heads of *Y. rigida* generally are only partially spherical. In flower the panicles of *Y. rigida* are at least partially within the leaves whereas the panicles of *Y. rostrata* are held on a stalk above the leaves. Some plants in the nursery trade appear to be hybrids between the two species.

USES: *Yucca rigida* is among the most attractive yuccas. It works well in natural and formal gardens and can be used in a variety of situations The very light bluish colored leaves provide a strong contrast to almost any other plants in the vicinity. *Yucca rigida* is a spectacular specimen plant in courtyards and near pools. If planted in partial shade, the plant's light bluish leaves seem to almost glow in the shadows. Because of its drought and cold tolerance, *Y. rigida* is an excellent ornamental plant for much of the desert regions of the southwestern United States.

Yucca rostrata Engelmann   PLATES 92, 93; FIGURE 2-4

COMMON NAME: Beaked yucca

SIZE: *Yucca rostrata* is a single-trunked species, 6–15 ft. (1.8–4.6 m) tall, often with one but sometimes with several heads of leaves. Very similar plants, which often are referred to as *Y. thompsoniana* Trelease, generally are smaller, 4–7.5 ft. (1.2–2.3 m) tall, and have several branches. These plants frequently are subsumed within *Y. rostrata*, but in many publications they remain as separate species. The plant's common named is derived from the distinctive beaklike appendages on the dried fruit.

LEAVES: The numerous leaves form nearly hemispherical heads and are narrow, approximately 1.25–2 ft. (0.4–0.6 m) long but only 0.5 in. (1.3 cm) wide. In the plants often referred to as *Y. thompsoniana* the leaves are shorter, only 9–18 in. (23–46 cm) long. The leaves of *Y. rostrata* are a light bluish green to bluish gray frequently with an attractive yellow marginal stripe. The leaves often have a slight twist or bend to them.

BLOOM: The inflorescence is a panicle 2 ft. (0.6 m) long. It usually is raised completely above the leaves. The flowers are bright white in color.

DISTRIBUTION: *Yucca rostrata* is found in northern Mexico in the states of Chihuahua and Coahuila and in the United States in Brewster County in western Texas. The plants referred to as *Y. thompsoniana* grow north of *Y. rostrata* in western Texas. As an ornamental plant *Y. rostrata* is planted in limited numbers throughout the southwestern United States. The plants referred to as *Y. thompsoniana* are popular ornamentals throughout much of the western half of Texas as well as into Oklahoma.

PROPAGATION: Propagation is by seed.

CULTURAL REQUIREMENTS: *Yucca rostrata* grows best in full sun in well-drained soils, but tolerates light or partial shade. It is very drought tolerant once it is established, needing only supplemental summer water in the most hot and dry climates. It is moderately cold tolerant, being able to withstand temperatures down to 5–10°F (–12 to –15°C). Plants referred to as *Y. thompsoniana* are likely to be even more cold tolerant, probably to –10°F (–23°C).

SIMILAR OR RELATED SPECIES: *Yucca rostrata* is most similar to *Y. rigida*, another arborescent yucca of similar stature with leaves having a bluish cast. *Yucca rostrata* has narrower and more numerous leaves than Y. *rigida*; they often are slightly twisted or drooping and are arranged in a dense hemispherical head. The leaves of Y. *rigida* are rigid and straight. When in bloom, the panicle of Y. *rostrata* usually is borne above the leaves while in Y. *rigida* it is hidden partially by the leaves.

USES: *Yucca rostrata* is a very attractive ornamental for either formal or natural plantings. The dense hemispherical head of leaves gives it a refined appearance when used as a specimen or focal plant for ornamental plantings. Its drought and cold tolerance allow it to be planted throughout much of the southwestern United States where it is a prized ornamental. Plants referred to as Y. *thompsoniana* also are popular and have been planted extensively throughout the south central United States in drought-tolerant gardens.

Yucca rupicola Scheele

SYNONYM: *Yucca tortifolia* Lindley ex Engelmann

COMMON NAME: Twisted leaf yucca

SIZE: *Yucca rupicola* is a relatively small, stemless species 10–30 in. (25–76 cm) tall, and 1.25–4 ft. (0.4–1.2 m) in diameter. Plants develop single rosettes or small open clumps of up to 15 rosettes with distinctive twisting, arching leaves.

LEAVES: The bright olive green leaves are 8–24 in. (20–61 cm) long and 0.5–2 in. (1.3–5 cm). wide. They are edged with minute teeth and a thin red, orange, or yellow marginal stripe. The most characteristic aspect of the leaves, and the one that gives the species its common name, are the distinctive twists and curves. The leaves end in a short, blunt yellow-brown terminal spine.

BLOOM: The inflorescence is an open, sparsely branched panicle that generally is 1.5–5 ft. (0.5–1.5 m) tall, but can be as much as 9 ft. (2.7 m) tall. The white to green-white attractive bell-shaped flowers are 2–3.25 in. (5–8.5 cm) long and pendant.

DISTRIBUTION: *Yucca rupicola* has a fairly restricted natural distribution in central Texas where it occurs on the Edwards Plateau west of Austin.

PROPAGATION: Propagation is by seed or by removal of the offsets.

CULTURAL REQUIREMENTS: *Yucca rupicola* tolerates a variety of growing conditions from full sun to moderately shaded areas, where soil drainage is good. It has a cold tolerance to approximately 0°F (−18°C) and perhaps lower.

SIMILAR OR RELATED SPECIES: The twisted and curved leaves of *Yucca rupicola* help distinguish it from other stemless yuccas. It bears some similarity to *Y. pallida* to which it probably is related closely, but the latter has flattened gray-green to blue-green leaves with a margin that sometimes is rolled inward, although the leaf itself is not twisted. Hybrids between the two species, which are sometimes seen in nature and in horticulture, can result in gray-blue twisted-leaved plants. *Yucca rupicola* might also be confused with *Y. filamentosa*, another common acaulescent species. *Yucca filamentosa* tends to have flat, dark green leaves with marginal filaments, while *Y. rupicola* has bright olive green strongly twisted leaves that lack filaments.

USES: *Yucca rupicola* is an attractive ornamental yucca for small spaces. Its tolerance of sun and shade allows it to be used in various conditions including underneath trees and in sunny borders of dryland perennials. Its attractive, pendant, bell-shaped flowers create a dramatic sight, especially for slightly shaded areas. *Yucca rupicola* is used as an ornamental in its natural range, but has considerable potential over larger areas. In desert areas of the southwestern United States, supplemental summer water is recommended. It could probably be used in well-drained sunny areas in the southeastern United States or other humid areas wherever winter temperatures are not too extreme.

Yucca schidigera Roezl ex Ortgies   PLATE 94

SYNONYMS: *Yucca californica* Nuttall ex Baker, *Yucca mohavensis* Sargent

COMMON NAME: Mohave yucca

SIZE: *Yucca schidigera* is an arborescent species, 3.25–16.5 ft. (1–5 m) tall, which occurs as a single trunk or as clustered multiple trunks. The trunks sometimes are branched near the top into a few branches.

LEAVES: The rigid leaves generally are yellow-green, but

blue-green forms are known. They range from 1 to 4.25 ft. (0.3–1.3 m) long but usually are around 2 ft. (0.6 m). They are 0.5–1.5 in. (1.3–3.8 cm) wide with the widest part at the midpoint. The leaves end in a sharp terminal spine, and the leaf margin is lined with abundant curled, white filaments.

BLOOM: The inflorescence is a dense, nearly rounded panicle that usually is entirely within the leaves or only up to half the panicle is raised above the leaves. The white or creamy flowers are often tinged with lavender or purple. They are 1.25–2 in. (3.2–5 cm) long and 0.5–0.75 in. (1.3–2 cm) wide and are completely or nearly sessile on the branches.

DISTRIBUTION: *Yucca schidigera* occurs primarily in the Mohave Desert in southern Nevada and northwestern Arizona into southern California. It also ranges into northern Baja California. It is used as an ornamental within the same area as its natural distribution and sparingly in desert areas to the east.

PROPAGATION: Propagation is by seed.

CULTURAL REQUIREMENTS: *Yucca schidigera* requires full sun with a well-drained soil. It is extremely drought tolerant, needing water only intermittently in the summer in the most arid areas. It also is relatively cold hardy, down to approximately 0°F (–18°C).

SIMILAR OR RELATED SPECIES: *Yucca schidigera* is similar to several other fleshy fruited yuccas. It differs from *Y. faxoniana* by having thinner trunks, generally shorter leaves, and sessile flowers that lack the distinctive floral tube found in *Y. faxoniana*. It differs from *Y. treculeana* primarily by its abundant curled filaments that are lacking in *Y. treculeana*. *Yucca schidigera* also is similar to *Y. torreyi*, but has shorter leaves, and smaller flowers that are sessile or nearly so, as opposed to the stalked flowers of *Y. torreyi*.

USES: *Yucca schidigera* was used by native peoples as a fiber source for making ropes and coarsely woven blankets. The small fleshy fruits were eaten raw or roasted, and the roots were used to produce a soap. Ornamentally, *Y. schidigera* is an excellent plant for low-maintenance desert gardens. It blends well with native shrubs and is relatively carefree in even the driest gardens.

Yucca schottii Engelmann   PLATE 95

COMMON NAME: Mountain yucca

SIZE: *Yucca schottii* is a medium-sized species, 6–20 ft. (1.8–6 m) tall, often with a single trunk that has a few simple branches. The dark brown trunk usually is 8–12 in. (20–30 cm) wide and may be clear of dead leaves.

LEAVES: The leaves are blue-green to gray-green in color, smooth to the touch, and slightly shiny. They are 1.5–3 ft. (0.5–1 m) long and 1–2.5 in. (2.5–6 cm) wide and usually are straight and rigid but can be curved slightly. They are concave in cross section and are lined with an attractive thin brown stripe. They end in a sharp light brown terminal spine.

BLOOM: The inflorescence is a nodding panicle 1–2.75 ft. (0.3–0.9 m) long. It is held at least partially above the leaves. The white, nearly spherical cup-shaped flowers are 1–2 in. (2.5–5 cm) long.

DISTRIBUTION: *Yucca schottii*, true to its common name, is a species of the foothills and mountains. It occurs in southeastern Arizona, southwestern New Mexico, and northern Mexico from 4000 to 7000 ft. (1200–2100 m) in elevation. It occurs in open, sunny, grassy areas and in the relatively deep shade of oaks and pines in mountain forests. It is an ornamental in its natural range and in the surrounding low desert.

PROPAGATION: Propagation is by seed.

CULTURAL REQUIREMENTS: *Yucca schottii* tolerates a wide array of growing conditions as long as none are too extreme. It tolerates full sun or partial shade, but if planted in full sun in extremely hot and dry areas it should be given supplemental water particularly in the summer. It tolerates cold, probably down to at least −10°F (−23°C). This species probably has more tolerance to moist shaded soils and dampness than most yuccas that occur in the southwestern United States. It has been experimentally grown with some success in North Carolina and coastal British Columbia.

SIMILAR OR RELATED SPECIES: *Yucca schottii* is similar to *Y. rigida* and *Y. rostrata*, but its thick concave leaves, smooth and shiny leaf surface, and thin brown marginal stripes help distinguish it from those species. A related species, *Y. jaliscensis*, is a much larger, branched tree yucca from the Mexican state of Jalisco. It has sometimes been referred to as *Y. schottii* var. *jaliscensis*. The leaves are very similar in appearance to those of *Y. schottii*.

USES: *Yucca schottii* is an excellent yucca for shaded areas throughout its natural range and into the surrounding low desert. Because of its greater tolerance of cold and damp conditions, it should be planted more in the southeastern Untied States and in parts of Europe. Its smooth light-colored leaves give the plant a clean refined look that allows it to be planted in either naturalistic plantings or more formal plantings where a moderate-sized focal plant is needed.

Yucca torreyi Shafer   PLATE 96

SYNONYMS: *Yucca baccata* var. *macrocarpa* Torrey, *Yucca macrocarpa* Coville ex Merriam, *Yucca crassifolia* Engelmann, *Yucca torreyi* f. *parviflora* McKelvey

COMMON NAMES: Torrey yucca, Spanish dagger

SIZE: *Yucca torreyi* is an arborescent species that ranges from 3 to 24 ft. (1–7.3 m) tall. It generally has one trunk but can have many. Very old plants can have several branches that diverge at sharp angles.

LEAVES: The leaves are rigid, ranging from 2 to 4.5 ft. (0.6–1.4 m) long and up to 2 in. (5 cm) wide. The living leaves often are arranged along the stem, forming an elongated rosette. Many of the leaves are upright, while others diverge at various angles. This trait combined with the fact that the dead leaves cling to the trunk gives *Yucca torreyi* what can best be described as a rather unkempt appearance. The leaves generally are dark yellowish green but an attractive blue-green form also exists. The leaf margin bears curly to straight persistent filaments.

BLOOM: The inflorescence is a panicle of which generally more than one-half is raised above the leaves. The flowers are large, 1.75–4 in. (4.4–10 cm), creamy white and often tinged with purple.

DISTRIBUTION: *Yucca torreyi* occurs naturally in northeastern Mexico, western Texas, and southeastern New Mexico. It is used as an ornamental within its natural range and to a lesser extent in the warm parts of the southwestern United States.

PROPAGATION: Propagation is by seed.

CULTURAL REQUIREMENTS: As with most western yuccas, *Yucca torreyi* requires full sun and well-drained soils. It is very drought tolerant, but supplemental summer water can be important when it is grown in extremely dry climates. It is hardy to at least 10°F (–12°C) and probably to 5°F (–15°C).

SIMILAR OR RELATED SPECIES: *Yucca torreyi* is distinguished from *Y. faxoniana* by its thinner, often leaning trunk, less regular head of leaves, smaller flowers, and its lack of a well-defined tube formed by the outer three tepals of the flowers. It differs from *Y. schidigera* by generally having longer leaves and flowers that have a distinct stalk as opposed to being sessile or nearly sessile on the panicle branches. *Yucca torreyi* is most similar to *Y. treculeana*, and many references subsume it into *Y. treculeana*. *Yucca torreyi*, however, has distinct and abundant curly filaments on the leaf margin while *Y. treculeana* has a smooth leaf margin or only light, straight filaments. *Yucca torreyi* has a more elongated and less regular head of leaves than *Y. treculeana*.

USES: The fleshy fruits of *Yucca torreyi* were eaten raw or toasted by native peoples in the area of natural distribution. The dried flowers were boiled for a tea and to make a remedy for cough. Ornamentally, *Y. torreyi* makes an excellent large drought-tolerant specimen plant. Because of its rather unkempt look, it tends to look best in gardens with a distinct natural or native look.

Yucca treculeana Carrière   PLATES 97, 98

SYNONYMS: *Yucca aspera* Regel, *Yucca longifolia* Buckley, *Yucca vandervinniana* Koch, *Yucca argospatha* Verlot, *Yucca contorta* Hort., *Yucca cornuta* Hort.

COMMON NAMES: Trecul yucca, Spanish dagger, Palma pita

SIZE: *Yucca treculeana* is an arborescent species, 5–25 ft. (1.5–7.6 m) tall, usually with a single trunk. The trunk often has several branches that can give older individuals the appearance of a giant candelabra. The trunk is a dark reddish brown in color with deep irregular furrows.

LEAVES: The leaves are borne on the end of the branches in hemispherical heads. The individual leaves are 2.5–4 ft. (0.8–1.2 m) long and 2–3.5 in. (5–9 cm) wide. The leaves are straight and slightly concave in cross section, ending in a dark brown or black terminal spine. Leaf color ranges from dark green to blue-green. The leaf margin generally is smooth or with a few straight, fine marginal filaments. An attractive brown line that sometimes has a white edge to it lines the leaf margin. Although dead leaves can hang down the trunk they often naturally fall away. A broad-leaved form, sometimes referred to as *Yucca treculeana* var. *canaliculata* (J. Hooker) Trelease (synonym *Y. canaliculata* J. Hooker), is particularly attractive.

BLOOM: The inflorescence is an elongated panicle 1.5–4 ft. (0.5–1.2 m) long, of which at least one-half is above the leaves. The small creamy white flowers are globose and 1–2 in. (2.5–5 cm) long.

DISTRIBUTION: *Yucca treculeana* is found in the Mexican states of Coahuila, Durango, Nuevo León, and Tamaulipas. In the United States it is limited to southern Texas from the lower Gulf Coast to the San Antonio area and west to approximately the Pecos River. Morphological differences are evident in the natural distribution range of the species. A coastal form has shorter leaves but a taller and more slender trunk than the inland form.

PROPAGATION: Propagation is by seed.

CULTURAL REQUIREMENTS: *Yucca treculeana* does best in full sun with well-drained soil. If planted in extremely dry areas, summer irrigation may be necessary to insure growth or survival. Although it tolerates temperatures down to at least 10°F (−12°C), it dies in extended extremely cold temperatures.

SIMILAR OR RELATED SPECIES: *Yucca treculeana* is similar to other arborescent fleshy fruited yuccas, such as *Y. faxoniana*, *Y. schidigera*, and *Y. torreyi*. It is separated from these species by its lack of abundant, curved or curled marginal leaf filaments. Some authorities group plants often referred to as *Y. torreyi* within *Y.*

treculeana, but in general *Y. treculeana* has a neat, symmetrical appearance, while the leaves of *Y. torreyi* present an asymmetrical, untidy look. Furthermore, the flowering panicle of *Y. treculeana* generally is held higher above the leaves than that of *Y. torreyi.* Where the two species overlap in their natural distribution, they hybridize, creating intermediate forms.

USES: Several traditional uses were developed for *Yucca treculeana.* The small fleshy fruits were fermented to create an intoxicating beverage. In Mexico terminal spines have been used to jab snakebite wounds to induce bleeding that would carry away the poison. The leaves have been used as thatching and leaf fibers for making twine and rope. *Yucca treculeana* is a very striking ornamental plant. The sturdy trunk, spreading branches, and the long flowering panicle have been admired for many years by gardeners in the United States and in Europe. As early as the 1860s, this species was used as an ornamental along the Mediterranean coast. William Robinson listed it as *Y. canaliculata* (now known as *Y. treculeana* var. *canaliculata*) in *The English Flower Garden,* his compendium of ornamental plants for English gardens published in numerous editions in the late nineteenth and early twentieth centuries. He suggested that it might be useful in "isolation or groups" for areas in England where the soils stayed warm in the winter. Within its natural range in Texas, *Y. treculeana* is an important ornamental yucca for its relatively large size and imposing presence. Its use should be encouraged in other parts of the American Southwest and warm parts of the Southeast.

Yucca whipplei Torrey   PLATE 99

SYNONYMS: *Hesperoyucca whipplei* (Torrey) Baker, *Yucca californica* Lemmon, *Yucca graminifolia* Wood, *Yucca newberryi* McKelvey, *Yucca nitida* C. Wright ex W. Watson

COMMON NAMES: Our Lord's candle, Chaparral yucca

SIZE: *Yucca whipplei* grows either as a single rosette, 2–3 ft. (0.6–1 m) wide, or in clumps of rosettes that are 3–6 ft. (1–1.8 m) wide. It is highly variable in form, and two broad varieties have been identified. The type has the larger rosettes and is solitary.

Yucca whipplei var. *caespitosa* M. E. Jones has smaller rosettes and is clump forming. *Yucca whipplei* is stemless but can branch from underground rhizomes or at ground level.

LEAVES: The rigid, sharp pointed leaves are 1.75–3 ft. (0.5–1 m) long and 0.5–0.75 in 1.3–1.9 cm) wide and lined with minute teeth. The finely striated leaves are thickened slightly in the middle, which gives them a three-sided appearance. The leaves are numerous and arranged into very regular and attractive hemispherical heads. Leaf color ranges from grayish green to bluish green. Some individuals have leaves that are very light gray in color.

BLOOM: *Yucca whipplei* has a unique blooming form and habit among the yuccas. The inflorescence can be up to 13 ft. (4 m) tall. It is a highly branched panicle and bears hundreds of flowers. The flowers are white and generally purple tipped. They are 1.25 in. (3.2 cm) long and have a distinctive bright green brushlike capitate stigma, which is unique among yuccas and distinguishes this species from all other yuccas. The rosettes are monocarpic and die after blooming. If plants are of a clustering form, the other rosettes continue to live until they bloom, thus keeping the clump alive in a similar fashion to clumping agaves that continue to survive despite the blooming and death of individual rosettes. Maturity often takes many years, with some plants known to bloom at over 50 years of age. When blooming does occur, the prodigious blooming stalk has been known to grow up to 14 in. (36 cm) per day and bear more than 600 flowers.

DISTRIBUTION: *Yucca whipplei* naturally occurs primarily in southern California and Baja California. Variety *whipplei* is a plant of the chaparral and coastal scrub. Variety *caespitosa* occurs on the edges of the Mojave Desert and has an interesting disjunct population in the Grand Canyon of Arizona. *Yucca whipplei* is cultivated in the southern parts of California, Nevada, and Arizona, and has been cultivated for years on the Mediterranean coast of Italy and France.

PROPAGATION: Propagation is by seed or by removal of the offsets.

CULTURAL REQUIREMENTS: *Yucca whipplei* is hardy down

to approximately 10°F (−12°C). It can also withstand the heat of the low desert, but should be planted with some shade for best performance in those climates. Since it naturally grows in areas of chaparral, which often can have a light tree cover, it tolerates light shade. It also tolerates soils that are richer and more loamy than those tolerated by most other yuccas native to the western United States. It has been successfully grown on an experimental basis in coastal British Columbia.

SIMILAR OR RELATED SPECIES: It is difficult to confuse *Yucca whipplei* with other yuccas. Its stiff, narrow, bluish green leaves combined with its trunkless habit separate it from other members of the genus. When they are young, *Y. rigida*, *Y. rostrata*, and *Y. schottii* are similar to *Y. whipplei*, but they often have a yellow or brown marginal stripe, which is lacking in *Y. whipplei*. The fine striations and the three-sided aspect of the leaves of *Y. whipplei* help to distinguish this species from other yuccas. *Yucca whipplei* could also be confused at a distance with *Dasylirion wheeleri*, but lacks the large curved teeth that line the leaves of the dasylirion. *Yucca whipplei* shows some similarities to *Agave stricta*, which also has striated blue-green leaves, but the leaves of the latter often have reddish or brownish highlights, are nearly round and narrow, and have no teeth. DNA research has shown that *Y. whipplei* is related closely to the genus *Hesperaloe*, with which it shares a very similar fruit. This very unique species in the Agavaceae shares traits with *Yucca* and several other genera in the family.

USES: The flowers of *Yucca whipplei* have been used by Mexicans and Native Americans as a food source. Young buds can be fried like potatoes, and the flowers can be toasted or used directly in salads. As an ornamental plant, *Y. whipplei* is outstanding for areas where a moderate-sized plant with strong color and texture contrast is desired. The regular arrangement of its narrow bluish gray leaves easily draws attention wherever the plant is grown. Because it can tolerate light shade, *Y. whipplei* is useful in somewhat shaded patios and under high canopy trees. Its cold tolerance and adaptation to winter rainfall suggest that it should be tried in cooler and wetter climates, where it might prove to be suitable.

Key to *Agave*

This key to the *Agave* species is based on vegetative character-istics. It is useful for separating most species, but it cannot truly replace the use of flowers and fruit in delimiting different species. Some species are just too similar vegetatively to easily separate, and hybrids make the task even more daunting. The key is meant to be a general help to get familiar with the plants and to ease identification.

1. Leaves without teeth, or if present minute, forming a serrate edge 2
1. Leaves with teeth. 19
2. Leaves without filaments. 3
2. Leaves with filaments. 13
3. Leaf margin smooth 4
3. Leaf margin serrate even if minutely so. 9
4. Leaves soft, pliable, or fleshy with a tender or absent terminal spine 5
4. Leaves hard, rigid, with a sharp, pungent terminal spine 7
5. Leaves wide, plants with a visible stem . . . . . *A. attenuata*
5. Leaves narrow, often recurved and curling, plants lack a visible stem 6
6. Leaves more than 24 in. (61 cm) long, plants up to 4 ft. (1.2 m) wide . . . . *A. vilmoriniana*
6. Leaves less than 24 in. (61 cm) long, plants much less than 3 ft. (1 m) wide . . . . *A. bracteosa*

277

7. Leaves thick and triangular, terminal spine short . . . .
. . . . *A. victoriae-reginae*

7. Leaves thin, flat, and stiff, terminal spine greater than 1.5 in. (3.8 cm) long 8

8. Leaf margin red-brown, flowers yellow . . . . *A. ocahui*

8. Leaf margin white, occasionally red-brown, flowers red. . .
. . . . *A. pelona*

9. Leaves very thin, round to rhomboid 10

9. Leaves lanceolate to oblanceolate, at least 3 in. (8 cm) wide
. . . . 11

10. Entire rosette appears as a tight sphere, leaves numerous .
. . . . *A. stricta*

10. Entire rosette appears less dense, leaves not numerous . . .
. . . . *A. striata*

11. Leaves sword-shaped, straight, typically without teeth . . .
. . . . *A. sisalana*

11. Leaves not sword-shaped 12

12. Border reddish, spine absent or a short tip, leaves bright green . . . . *A. ellemeetiana*

12. Border green, spine to 1 in. (2.5 cm) long, leaves fleshy, glaucous green . . . . *A. desmettiana*

13. Leaves with a distinct white bud imprint 14

13. Leaves without a distinct bud imprint. 16

14. Leaves flat, more than 12 in. (30 cm) long, straight 15

14. Leaves incurved, less than 12 in. (30 cm) long . . . .
. . . . *A. toumeyana*

15. Leaves thin, filaments coarse, plants usually solitary. . . . .
. . . . *A. schidigera*

15. Leaves thicker, filaments very fine, plants with numerous offsets . . . . *A. filifera*

16. Leaves numerous, more than 200 17

16. Leaves much less numerous 18

17. Leaves to 24 in. (61 cm) long, round to rhomboid, spine flat, gray, and less than 0.25 in. (0.6 cm) long . . . *A. geminiflora*

17. Leaves to 31 in. (79 cm) long, spine flat, green, pliant, and 0.5 in. (1.3 cm) long. *A. multifilifera*

18. Leaf filaments numerous, leaves scabrous . . . . . . *A. felgeri*

18. Leaf filaments sparse, leaves smooth. . . . . *A. schottii*

19. Terminal spine not decurrent, or barely so 20
19. Terminal spine decurrent. 32
20. Leaf margin straight 21
20. Leaf margin undulate or mammillate, even slightly 26
21. Leaves with a strong white bud imprint 22
21. Leaves without a white bud imprint 23
22. Flowers yellow. . . . . *A. parviflora*
22. Flowers pink to red . . . . *A. polianthiflora*
23. Leaves small and blue-gray . . . . *A. macroacantha*
23. Leaves otherwise 24
24. Leaves striate on back, less than 20 in. (51 cm) long . . . . . .
. . . . *A. lechuguilla*
24. Leaves not striate, much more than 20 in. (51 cm) long . . .
. . . . 25
25. Leaves flat. . . . . *A. angustifolia*
25. Leaves guttered . . . . *A. fourcroydes*
26. Leaves dark green to yellow green, occasionally purple or
gray. 27
26. Leaves gray, blue-gray, white often crossbanded 28
27. Leaves with a distinct gray border. . . . . *A. lophantha*
27. Leaves fleshy, spine conic and dark . . . . *A. decipiens*
28. Leaves thick at base with a horny border. . . . . . *A. titanota*
28. Leaves without a horny border 29
29. Leaves few, wide, ovate, with a slightly rough surface . . . .
. . . . *A. colorata*
29. Leaves otherwise 30
30. Leaves flat, mammillate, crossbanded . . . . . *A. marmorata*
30. Leaves concave, even slightly, not crossbanded. 31
31. Leaves oblong to ovate, numerous. . . . . . *A. guadalajarana*
31. Leaves lanceolate, many to few . . . . *A. subsimplex*
32. Leaf margin straight, occasionally or only slightly undulate
. . . . 33
32. Leaf margin undulate or strongly mammillate. 53
33. Leaves with a horny border 34
33. Leaves without a horny border 36
34. Teeth only on lower two-thirds of leaf, border continuous
. . . . *A. ghiesbreghtii*
34. Teeth on all or half the leaf 35

35. Border white, teeth very far apart, leaves thin and gray . . .
. . . . *A. albomarginata*
35. Border gray or brown, teeth on at least half the leaf, border discontinuous . . . . *A. neomexicana*
36. Teeth encircled by a dark ring at the base 37
36. Teeth without a dark ring at the base. 38
37. Leaves with regularly spaced small teeth, less than 1.25 in. (3.2 cm) wide, dark gray to gray-green . . . . *A. utahensis*
37. Leaves with irregularly spaced small teeth, more than 1.5 in. (3.8 cm) wide, yellow-green to gray-green. . . *A. cerulata*
38. Teeth on half the length of the margin, or absent . . *A. weberi*
38. Teeth on the entire length of the margin. 39
39. Leaves large, usually blue-gray to white, plants very large. 40
39. Leaves moderate to small, color variable, plants moderate to small 41
40. Teeth prominent from a wide base, leaves scabrous, spine without a groove . . . . *A. franzosinii*
40. Teeth widely spaced and variable, leaves smooth, spine with a definite groove . . . . *A. americana*
41. Leaves soft, fleshy or succulent. 42
41. Leaves hard, rigid or straight 44
42. Leaves blue-gray, teeth irregular. . . . . *A. guiengola*
42. Leaves green to blue-gray, teeth very regular 43
43. Teeth bicuspid, spine weak . . . . *A. celsii*
43. Teeth uniform, spine strong. . . . . *A. chiapensis*
44. Leaves less than 14 in. (36 cm) long 45
44. Leaves much more than 14 in. (36 cm) long 46
45. Leaves ovate, blue-gray, tightly held . . . . *A. parrasana*
45. Leaves linear, gray-green, erect . . . . *A. mckelveyana*
46. Leaves at least eight times longer than wide 47
46. Leaves much less than eight times longer than wide . . . 49
47. Terminal spine short, leaves flat to concave. 48
47. Terminal spine long, leaves deeply guttered . . . . *A. datylio*
48. Leaves long, thin, rigid, and held upright, terminal spine 0.25 in. (0.6 cm) long or less. . . . . *A. tequilana*
48. Leaves lanceolate, thick, flat then guttered at tip, terminal spine greater than 0.25 in. (0.6 cm) long . . . . . . *A. murpheyi*

49. Teeth small, regularly spaced, plants less than 20 in. (51 cm) tall . . . . *A. deserti*

49. Teeth small or large, variable or regular, plants more than 20 in. (51 cm) tall 50

50. Leaves numerous, terminal spine stout, less than 1 in. (2.5 cm) long . . . . *A. parryi*

50. Leaves few to moderate in number, spine various forms but greater than 1 in. (2.5 cm) long 51

51. Plants less than 3 ft. (1 m) tall, teeth noticeably larger toward tip . . . . *A. havardiana*

51. Plants more than 3 ft. (1 m) tall, teeth similar along the length 52

52. Terminal spine needlelike, plant generally 3–4 ft (1–1.2 m) tall, teeth small and close . . . . *A. palmeri*

52. Terminal spine heavy, plant generally 2–3 ft. (0.6–1 m) tall, teeth large and far apart . . . . *A. chrysantha*

53. Leaves smooth 56

53. Leaves scabrous, even slightly 54

54. Leaves less than 4 in. (10 cm) wide, teeth small, flat . . . . *A. sobria*

54. Leaves more than 4 in. (10 cm) wide, teeth large, various . . 55

55. Leaves strongly crossbanded, teeth for entire leaf length, spine long and straight . . . . *A. zebra*

55. Leaves not crossbanded, teeth from middle of leaf to the base, spine long and recurved . . . . *A. scabra*

56. Leaves very large, 8 in. (20 cm) wide or more, spine long decurrent and curved . . . . *A. salmiana*

56. Leaves less than 8 in. (20 cm) wide, often much less, spine various 57

57. Leaves green, sometimes glossy 58

57. Leaves glaucous gray, gray-green to blue-green 60

58. Leaves markedly wider in midleaf, teeth highly variable . . . . *A. bovicornuta*

58. Leaves lanceolate to linear 59

59. Teeth uniform . . . . *A. shawii*

59. Teeth irregular . . . . *A. xylonacantha*

60. Leaves ovate, truncate, succulent or fleshy 61

60. Leaves linear to lanceolate, fleshy or not 63

61. Leaves small, generally less than 11 in. (28 cm) long, teeth small, closely spaced and downcurved, spine shortly decurrent .... *A. pygmae*

61. Leaves generally greater than 11 in. (28 cm) long, teeth variable but usually straight, spine long decurrent 62

62. Leaves usually glaucous gray-green or white, teeth reddish, margin extremely mammillate .... *A. potatorum*

62. Leaves usually glaucous green to green-yellow, teeth dark brown on low teats .... *A. seemanniana*

63. Leaves with extremely mammillate margins, teeth highly variable, large and widely spaced .... *A. gigantensis*

63. Leaves with undulate to slightly mammillate margins, teeth variable, small and closely spaced ....
.... *A. avellanidens*

Key to *Yucca*

1. Marginal fibers present. 13
1. Marginal fibers absent. 2
2. Leaves straight, rigid. 8
2. Leaves curved, bent, wavy with or without a terminal spine
. . . . 3
3. Trunk absent or hidden by the leaves 4
3. Trunk visible, usually more than 3 ft. (1 m) tall. 5
4. Flowers few on tall stalk, leaves more or less flat, occasionally inrolled . . . . *Y. pallida*
4. Flowers numerous on tall stalk, leaves rolled and twisted,
never flat . . . . *Y. rupicola*
5. Plants solitary, leaves 0.5 in. (1.3 cm) or less wide. . . . .
. . . . *Y. rostrata*
5. Plants multitrunked, leaves 1.5 in. (3.8 cm) or greater wide
. . . . 6
6. Leaf margin with minute serrations . . . . *Y. gloriosa*
6. Leaf margin smooth 7
7. Marginal stripe yellow or brown, plants multitrunked, 6–10
ft. (1.8–3 m) tall. . . . . *Y. recurvifolia*
7. Marginal stripe absent, plants multitrunked, 10–30 ft. (3–9
m) tall. . . . . *Y. elephantipes*
8. Trunk absent . . . . *Y. whipplei*
8. Trunk visible 9
9. Leaves 0.5 in. (1.3 cm) wide, usually less than 12 in. (30 cm)
long. . . . . *Y. brevifolia*
9. Leaves 1 in. (2.5 cm) wide, 12 in. (30 cm) long or more . . 10

10. Leaf margin smooth 11
10. Leaf margin serrated 12
11. Leaves smooth, light green .... *Y. schottii*
11. Leaves scabrous, dark green .... *Y. treculeana*
12. Leaves powdery blue to gray, margin yellow ..... *Y. rigida*
12. Leaves green to purple, no separate margin .... *Y. aloifolia*
13. Trunk absent or hidden by the leaves 14
13. Trunk visible 17
14. Marginal stripe present............................ 15
14. Marginal stripe absent 16
15. Marginal stripe white .... *Y. glauca*
15. Marginal stripe tan or brown .... *Y. harrimaniae*
16. Leaves lanceolate, generally recurved, straight fibers .....
.... *Y. flaccida*
16. Leaves spatulate, generally straight, curled fibers ....
.... *Y. filamentosa*
17. Leaves less than 0.25 in. (0.6 cm) wide .... *Y. elata*
17. Leaves greater than 1 in. (2.5 cm) wide 18
18. Leaf filaments few, straight and fine, generally only at the
base .... *Y. grandiflora*
18. Leaf filaments many, coarse, occurring along the leaf.....
....19
19. Flower head pendulous, held outside the head of leaves...
.... *Y. filifera*
19. Flower head upright, held either inside or outside the head
of leaves... 20
20. Flower head entirely or mainly within the head of leaves,
flowers less than 2 in. (5 cm) long, sessile ... *Y. schidigera*
20. Flower head mainly or entirely outside the head of leaves,
flowers more than 2 in. (5 cm) long on a pedicel 21
21. Flowers with a distinct floral tube .... *Y. faxoniana*
21. Flowers without a distinct floral tube 22
22. Plants generally solitary or few trunks, leaves held in irregular rosette, generally more than 10 ft. (3 m) tall ....
....*Y. torreyi*
22. Plants generally multitrunked, often forming extensive
clumps, leaves held in very symmetrical rosettes, rarely
more than 8 ft. (2.4 m) tall.................. *Y. baccata*

Plants Suitable for Humid Gardens

Although nearly all the plants described in this book grow well in either warm desert or Mediterranean climates, many may also be used in warm, humid regions. The following list is a compilation based on the experiences of Tony Avent of Plants Delight Nursery in Raleigh, North Carolina, and Carl Schoenfeld of Yucca Do Nursery in Hempstead, Texas. It shows the plants being grown at one or both locations. Raleigh is in USDA zone 7b, with winter lows of 5–10°F (–15 to –6°C). Hempstead is in zone 8b, with winter lows of 15–20°F (–9 to –7°C). Both cities have humid climates with regular summer rainfall.

Species	Location[a]	Comment
Agave americana	NC	Marginal, needs to be kept dry in winter
Agave bracteosa	TX	
Agave celsii	TX	Needs protected location
Agave deserti subsp. simplex	TX	Poor performer in winter
Agave filifera	TX	
Agave havardiana	NC, TX	
Agave lechuguilla	NC	Marginal, needs to be kept dry in winter
Agave lophantha	NC, TX	
Agave mckelveyana	NC, TX	Needs to be kept dry in TX
Agave neomexicana	NC, TX	

Species	Location[a]	Comment
Agave ocahui	NC	Marginal, needs to be kept dry in winter
Agave palmeri	NC, TX	
Agave parryi	NC	
Agave parryi var. *couesii*	TX	
Agave parryi var. *huachucensis*	NC, TX	
Agave parviflora	NC	Marginal, needs to be kept dry in winter
Agave potatorum	TX	Damaged at 17°F (−8°C)
Agave salmiana	NC	Marginal, needs to be kept dry in winter
Agave scabra	NC	
Agave schidigera	TX	
Agave schottii	TX	
Agave striata	NC, TX	Marginal, needs to be kept dry in winter in NC
Agave striata subsp. *falcata*	NC, TX	
Agave stricta	NC, TX	Marginal, needs to be kept dry in winter in NC
Agave toumeyana	NC, TX	Marginal, needs to be kept dry in winter in NC
Agave utahensis	NC, TX	Lost in TX to excessive moisture
Agave victoriae-reginae	NC, TX	Marginal, needs to be kept dry in winter in NC
Agave weberi	TX	
Beschorneria septentrionalis	NC, TX	
Beschorneria yuccoides	NC	Tender to cold in NC; hardy in TX
Calibanus hookeri	TX	Survived 17°F (−8°C) outdoors
Dasylirion acrotriche	TX	
Dasylirion leiophyllum	NC, TX	
Dasylirion quadrangulatum	NC, TX	Tender to cold in NC; hardy to normal cold in TX
Dasylirion texanum	NC, TX	
Dasylirion wheeleri	NC, TX	
Hesperaloe campanulata	NC, TX	
Hesperaloe funifera	TX	
Hesperaloe nocturna	TX	
Hesperaloe parviflora	NC, TX	

Species	Location[a]	Comment
Manfreda maculosa	NC, TX	
Manfreda undulata	NC, TX	
Manfreda variegata	TX	
Manfreda virginica	NC	
Nolina beldingii	TX	
Nolina bigelovii	TX	Needs to be kept dry
Nolina lindheimerana	TX	
Nolina longifolia	NC, TX	
Nolina matapensis	TX	
Nolina microcarpa	NC, TX	
Nolina nelsoni	NC, TX	
Nolina texana	NC, TX	
Polianthes geminiflora	TX	
Polianthes howardii	TX	
Polianthes pringlei	TX	
Polianthes tuberosa	NC	Marginal, survives only five to seven years
Yucca aloifolia	NC, TX	
Yucca baccata	NC, TX	Dies from excessive moisture even in sand beds in NC; hardy in TX
Yucca elata	NC, TX	
Yucca filamentosa	NC, TX	
Yucca flaccida	NC	
Yucca glauca	TX	
Yucca harrimaniae	TX	
Yucca pallida	NC, TX	
Yucca rostrata	NC, TX	
Yucca rupicola	TX	
Yucca schottii	NC, TX	
Yucca torreyi	TX	
Yucca treculeana	NC, TX	

[a] NC = Plants Delight Nursery, Raleigh, North Carolina; TX = Yucca Do Nursery, Hempstead, Texas

Map of Mexico and Adjacent Areas

1 Distrito Federal
2 Morelos
3 Tlaxcala
4 Querétaro
5 Aguascalientes
6 Colima
7 Tiburôn

Adapted from *Atlas of United States Trees*, Elbert L. Little Jr., U.S.D.A., Forest Service, Miscellaneous Publication No. 1146 (Washington, D.C., 1971).

Glossary

Acaulescent. Lacking a visible stem

Bud imprint. The outline of the margins and teeth of one leaf upon another leaf while the leaves were in the bud and remaining on the leaf after opening

Bulbil. A small clonal plant produced on the inflorescence

Caespitose. Arising from an aboveground stem or the base of a plant, usually in reference to offsets or suckers

Capsule. A multi-chambered fruit with many seeds per chamber

Clone. A plant that is genetically identical to the parent plant as in offsets, bulbils, or cuttings

Crenation. Applied to leaf, strongly undulate, scalloped, with large teats

Crossbanding. A slight color variation that is horizontal on the leaf, usually in reference to *Agave* leaves

Decurrent. The extension of the terminal spine down the margin of the leaf

Dioecious. Having male and female flowers on separate plants

Endemic. Originating from a specific, usually small, geographic area

Etiolate (etiolation). Leaves or stems that are unnaturally long, often with a change of color or texture due to a lack of light

Exserted. Stamens or pistils that exceed the length of the tepals

Glabrous. Without hair, usually in reference to the surface of a leaf

Glaucous. Covered with a blush or waxy bloom, usually in reference to the surface of a leaf often whitish blue-green or whitish blue in color

Guttered. Leaf margins that are folded more or less inward, leaf shaped like a gutter in cross section

Inflorescence. An arrangement of flowers on a stalk

Keeled. Having a ridge running along the length of a leaf, stem, or flower part

Lanceolate. Lance-shaped, much longer than wide and tapering from at least the midpoint to the tip and more abruptly to the base

Mammillate. Extremely undulate, exaggerated, and breast-shaped

Mescal. A distilled liquor made from *Agave* species, a common name in Mexico for certain agaves

Monocarpic. A plant that flowers only once in its lifetime and then dies

Monocotyledons (monocots). A large group of flowering plants with one cotyledon that initially emerges from a germinated seed as opposed to dicotyledons, which have two cotyledons that initially emerge from the seed

Oblanceolate. Inversely lanceolate

Offset. A plant or plants that arise from and remain connected to another plant, typically from rhizomes, stems, or tubers

Panicle (paniculate). A branched inflorescence

Pedicel. A short stalk that connects flowers to the main stem of the plant or branches of the inflorescence

Petal. A part of a flower that is a modified leaf, usually colored and located in proximity to the pistils and stamens and above the sepals

Polycarpic. A plant that flowers more than once during its lifetime

Pups. An offset, often used in reference to agaves and bromeliads

Raceme. An unbranched inflorescence with flowers attached by pedicels to a main stalk

Rhizome. A stem that grows underground and from which arise aerial stems or leaves

Rosette. A tight cluster of leaves that are arranged around a central apex and grow outward to form a radially symmetrical pattern

Scabrous. Rough, usually in reference to the surface of a leaf, caused by tubercles, hairs, or other structures on the leaf

Segment. An individual division of a flower, like a tepal

Sepal. A modified leaf that is part of a flower, usually colored and located in proximity to the pistils and stamens and below the petals

Sessile. Attached directly to a stalk, as in flowers directly attached to the inflorescence

Spatulate. Shaped like a spatula; broadened toward the tip

Spike (spicate). An unbranched inflorescence with the flowers attached directly to the main stalk

Spine. A narrow, sharp, and pointed woodlike structure on a leaf, branch, or stem

Stem. The main aerial axis of a plant from which branches and or leaves arise. In trees and shrubs the stem is made of woody material.

Subtend. Located closely below, as in bracts below the flower bud

Taxon (plural taxa). Any taxonomic division of plants such as the family, genus, species, or variety

Teats. Teeth-bearing, rounded prominences along the margins of a leaf, as in agaves

Teeth. Small, sharp, pointed, more or less triangular structures that arise on the margins of leaves

Tepal. A part of the flower that cannot be distinguished as either a sepal or a petal, as in the flowers of agave

Terminal spine. The spine located at the end of a leaf

Truncate. Ending abruptly, usually in reference to the end of a leaf

Trunk. A woody stem from which branches and or leaves arise

Tube. A narrow structure formed by the fusion of the tepals, as in the flowers of agave

Umbels. A cluster of flowers with pedicels arising more or less from a central point, like an upturned umbrella

Variety. A naturally occurring taxonomic subdivision of a species that represents individuals with recognizable but minor variations in selected characteristics

Bibliography

Alvarez de Zayas, Alberto. 1996. El Genero Furcraeae (Agavaceae) en Cuba. *Anales del Instituto de Biologia, Universidad Nacional Autonoma de Mexico,* ser. bot., 67: 329–346.

Arnott, Howard J. 1962. *The Seed, Germination and Seedling of* Yucca. University of California Publications in Botany 35(1): 1–164.

Bailey, L. H. 1947. *The Standard Cyclopedia of Horticulture.* 3 vols. New York. The MacMillan Company.

Baker, J. G. 1888. *Handbook of the Amaryllidaceae.* London: George Ball and Sons.

Baker, J. G. 1896. *Agaves and Arborescent Liliaceae on the Riviera.* Royal Gardens Kew, Bulletin of Miscellaneous Information 61.

Benson, Lyman, and Robert A. Darrow. 1981 *Trees and Shrubs of the Southwestern Deserts.* 3rd ed. Tucson, Arizona: The University of Arizona Press.

Blessington, Thomas M., and David L. Clement. 1997. Production/Postproduction Factors for Maintaining High-Keeping Quality of *Beaucarnea. Maryland Cooperative Extension Service Nurseryman's News* 59: 1.

Bogler, David John. 1994. *Taxonomy and Phylogeny of* Dasylirion *(Nolinaceae).* Ph.D. thesis, The University of Texas.

Botkin, C. W., L. B. Shires, and E. C. Smith. 1943. *Fiber of Native Plants in New Mexico.* Bulletin 300, Agricultural Experiment Station of the New Mexico College of Agriculture and Mechanic Arts, State College, New Mexico.

Breitung, August J. 1968. *The Agaves.* Eds. Charles Glass and Robert Foster. Reseda, California: Abbey Garden Press.

Clary, Karen H. 1997. *Phylogeny, Character Evolution and Biogeography of* Yucca *L. (Agavaceae) as Inferred from Plant Morphology and Sequences of the Internal Transcribed (ITS) Region of the Nuclear Ribosomal DNA.* Ph.D. thesis, The University of Texas.

Clary, Karen H., and Beryl B. Simpson. 1995. Systematics and Character Evolution of the Genus *Yucca* L. (Agavaceae): Evidence from Morphology and Molecular Analysis. *Boletín de la Sociedad Botánica de México* 56: 77–86.

Correll, Donovan Stewart, and Marshall Conring Johnston. 1979. *Manual of the Vascular Plants of Texas.* Richardson, Texas: The University of Texas at Dallas.

Dahlgren, R., H. Clifford, and P. Yeo. 1985. *The Families of Monocotyledons.* New York: Springer-Verlag.

Davidse, Gerrit, Mario Sousa S., and Arthur O. Chater, eds. 1994. *Flora Mesoamericana.* Vol. 6, *Alismataceae a Cyperaceae.* Mexico City: Universidad Nacional Autonoma de Mexico; St. Louis: Missouri Botanical Garden; London: The Natural History Museum.

Drummond, J. R. 1907. The Literature of *Furcraea* with a Synopsis of the Known Species. Eighteenth Annual Report of the Missouri Botanical Garden.

Everett, Thomas H., ed. 1981. *The New York Botanical Garden Illustrated Encyclopedia of Horticulture.* New York: Garland Publishing.

Fish, Suzanne K., Paul R. Fish, Charles Miksicek, and John Madsen. 1985. Prehistoric *Agave* Cultivation in Southern Arizona. *Desert Plants* 7: 107–112.

Ferguson, Dave J. 1998. Mesembs and Re: *Dasylirion.* E-mail posting on cacti_etc. Usenet mailing list.

García-Mendoza, Abisaí. 1987. *Monografia del genero* Beschorneria *Kunth. Agavaceae.* Thesis, Universidad Nacional Autonoma de Mexico.

García-Mendoza, Abisaí, and Raquel Galván. 1995. Riqueza de las familias Agavaceae y Nolinaceae en Mexico. *Boletín de la Sociedad Botánica de México* 56: 7–24.

Gentry, Howard Scott. 1972. *The Agave Family in Sonora.* Agriculture Handbook No. 399, Agricultural Research Service, United States Department of Agriculture.

Gentry, Howard Scott. 1982. *Agaves of Continental North America.* Tucson, Arizona: The University of Arizona Press.

Hatfield, Miles. 1955. *Pioneers in Gardening.* Rpt., 1996. London: Bloomsbury Publishing.

Hernández, Luis Gerardo. 1993. *Cladistic Analysis of the American Genera of Asparagales and the Systematic Study of* Beaucarnea *(Nolinaceae) and* Hemiphyacus *(Hyacinthaceae).* Ph.D. thesis, The University of Texas.

Hessayon, D. G. 1995. *The Bulb Expert.* London: Transworld Publishers.

Hickman, James C., ed. 1993. *The Jepson Manual, Higher Plants of California.* Berkeley, California: The University of California Press.

Hobhouse, Penelope. 1992. *Gardening Through the Ages.* New York: Simon and Schuster.

Hodgson, Wendy. *Food Plants of the Sonoran Desert.* Manuscript, Desert Botanical Garden, Phoenix, Arizona.

Hodoba, Theodore B. 1995. *Growing Desert Plants: From Windowsill to Garden.* Santa Fe, New Mexico: Red Crane Books.

Jacobsen, Hermann. 1960. *A Handbook of Succulent Plants.* 3 vols. London: Blandford Press.

Jones, J. M., and A. B. Conner. 1918. *The Utilization of* Yucca *for the Maintenance of Cattle.* Bulletin No. 240, Texas Agricultural Experiment Station, College Station, Texas.

Kearney, Thomas H., Robert H. Peebles, and collaborators. 1960. *Arizona Flora.* 2nd ed. Berkeley, California: The University of California Press.

Lenz, Lee W., and John Dourley. 1981. *California Native Trees and Shrubs.* Claremont, California: Rancho Santa Ana Botanic Garden.

Mason, Charles T., and Patricia B. Mason. 1987. *A Handbook of Mexican Roadside Flora.* Tucson, Arizona: The University of Arizona Press.

Mathew, Brian. 1997. *Growing Bulbs: The Complete Practical Guide*. Portland, Oregon: Timber Press.

Matuda, Eizi, and Ignacio L. Piña. 1980. *Las Plantas Mexicanas del Genero Yucca*. Toluca, Estado de Mexico: Coleccion Miscelanea Estado de Mexico, Serie Fernando de Alva Ixtlilxochitl.

McDaniel, J. C. 1975. The typical *Yucca filamentosa*. *Cactus and Succulent Journal* 67: 110–111.

McKelvey, Susan D. 1947. *Yuccas of the Southwestern United States*. Jamaica Plain, Massachusetts: The Arnold Arboretum of Harvard University.

Michigan State University Extension. 1998. *Yucca filamentosa*. Ornamental Plants Bulletin.

Mielke, Judy. 1993. *Native Plants for Southwestern Landscapes*. Austin, Texas: The University of Texas Press.

Nokes, Jill. 1986. *How to Grow Native Plants of Texas and the Southwest*. Austin, Texas: Texas Monthly Press.

Ogden, Scott. 1994. *Garden Bulbs for the South*. Dallas, Texas: Taylor Publishing Company.

Piña, Ignacio L. 1980. Geographic Distribution of the Genus *Yucca*. *Cactus and Succulent Journal* 52: 277–281.

Powell, A. Michael. 1988. *Trees and Shrubs of Trans-Pecos Texas*. Big Bend National Park, Texas: Big Bend Natural History Association.

Rademacher, Janet. 1995. Agaves, Yuccas. . . . Paper presented at the Desert Horticulture Conference. 18 May 1995, Tucson, Arizona.

Ramsay, Marylee, and John R. Schrock. 1992. The Yucca Plant and the Yucca Moth. *The Kansas School Naturalist* 38: 2.

Raulston, J. C. 1996. North Carolina State University Arboretum Newsletter No. 27 (July).

Ricketts, Harold W. 1970. *Wildflowers of the United States*. Vol. 3, *Texas*. New York: McGraw-Hill Book Company.

Ricketts, Harold W. 1970. *Wildflowers of the United States*. Vol. 4, *Southwestern United States*. New York: McGraw-Hill Book Company.

Roberts, Norman C. 1989. *Baja California Plant Field Guide*. La Jolla, California: Natural History Publishing Company.

BIBLIOGRAPHY

Schmidt, Marjorie G. 1980. *Growing California Native Plants.* Berkeley, California: The University of California Press.

Shistovksy, W. 1997. A Few Observations on Yuccas and Agaves. *Hardy Palm International* (May).

Slausen, L. A. 1996. *Amorphometric and pollination ecology study of* Agave chrysantha *Peebles and* Agave palmeri *Engelmann (Agavaceae).* Ph.D. thesis, Arizona State University.

Starr, Greg. 1995. *Hesperaloe:* Aloes of the West. *Desert Plants* 11(4): 3–8.

Starr, Greg. 1996. Agaves for the Landscape. Paper presented at the Xeriscape Conference, Phoenix, Arizona.

Standley, Paul C. 1920. *Trees and Shrubs of Mexico.* Contributions from the United States National Herbarium, Vol. 23, part 1. Washington D.C.: Smithsonian Institution, United States National Museum.

Thorne, Francis M. 1965. *The Taxonomy of the Genus* Nolina *Michx. (Agavaceae) in the Southeastern United States.* Ph.D. thesis, The University of Georgia.

Turner, Raymond M., Janice E. Bowers, and Tony L. Burgess. 1995. *Sonoran Desert Plants: An Ecological Atlas.* Tucson, Arizona: The University of Arizona Press.

Trelease, William. 1893. *Further Studies of* Yucca. Fourth Report of the Missouri Botanical Garden.

Trelease, William. 1902. *The Yuccae.* Thirteenth Report of the Missouri Botanical Garden.

Trelease, William. 1907. The Century Plant. *Popular Science Monthly* 70: 14

Verhoek-Williams, Susan E. 1975. *A Study of the Tribe Poliantheae (including* Manfreda*) and Revision of* Manfreda *and* Prochnyanthes *(Agavaceae).* Ph.D. thesis, Cornell University.

Wasowski, Sally, and Andy Wasowski. 1988. *Native Texas Plants.* Austin, Texas: Texas Monthly Press.

Watson, W. 1889. *Cool Cultivation of Tropical and Subtropical Plants.* Royal Gardens Kew, Bulletin of Miscellaneous Information.

Webber, John M. 1953. *Yuccas of the Southwest.* Agriculture Monograph 17, United States Department of Agriculture.

Index

Bold-faced page numbers indicate the main entries.